Python Graphics for Game Creation # 1:

Python Line, Shape and Color

Recipes and techniques for creating 2D images using Python.

Mike Ohlson de Fine

Python Graphics for Game Creation 1: Python Line, Shape and Color

Mike Ohlson de Fine

First published: March, 2015

Published by Mike Ohlson de Fine.
Mike.ohlsondefine@gmail.com

ISBN 978-0-620-56642-1

Dedication

I humbly dedicate this book to my wife Suzy, and my daughter Candace.

Suzy for love, forbearance and starting the whole shebang that resulted in my daughter Candace. I am also very grateful to Guido von Rossum who, with his clarity of thought gave us that almost impossible treasure, a pain free computer language.

Table of Contents

Preface

This is the first of a series of books titled *Python Graphics for Games* whose aim is to provide tools to help you develop your ideas for making games and simulations.
The tools are constructed using code of the Python language. The Python code is printed out in full in the book. It is yours to use any way you like – just do not be nasty and prevent others from doing the same.
The Python programming language has been selected because it is easy to learn, cleanly elegant, versatile, widely known and loved, well supported and is open source. When you know Python you know programming. It is easier to learn other languages when the ideas and concepts of programming are clear in your head. C++ and Java are commercially good languages to know but they can be messy and weighed down by the cumbersome and artificial compulsion to use classes unnecessarily. Trying to be creative with them is like using pneumatic hammers to build delicate furniture – noisy, distracting and likely to damage your best raw material.

This particular book *Line, Shape and Color* is a carefully trimmed collection of code recipes and illustrative screenshots for developing vector graphic pictures and objects. All the code has been successfully run on Python version 2.7.2 and version 3.2.3

The book is intended to serve the following purposes:

- present the simplest programs to drawing, line, circles, ellipses, rectangles and complex shapes.
- Provide a solid capability of controlling color in vector graphic objects.
- Develop more advanced skills in vector image

manipulation and control.
- Lay a foundation or the development of games, dynamic cartooning and simulations which are covered in subsequent books in this series.

What you need for this book

To run the code in this book, the reader will need a Linux operating system or Microsoft Windows and some way of downloading Python from the internet. Although not *necessary* it is useful to have a copy of Inkscape available on your computer. Inkscape is a very good open source drawing package.

The code in this book was developed on various versions of Linux Ubuntu and Mint as well as Microsoft Windows 7 and XP.

What the book covers

Chapter 1, Lines and Rectangles.
This chapter explains how to create lines and rectangle to create lines and rectangles and control all aspects like color, thickness, style and end features like arrows and rounded end caps.
It gradually introduces strategies for creating re-usable code in a simple way.

Chapter 2, Ovals.
This chapter explains how to create circles, ellipses ovals) and arcs.
Starting with short and simple programs more complicated images are produced using programming loops.

Chapter 3, Color Control.
This chapter explains how color is controlled using Python

instructions.
The confusing choice of hundreds of colors with names is reduced to smaller, more useful palettes. Complete control of color is shown using the arithmetic and string handling capabilities of Python.

Chapter 4, Polygons.
This chapter starts with how to draw simple polygons like triangles and progresses to intricate shapes. The programs are more complex and attention is devoted to debugging methods. Programs for transforming the size, position and rotation of complex shapes are developed. Also methods of filling in colored areas with shaded blends of colors are shown.

Chapter 5, Textured Color.
This chapter concentrates on how texture and color can be used to fill in geometric shapes and polygons. Geometry is used fill in polygons and whole groups or arrays of polygons with a variety of graphic elements. Some problems and their solutions arising from coloring complex shapes are shown. The use of randomly varying elements to produce novel textures are shown.

Chapter 6, Text Control.
All aspects of text control in the Python vector graphics environment are explored. Control of font style, size, position and color using operating system supplied typefaces are dealt with. In addition methods of acquiring and creating new fonts are covered.

Appendix, How to acquire and install Python and other tools.

The code is available at Github at mikeodf/Python_Line_Shape_Color.

1

Graphic Elements: Lines

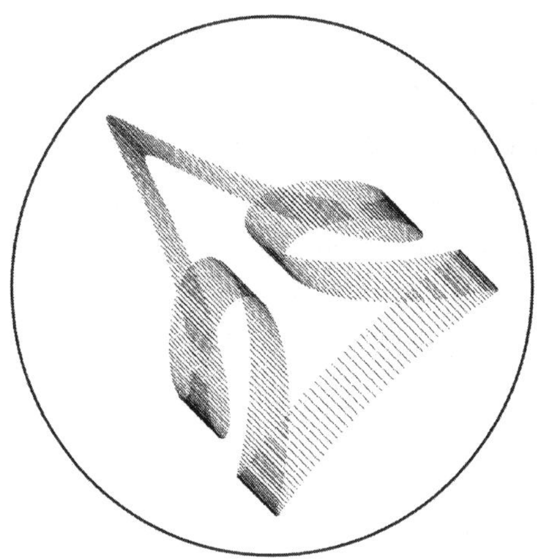

In this chapter we will cover the drawing of:

- a straight line on a canvas
- a dashed line.
- lines of various styles on the same canvas.
- lines with arrows
- lines with rounded end caps
- lines of more than one segment
- segmented lines made into smooth curves

- rectangles
- concentric squares
- overlapping rectangles
- stipple fill patterns
- stipple fill with dominant borders

The emphasis in this book is on giving to you, dear reader, Python programs that just work. The principle we follow is "bare metal" and "batteries included", the design principle of the wise Python sages on mount Python. Bare metal means that we try to use standard Python commands, rather than packages that separate us from the code, whenever practical. Because we are using graphics we invoke the Tkinter (tkinter, no capital letter, in Python 3.xx versions) module which is regarded as a just one of Python's standard libraries like the math library. Using packages like Pygame are avoided if we can achieve the same results using basic Python. We do this because it keeps our options and creativity wide open and not confined to the mindset of the writers of the wrapper packages. "Batteries included" means that you do not need to add anything to the code to get it to run. You can just copy and paste the code into a Python interpreter and it will execute.
A strategy followed in the book is to start with the absolute simplest or shortest code needed to demonstrate a particular graphic function and then add-on increasing complexity in progressive stages. This way when something does not work as expected we can go back one step to where everything DID work AND where we could understand how things worked. The re-starting from the last step that worked we can edge forward again onto paths less familiar.

This brings us to:
Programming Tip No. 1.
When writing code for a program only make one change at a

time then test your code. This way, if it does not work you know exactly what caused the problem. This is the dazzling and peerless beauty of interpreted languages like Python. Testing is so very easy and convenient.

You are encouraged to experiment with the code. It is yours to use anyway you want. Keep the lawyers out of it. No anti-hacking rules here. Change something and watch the result change.
You are legally free to copy, chop, splice and extend the code presented in this book in any way. It is free and open. You can use it anywhere you want but do not restrict anybody else from the same freedom. Please. We are all nice humans here.

The engine of Python graphics is the Tkinter graphics library.
For a Linux (Debian, Ubuntu, Mint flavours) operating systems you need to run **Sudo apt-get install python-tk** in a terminal.
This will download and install the Tkinter graphics functions we need for all our graphics work.

Draw a Straight Line

Canvas(...) and create_line(...) are both functions from the Tkinter library. **Canvas(root, width=200, height=200)** sets up an area on your monitor screen to contain drawn shapes. This digital canvas is 200 pixels wide and 200 pixels high. In this example the shape is a line starting from the point x=10, y=20 and going to the point x=50, y=100.

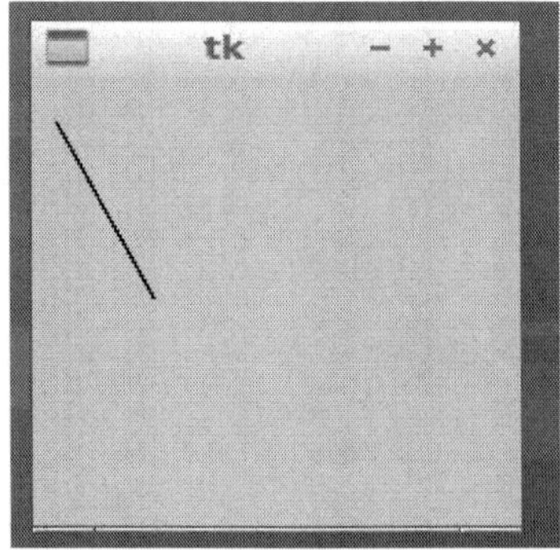


```
"""
Program name: line_1.py
Objective: Draw a straight line on a canvas.

Keywords: canvas, line, default
==================================================================
Comments: When drawing lines you MUST specify the start and end points.
Other properties like color and line width may also be specified, but you don't
HAVE to. Default values will be used if none are explicitly stated.

Tested on: Python 2.6,  Python 2.7 and Python 3.2.3
Author: Mike Ohlson de Fine
"""
# >>>>>>>>>>>>>>>>>>>>>>>>>>>>>>>>>>>>>>>>>>>>>>>>>>>>>>>>>>>>>>>>>
from Tkinter import *   # For Python 3.2 change Tkinter to tkinter, as shown
below.
#from tkinter import *
root = Tk()

canvas_1 = Canvas(root, width=200, height=200)
canvas_1.grid(row=0, column=1)

canvas_1.create_line(10, 20, 50, 100)

root.mainloop()
# >>>>>>>>>>>>>>>>>>>>>>>>>>>>>>>>>>>>>>>>>>>>>>>>>>>>>>>>>>>>>>>>>
```

Points to note

- Only the code between the two herring-bone dividers is needed to make the program.
- The code between the “”” markers is just explanatory text that does not get executed. This is used to explain what the code is

for and which version of Python it was tested on.

- Python 2.x code will not in general run on Python 3.x. You need to make a modification. The line in red above must be used in Python 3.xx code. Just put a “#” character at the front of the “fron Tkinter import*” line and remove the leading “#” from the next line. See Sidebar 1.

Sidebar 1

Python 2.6, Python 2.7 code will not generally run on Python 3.2 and Python 3.3 and higher. This is because some changes were made to the Python 3.x series that are not backwards compatible to the earlier versions like Python 2.7. This is mostly a good thing because there were some things in the earlier Python versions that were incorrect or inconsistent. Some differences were small such as a change in the use of capital 't' in **Tkinter** used in Python 2.x programs and lowercase **tkinter** used in Python 3.x.

In this book the changes needed to make the code run on Python 3.2 are shown as comments in red type.
For example to modify the code in example 1 above for Python 3.2, the word **Tkinter** must be replaced by **tkinter** as follows.

```
# >>>>>>>>>>>>>>>>>>>>>>>>>>>>>>>>>>>>>>>>>>>>>>>>>>>>>>>>>>>>
from tkinter import *  # For Python 3.2 and higher versions.
root = Tk()

canvas_1 = Canvas(root, width=200, height=200)
canvas_1.grid(row=0, column=1)

canvas_1.create_line(10, 20, 50, 100)

root.mainloop()
# >>>>>>>>>>>>>>>>>>>>>>>>>>>>>>>>>>>>>>>>>>>>>>>>>>>>>>>>>>>
```

Discussion

The command *canvas_1.create_line(10, 20, 50, 100)* says the following:
- place the 'pen' at the position x= 10 and y = 20 on the canvas and draw a line to x= 50 and y = 10.

If we want to add another segment to the line all we need do is add another point x,y directing the pen to the new position. We could make the line go on forever snaking all over the canvas.

Points to note

It is important to note that the 'computer-graphics' way of locating positions on a drawing area using pairs of x, y coordinates has the world turned upside down. When the y (vertical) values get larger the locations of points move downwards as shown in the accompanying pictures.

An artist would find the coordinates used for Tkinter confusing – the picture would be upside down.

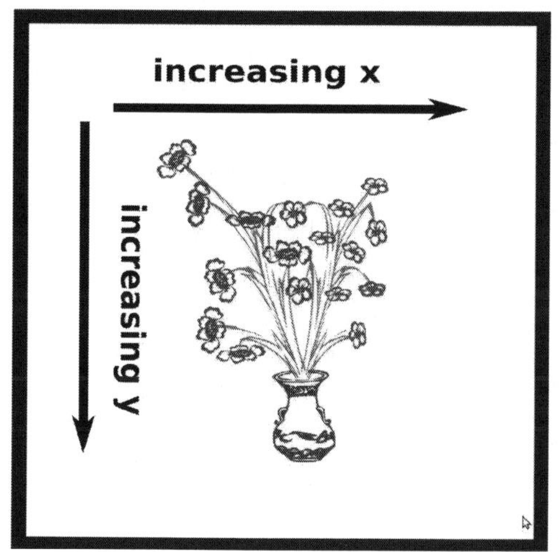

The Tkinter canvas widget has the x=0, y=0 point starting at the top left of the canvas.

What next?

Next we need to know how the character of lines can be changed by means of properties like, color, dashes, arrows or rounded ends.

Draw a Dashed Line

Now we draw three lines each with a different line-and-space pattern.
The parameter **dash=(1,11)** specifies that the visible line segment is one pixel long while the blank gap is 11 pixels long. This pattern is repeated along the length of the line. This example also specifies the x and y coordinates of the line as named variables. That is, we use a name instead of a value.

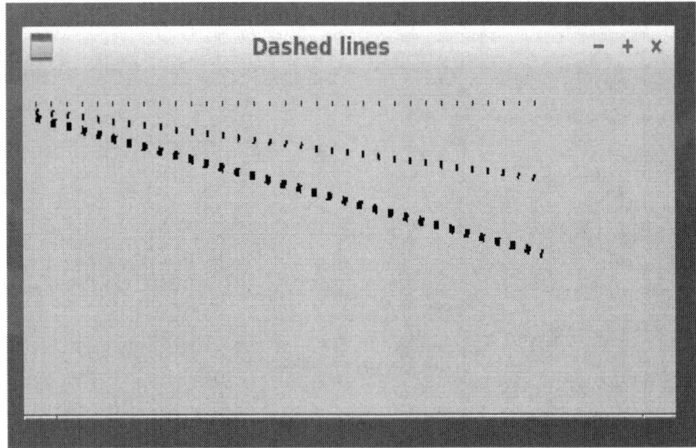


```
"""
Program name: dashed_line_1.py
Objective: Draw some straight dashed lines on a canvas.

Keywords: canvas, line, , dashed line, default
=====================================================
Comments: Start and end points need to be specified explicitly.
Here we also specify three dashed lines as follows:
Firstly line: Dashed with one solid pixels followed by 11 blank pixels.
Repeated till the end of the line is reached.
The second line has 2 solid pixels followed by 10 blank.
The third line has four solid black followed by 8 blank.
In all cases the total pixels in each repeated pattern is 12 pixels.

Here variable names are used instead of numerical values.
Tested on: Python 2.6, Python 2.7.3, Python 3.2.3
Author:       Mike Ohlson de Fine
"""
# >>>>>>>>>>>>>>>>>>>>>>>>>>>>>>>>>>>>>>>>>>>>>>>>>>>>>
from Tkinter import *
#from tkinter import *  # For Python 3.2.3 and higher.
root = Tk()
root.title('Dashed lines')

cw = 500                          # canvas width
ch = 200                          # canvas height
canvas_1 = Canvas(root, width=cw, height=ch)
canvas_1.grid(row=0, column=1)
```

```
x_start = 10
y_start = 20
x_end = 400
y_end = 20
canvas_1.create_line(x_start, y_start, x_end,y_end, dash=(1,11), width = 3)
y_end += 40
canvas_1.create_line(x_start, y_start+4, x_end,y_end+4, dash=(2,10), width = 4)
y_end += 40
canvas_1.create_line(x_start, y_start+8, x_end,y_end+8, dash=(4,8), width = 5)

root.mainloop()
# >>>>>>>>>>>>>>>>>>>>>>>>>>>>>>>>>>>>>>>>>>>>>>>>>>>>>
```

Discussion

What we have done differently here is to use symbolic values in the *canvas_1.create_line(a, b b, d, ...)* when specifying the position of the start and end of the line. This makes our code re-usable and more flexible.

Programming Tip No. 2. Use symbolic variables (named variables) in code. It makes the code completely flexible and re-usable.

Points to note

You may feel we are using variable names that are unnecessarily long. Why not make our code short and neat by using x0, y0 instead of x_start and y_start? The reason we do this is for **future readability.** This comes from painful lessons learned thorough bitter experience. We should always write code as if we want a dear, but not too bright friend with a poor memory, to be able to take our code and use it. Here is the shocker: that dear friend is actually ourself about three months in the future. Trust me on this. About three months after we have completed a batch of code we will have forgotten how we were thinking when we wrote it. Software programmers often find themselves saying “Why did I do that?” before they have learned the lesson.
The famous Python Enhancement Proposals (PEPs) states the following very wise words:

" Explicit is better than implicit.

Simple is better than complex.

...

Readability counts."

Tim Peters, PEP20 aka The Zen of Python

Other new things that have been added in this program are:

- The width of the lines has been increased to 3, 4 and 5 pixels.
- The statement **root.title('Dashed lines')** places a text title in the bar above the canvas.
- The ending y coordinate is increased from one line to the next by adding 40 pixels to the previous value of the coordinate using *y_end += 40.*

What next?

As the actions of our code become more and more complicated we need to work harder at keeping our code simple, explicit and readable. It is a persistent challenge and we seldom do a perfect job. But is is well worth the effort of trying.

Specify Line Color and Width

We now see that all the properties of lines can be controlled.

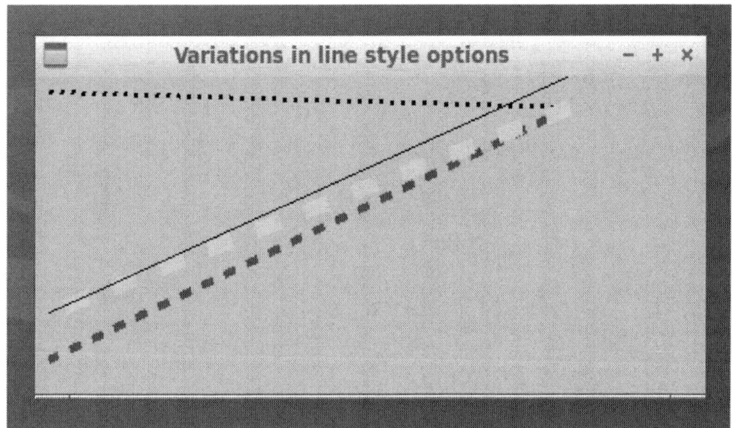


```
"""
Program name: line_styles_1.py
Objective: Four straight lines, different styles on a canvas.

Keywords: canvas, line, , color, dashed line, default
==================================================================
Comments: When drawing lines you MUST specify the start and end points.
Different colors, line widths and styles have been used here.
Variable names are used instead of numerical values.

Tested on: Python 2.6, Python 2.7.3, Python 3.2.3
Author:    Mike Ohlson de Fine
"""
#>>>>>>>>>>>>>>>>>>>>>>>>>>>>>>>>>>>>>>>>>>>>>>>>>>>>>>>>>>>>>>>>>>
>>
from Tkinter import *
#from tkinter import *  # For Python 3.2.3 and higher.
root = Tk()
root.title('Variations in line options')
cw = 500                         # canvas width
ch = 200                         # canvas height
canvas_1 = Canvas(root, width=cw, height=ch, background="pink")
canvas_1.grid(row=0, column=1)

x_start = 10
y_start = 10
x_end = 400
y_end = 20
canvas_1.create_line(x_start, y_start, x_end, y_end, dash=(3,5), width = 3)
```

```
x_start= x_end
y_start= y_end
x_end= 10
y_end= 180
canvas_1.create_line(x_start, y_start, x_end, y_end, dash=(9,), width = 5, fill=
"red")

y_end= 150
canvas_1.create_line(x_start, y_start, x_end, y_end, dash=(19,),width= 10, fill=
'yellow')

y_start= 0
# If not explicitly specified line style reverts to default width = 1,
# and default color = 'black'.
canvas_1.create_line(x_start, y_start, x_end,y_end)

root.mainloop()
#>>>>>>>>>>>>>>>>>>>>>>>>>>>>>>>>>>>>>>>>>>>>>>>>>>>>>>>>
>>>>>>>
```

Discussion

Note that the first 'draw-a-line' instruction could have been written:
canvas_1.create_line(10, 10, 400, 20, dash=(3,5), width = 3)
instead of
canvas_1.create_line(x_start, y_start, x_end, y_end, dash=(3,5), width = 3) which seems long winded. However the terms *x_start, y_start, x_end, y_end* are self-explanatory and therefore make the code easier to understand. Also, as demonstrated in the program, we repeat the same instruction four times.

Points to note

Using symbols like *x_start* instead of explicit numbers like 10 is essential when we start to create re-usable functions. When programs are longer than about 150 lines it becomes insane not to use functions. Although we never see it mentioned much, one of the BEST reasons for using functions is that we only ever need to debug the sequence of code in the function once and never again.

Place Arrowheads on Lines

Up to now we have ignored ways of using the ends of lines to serve a purpose.
There are three ways to start and end lines: chopped-off square, with arrows or rounded.

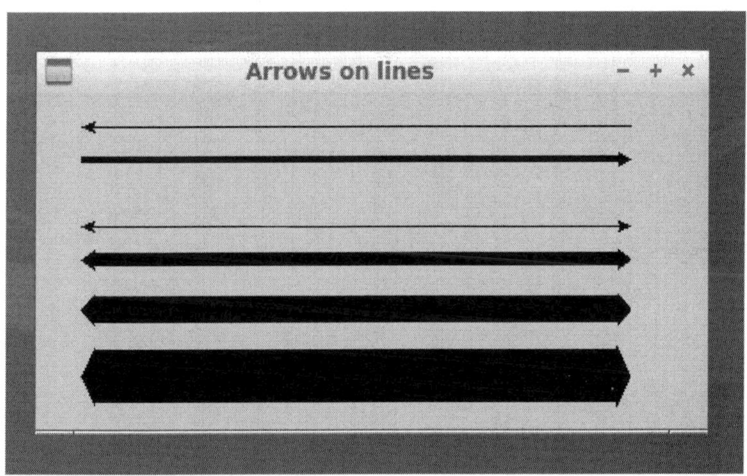


```
"""
Program name: arrowed_line_1.py
Objective: Draw straight with arrowheads at ends specified.

Keywords: canvas, line, , arrowed line, default
=================================================================
Comments: You specify at which end of the line the arrow goes:
"first" = the start, "last" = the end, "both" = each end
The size of the arrow is modified by the line width.  Tkinter does this
automatically.

Tested on: Python 2.6, Python 2.7.3, Python 3.2.3
Author:  Mike Ohlson de Fine
"""
# >>>>>>>>>>>>>>>>>>>>>>>>>>>>>>>>>>>>>>>>>>>>>>>>>>>>>>>>>>>>
from Tkinter import *
```

```
#from tkinter import *  # For Python 3.2.3 and higher.
root = Tk()
root.title('Arrows on lines')
cw = 450                              # canvas width
ch = 200                              # canvas height
canvas_1 = Canvas(root, width=cw, height=ch)
canvas_1.grid(row=0, column=1)

x_start = 30
y_start = 20
x_end = 400
y_end = 20
canvas_1.create_line(x_start, y_start,         x_end,  y_end,            arrow =
"first",   width = 1)
canvas_1.create_line(x_start, y_start+20,    x_end,  y_end+20,      arrow =
"last",    width = 4)
canvas_1.create_line(x_start, y_start+60,    x_end,  y_end+60,      arrow =
"both",    width = 1)
canvas_1.create_line(x_start, y_start+80,    x_end,  y_end+80,      arrow =
"both",    width = 8)
canvas_1.create_line(x_start, y_start+110,  x_end,  y_end+110,    arrow =
"both",    width = 16)
canvas_1.create_line(x_start, y_start+150,  x_end,  y_end+150,    arrow =
"both",    width = 32)

root.mainloop()
# >>>>>>>>>>>>>>>>>>>>>>>>>>>>>>>>>>>>>>>>>>>>>>>>>>>>>>>>>>>
```

Discussion

In the *create_line* instructions above, the attribute of the line *arrow='first'* means
"place an arrow-head at the line-start".

Points to note

The size and shape of the arrow are determined by the line width in Tkinter. We have no control over it. If we want a style of arrow that is different we would need fashion our own using the *create_polygon* instruction as shown later.

Put Rounded End-caps on Lines

Thick lines with rounded end have a pleasing and professional polish.

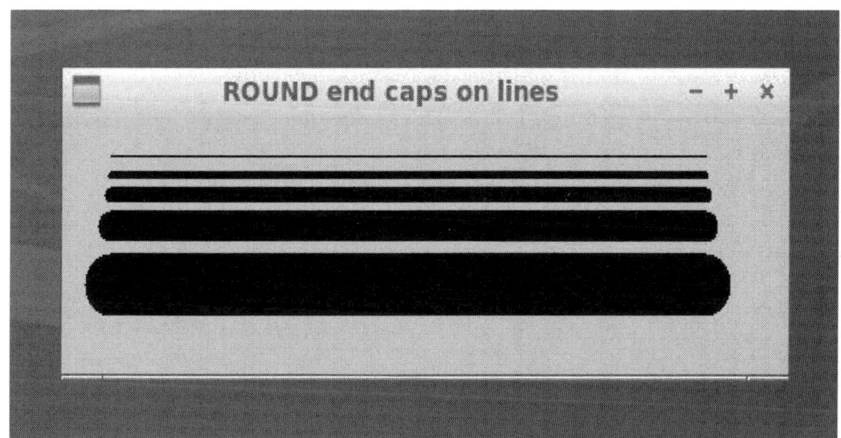


```
"""
Program name: roundcap_line_1.py
Objective: Draw straight with rounded ends.

Keywords: canvas, line, , arrowed line, default
=====================================================
Comments: You specify capstyle=ROUND.
The rounded bit is at bot start and finish of the line.

Tested on: Python 2.6, Python 2.7.3, Python 3.2.3
Author:  Mike Ohlson de Fine
"""
# >>>>>>>>>>>>>>>>>>>>>>>>>>>>>>>>>>>>>>>>>>>>>>>>>>>>>
from Tkinter import *
#from tkinter import *  # For Python 3.2.3 and higher.
root = Tk()
root.title('ROUND end caps on lines')
cw = 450                              # canvas width
ch = 130                              # canvas height
canvas_1 = Canvas(root, width=cw, height=ch)
canvas_1.grid(row=0, column=1)
```

```
x_start = 30
y_start = 20
x_end = 400
y_end = 20
canvas_1.create_line(x_start, y_start,    x_end,y_end,         capstyle= ROUND,
width = 1)
canvas_1.create_line(x_start, y_start+10, x_end,y_end+10, capstyle= ROUND,
width = 4)
canvas_1.create_line(x_start, y_start+20, x_end,y_end+20, capstyle= ROUND,
width = 8)
canvas_1.create_line(x_start, y_start+36, x_end,y_end+36, capstyle= ROUND,
width = 16)
canvas_1.create_line(x_start, y_start+66, x_end,y_end+66, capstyle= ROUND,
width = 32)
root.mainloop()
# >>>>>>>>>>>>>>>>>>>>>>>>>>>>>>>>>>>>>>>>>>>>>>>>>>>>>>>
```

Note

By default, when we don't specify anything, the ends of lines are square and only an explicit *capstyle= ROUND* parameter specification will override the default.

Draw a Two Segment Line

Lines made up of many segments joined end-to-end are how we can draw practically anything no matter how complicated. It is important that we start off with the simplest example which is a line of two segments.

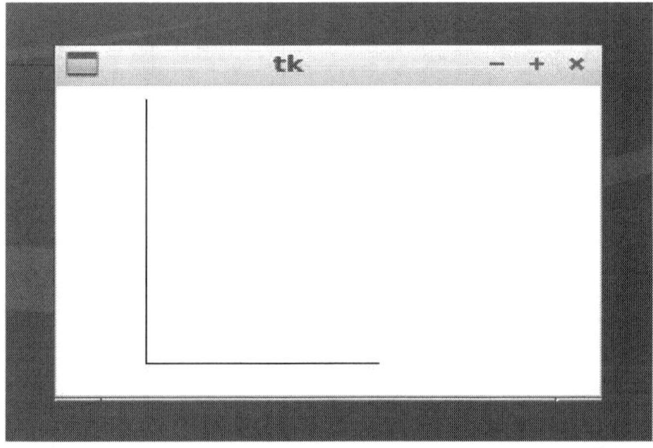


```
"""
Program name: segmented_line_1.py
Objective: Draw a line with a sharp bend on a canvas.

Keywords: canvas, bent line , segmented line
=============================================================
Comments: When drawing lines with many segments you specify location of
each segment. The end of one segment is the start of the next.

Tested on: Python 2.6, Python 2.7.3, Python 3.2.3
Author:    Mike Ohlson de Fine
"""
from Tkinter import *
#from tkinter import *  # For Python 3.2.3 and higher.
root = Tk()

cw = 300                                   # canvas width
ch = 200                                   # canvas height
canvas_1 = Canvas(root, width=cw, height=ch, background="white")
canvas_1.grid(row=0, column=1)

x1 = 50
y1 = 10

x2 = 50
y2 = 180

x3 = 180
y3 = 180

canvas_1.create_line(x1,y1,  x2,y2,  x3,y3)
```

```
root.mainloop()
```

Points to note

As we have done previously we express our *create_line* instruction with symbols rather than explicit numbers. But now there is something new to consider: the arguments (that is, the parameters or attributes) are just a list of numbers *x1,y1, x2,y2, x3,y3.*
That list could be written *my_line = [x1, y1. x2, y2, x3, y3].* Then instruction could have been written *canvas_1.create_line(my_line)* . This is very clear, short and neat.

What next?

Later on in this book, and in other books in this series, this form of line creation is used again and again. The Python list *some_name = [x1, y1, ...]* can consist of many thousands of numbers. We can have a big library of interesting and useful drawings stored on our hard drive to use for a variety of purposes.

There are several neat ways to make complicated drawings using mouse clicks and turn them into named lists that can simply be placed in a *create_line(some_name)* type of statement that will make it appear on a canvas. There are also ways of animating such line drawings by changing their shape, orientation and color but these are topics for later chapters.

Draw a Smooth Curve

The basic two-segment line demonstrated above can be

simply transformed into a smooth curve by including the parameter *smooth="true"* in the *create_line* instruction.

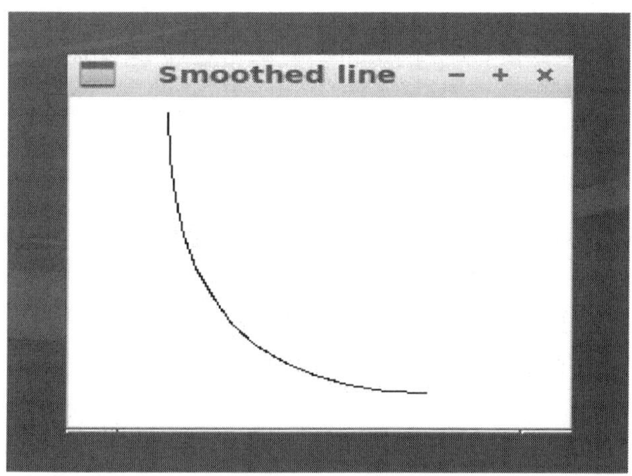


```
"""
Program name: smoothed_line_1.py
Objective: Draw a line with a smooth bend on a canvas.

Keywords: canvas, bent line, curve, smooth line
==================================================
Comments: When drawing lines with many segments you specify location of
each segment. The end of one segment is the start of the next.
In addition choosing the option "smooth="true" gets the line smoothed into a
curve.
The amount of smoothness in the curve is determined by the number of spline
steps. High numbers give a smoother curve.
In this example the default number of splinesteps is in effect.

Tested on: Python 2.6, Python 2.7.3, Python 3.2.3
Author:    Mike Ohlson de Fine
"""
from Tkinter import *
#from tkinter import *  # For Python 3.2.3 and higher.
root = Tk()
root.title('Smoothed line')
cw = 250                                  # canvas width
ch = 200                                  # canvas height
canvas_1 = Canvas(root, width=cw, height=ch, background="white")
canvas_1.grid(row=0, column=1)
```

```
x1 = 50
y1 = 10
x2 = 50
y2 = 180
x3 = 180
y3 = 180

canvas_1.create_line(x1,y1,  x2,y2,  x3,y3, smooth="true")

root.mainloop()
```

Points to note

The way Tkinter transforms two straight line segments into a curve is to break the line into many short lengths and fit them end to end to approximate a perfectly smooth curve. By default the number of short segments used is 12. We can change that by using the parameter *splinesteps = N* where N is the number of straight pieces approximating the curve.

What next?

Choice of the number of steps can present a dilemma. How smooth is smooth enough?
The next example experiments with the number of steps. It appears that 12 steps, the default, is good enough to make a curve that looks good. There are no visible angles or flats.

Vary the Smoothness of Curves

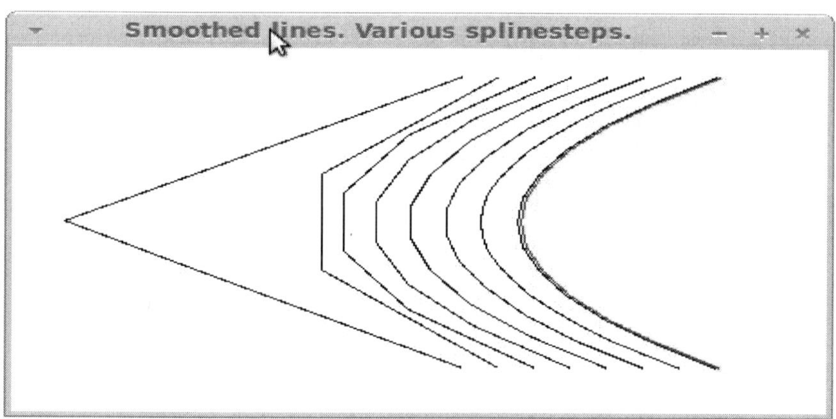

Sometimes we want to alter the smoothness of a curve. This is achieved by giving explicit values to the *splinesteps* parameter associated with the smooth='true' specification.

```
"""
Program name: smoothed_lines_splinesteps_1.py
Objective: Draw a family of lines with a progressive smoothness.

Keywords: canvas, bent line, curve, splinesteps, smooth line
=============================================================
Comments: The amount of smoothness in the curve is determined
by the number of spline steps. High numbers give a smoother curve.
In this example we vary the number of segments in the smoothed curve.

Tested on: Python 2.6, Python 2.7.3, Python 3.2.3
Author:    Mike Ohlson de Fine
"""
from Tkinter import *
#from tkinter import *  # For Python 3.2.3 and higher.
root = Tk()
root.title('Smoothed lines. Various splinesteps.')
cw = 450                          # canvas width
ch = 250                          # canvas height
canvas_1 = Canvas(root, width=cw, height=ch, background="white")
canvas_1.grid(row=0, column=1)

offset = 0.0
x1 = 250+offset
y1 = 20
```

```
x2 = 30+offset
y2 = 120
x3 = 250+offset
y3 = 220
my_line = [ x1, y1, x2, y2, x3, y3 ]

canvas_1.create_line(x1,y1,  x2,y2,  x3,y3, smooth="false")
offset += 20.0
x1, x2, x3 = 250+offset, 30+offset, 250+offset
canvas_1.create_line(x1,y1,  x2,y2,  x3,y3, smooth="true", splinesteps = 3)
offset += 20.0
x1, x2, x3 = 250+offset, 30+offset, 250+offset
my_line = [ x1, y1, x2, y2, x3, y3 ]
canvas_1.create_line(x1,y1,  x2,y2,  x3,y3, smooth="true", splinesteps = 5)
offset += 20.0
x1, x2, x3 = 250+offset, 30+offset, 250+offset
my_line = [ x1, y1, x2, y2, x3, y3 ]
canvas_1.create_line(x1,y1,  x2,y2,  x3,y3, smooth="true", splinesteps = 7)
offset += 20.0
x1, x2, x3 = 250+offset, 30+offset, 250+offset
my_line = [ x1, y1, x2, y2, x3, y3 ]
canvas_1.create_line(x1,y1,  x2,y2,  x3,y3, smooth="true", splinesteps = 9)
offset += 20.0
x1, x2, x3 = 250+offset, 30+offset, 250+offset
my_line = [ x1, y1, x2, y2, x3, y3 ]
canvas_1.create_line(x1,y1,  x2,y2,  x3,y3, smooth="true", splinesteps = 11)
offset += 20.0
x1, x2, x3 = 250+offset, 30+offset, 250+offset
my_line = [ x1, y1, x2, y2, x3, y3 ]
canvas_1.create_line(x1,y1,  x2,y2,  x3,y3, smooth="true", splinesteps = 20)
offset += 20.0
x1, x2, x3 = 250+offset, 30+offset, 250+offset
my_line = [ x1, y1, x2, y2, x3, y3 ]
canvas_1.create_line(x1,y1,  x2,y2,  x3,y3, smooth="true", splinesteps = 12)
offset += 2.0
x1, x2, x3 = 250+offset, 30+offset, 250+offset
my_line = [ x1, y1, x2, y2, x3, y3 ]
canvas_1.create_line(x1,y1,  x2,y2,  x3,y3, smooth="true", fill='red')

root.mainloop()
```

Discussion

We have drawn a series of lines starting at the left with no smoothness specified and then with increasing smoothness from *splinesteps = 3* up to *splinesteps = 20*. The last two lines on the right are the default (red line) and splinesteps = 12. They have identical smoothness. The line with splinesteps = 11 is too rough for most purposes and going beyond splinesteps = 20 does make a noticeable improvement, particularly at the apex of the curve (the sharpest portion).

The code used to draw each curve has been put down separately in order to show clearly how each curve differs from its neighbors. It could be achieved more compactly if the sequence if instructions:
offset += 20.0
x1, x2, x3 = 250+offset, 30+offset, 250+offset
canvas_1.create_line(x1,y1, x2,y2, x3,y3, smooth="true", splinesteps = 3)
were written as a function. At this stage we do not want to burden the reader with a side trip about functions. We need to focus on the curve drawing effect.

Point to note

The statement *offset += 20.0* means "take the current value of the variable *offset* and add 20 to it and assign this as the new value of *offset.*

Draw a Rectangle

Now we draw rectangles and squares.

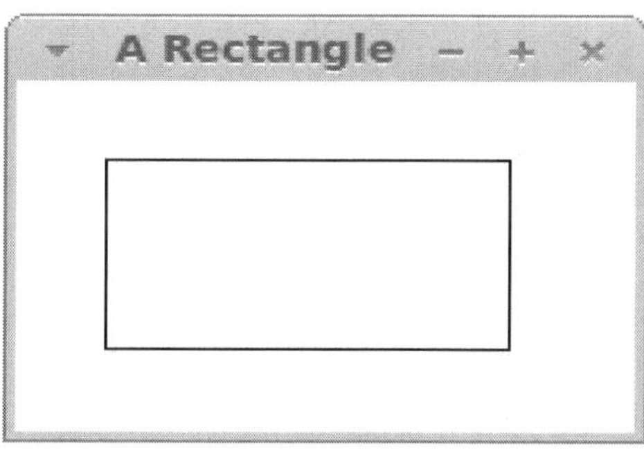

```
"""
Program name: rectangle_1.py
Objective: A rectangle.

Keywords: canvas, rectangle
==================================================
Comments: A rectangle is specified by two points:
The top left corner (30, 30) and the bottom right (80, 120).

Tested on: Python 2.6, Python 2.7.3, Python 3.2.3
Author:  Mike Ohlson de Fine
"""
#>>>>>>>>>>>>>>>>>>>>>>>>>>>>>>>>>>>>>>>>
from Tkinter import *
#from tkinter import *  # For Python 3.2.3 and higher.
root = Tk()
root.title('A Rectangle')

cw = 200                              # canvas width
ch = 130                              # canvas height
canvas_1 = Canvas(root, width=cw, height=ch, background="white")
canvas_1.grid(row=0, column=1)

canvas_1.create_rectangle( 30, 30, 160, 100 )
root.mainloop()
#>>>>>>>>>>>>>>>>>>>>>>>>>>>>>>>>>>>>>>>>
```

Discussion

Drawing rectangle by starting at the top left corner is not always convenient. If we needed to use a colored rectangle to represent the level of liquid in a tank we would want to fixt the position of the bottom and have the top rise and fall to represent liquid level. The next couple of examples explore ways to solve this problem.

Points to note

There is no special function for drawing squares. A square is just a rectangle whose height and width are equal.

What next?

The position of the starting point of drawn shapes like rectangles, ellipses or more complex polygons is something that will often make us scratch our heads because there is never a best choice. Later we will discover how to rotate, shift, expand, shrink and distort shapes. The best position for fixed anchor points of the shape will depend on what we plan will happen afterward. A bouncing ball hitting a wall should be anchored to the wall until it has bounced free. This actual position of this anchor point will change depending on whether the ball is striking the left-hand or right-hand wall. Or whether it is striking the ceiling or floor. We look at these problems in chapter 4 where we transform the shape of complex polygons.

Draw a Square

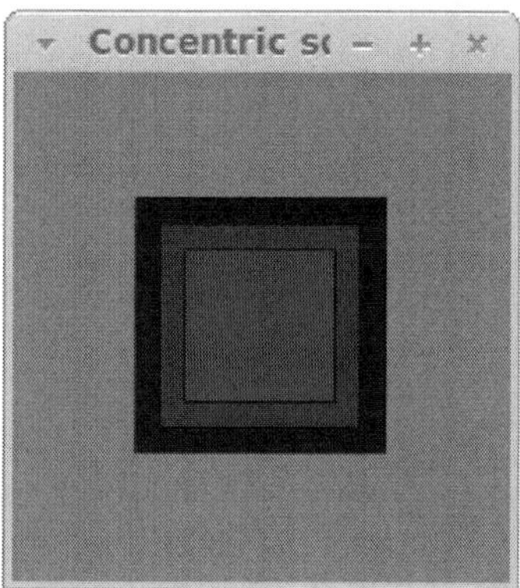


```
"""
Program name: concentric_squares_1.py
Objective: Draw sets of squares all with the same center..

Keywords: rectangle, square, concentric
==================================================
Comments: A square is just a rectangle with height equal to width.
```

```
To place each square on the same center we use  some arithmetic using
center and width/height values.
This has an advantage, to seen later, of making each 'create_rectangle
command identical.

Tested on: Python 2.6, Python 2.7.3, Python 3.2.3
Author:         Mike Ohlson de Fine
"""
# >>>>>>>>>>>>>>>>>>>>>>>>>>>>>>>>>>>>>>>>>>>>>>>>>>>>>>>
from Tkinter import *
#from tkinter import *  # For Python 3.2.3 and higher.
root = Tk()
root.title('Concentric squares')
cw = 200                                # canvas width
ch = 400                                # canvas height
canvas_1 = Canvas(root, width=cw, height=200, background="green")
canvas_1.grid(row=0, column=1)

# dark blue
x_center = 100
y_center = 100
x_width  = 100
y_height = 100
kula = "darkblue"
canvas_1.create_rectangle( x_center - x_width/2,  y_center - y_height/2,
x_center + x_width/2,  y_center + y_height/2, fill=kula)

#dark red
x_width  = 80
y_height = 80
kula ="darkred"
canvas_1.create_rectangle( x_center - x_width/2,  y_center - y_height/2,
x_center + x_width/2,  y_center + y_height/2, fill=kula)

#dark green
x_width  = 60
y_height = 60
kula ="darkgreen"
canvas_1.create_rectangle( x_center - x_width/2,  y_center - y_height/2,
x_center + x_width/2,  y_center + y_height/2, fill=kula)

root.mainloop()
root.destroy() # optional; see description below
```

Discussion

Rectangles and squares are well behaved shapes. Irregular triangles and other polygons are more difficult. For triangles we would need to calculate the center as being where the lines that go from each tip to the middle of the opposite side intersect. Relax. We are not going to go there. For awkward shapes we will use the idea of a bounding box to simplify our job. A bounding box is the rectangle into which our shape will fit exactly. Once we have this box we can choose our anchor reference positions to be any of the four corners or the middle. This is dealt with in chapter 4.

Points to note

We have started to use color for the first time. This adds a new dimension to our creative expression. Color makes a dramatic difference to drawn shapes. The choice of background color above seems particularly jarring. The loud green just does not blend well with the dark muted squares. We can almost hear a discordant noise when we see the picture. Effective color combinations tap into our subconscious emotional response. At this stage we just need to be aware of this fact. In chapter 3 we examine color.

What next?

In the next image a calmer background color has been used with the same three rectangle colors. It is not the best but it seems calmer.

Draw a Set of Overlapping Rectangles

When we draw several objects on a Tkinter canvas we need to know how execution order or sequence affects the arrangement and layout of objects. As each object is created Tkinter assigns it a sequential *item number*, also called an *item handle* which is an integer. They are drawn on the canvas in the sequence they are created – the objects created first go to the bottom. There are ways of changing the sequence after initial execution but we will not use them here.

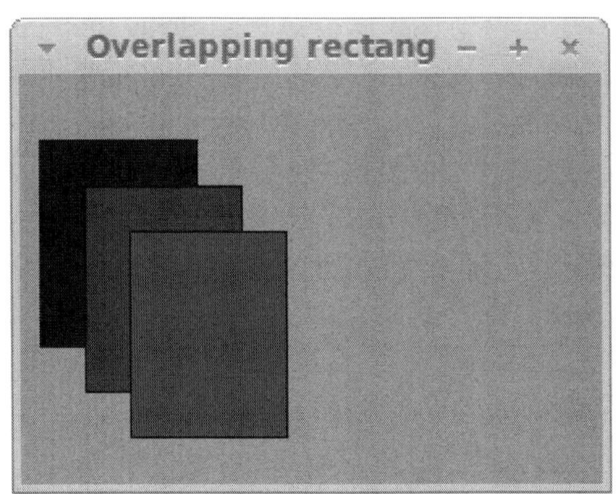


```
"""
Program name: overlap_rectangles_1.py
Objective: A set of overlapping rectangles.

Keywords: canvas, rectangles, overlap
=====================================================
Comments: Overlapping rectangle are placed down on the canvas in the
same sequence that they appear in the code. That is, the last one is on top.

Tested on: Python 2.6, Python 2.7.3, Python 3.2.3
Author:          Mike Ohlson de Fine

"""
#>>>>>>>>>>>>>>>>>>>>>>>>>>>>>>>>>>>>>>>>>>
from Tkinter import *
#from tkinter import *  # For Python 3.2.3 and higher.
root = Tk()
root.title('Overlapping rectangles')

cw = 260                              # canvas width
ch = 180                              # canvas height
canvas_1 = Canvas(root, width=cw, height=ch, background="turquoise")
canvas_1.grid(row=0, column=1)
```

```
# dark blue rectangle - painted first therefore at the bottom
x_start = 10
y_start = 30
x_width =70
y_height = 90
kula ="darkblue"
canvas_1.create_rectangle( x_start,  y_start,\
                    x_start + x_width, y_start + y_height,\
                    fill=kula)

#dark red rectangle - second therefore in the middle
x_start = 30
y_start = 50
kula ="darkred"
canvas_1.create_rectangle( x_start,  y_start,\
                    x_start + x_width, y_start + y_height,\
                    fill=kula)

#dark green rectangle - painted last therefore on top of previous ones.
x_start = 50
y_start = 70
kula ="darkgreen"
canvas_1.create_rectangle( x_start,  y_start,\
                    x_start + x_width, y_start + y_height,\
                    fill=kula)
root.mainloop()
```

Discussion

Order if instruction execution determines the layering sequence of shapes on a canvas. A large shape could be used to hide smaller shapes. This is wasteful of computer resources and there are better ways to control which objects are visible. The is a parameter in all the Tkinter line, rectangle, oval and polygon instructions called *tagname.* Tagnames can be used to delete or re-paint objects selectively. We do not need to do any of this in this book but is needed in animation as can be seen in book 2.

Points to note

We have established a convention so far of using the labels

x_start, y_start to denote the first coordinate position of any drawn object. It follows that x_end, y_end would denote the position of the end point, particularly of lines. Throughout this book we have chosen to use longer but explicit names for variables. Explicit and clear is always good.

What next?

We started to use color in the previous two programs. The colors have been solid and opaque. Does Python allow us to use semi-transparent colors? It doe to a limited extent in vector graphics. The partial transparency is through the use of a *stipple* parameter specification. See the next example.

Draw Rectangles with Stipple Fill

When we need to make semi-transparent objects the stipple fill parameter can provide this.
The definition of stipple is “to draw with dots instead of lines”. Tkinter pre-defines four values of stipple: gray12, gray25, gray50 and gray70. With gray 12 only 12% of the area is covered with dots while with gray75, 75% of the area is covered.

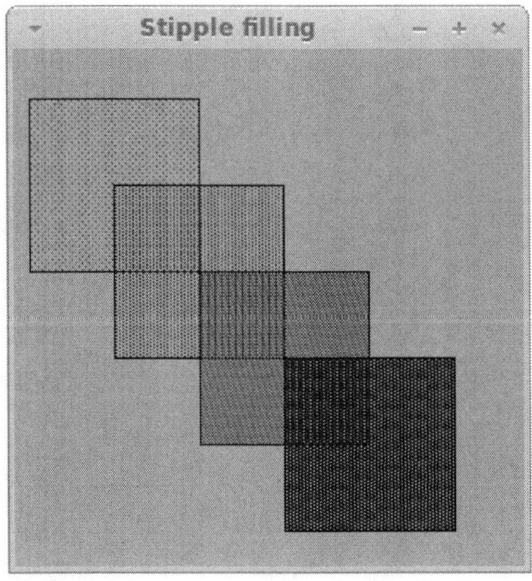

```
"""
Program name: stipple_fill_1.py
Objective: Make semi-transparent objects using stipple filling.
Stipplebrush: stipple values: "gray12", "gray25", "gray50", or "gray75

Keywords: canvas, rectangles, overlapp, stipple fill
=========================================================
Comments: Overlapping rectangles are placed down on the canvas in the
same sequence that they appear in the code. With stipple filling this does have an
influence on the final impression of color.

Tested on: Python 2.6, Python 2.7.3, Python 3.2.3
Author:         Mike Ohlson de Fine
"""
#>>>>>>>>>>>>>>>>>>>>>>>>>>>>>>>>>>>>>>>>>>>
from Tkinter import *
#from tkinter import *  # For Python 3.2.3 and higher.
root = Tk()
root.title('Stipple filling')

cw = 300                                      # canvas width
ch = 300                                      # canvas height
canvas_1 = Canvas(root, width=cw, height=ch, background="black")
canvas_1.grid(row=0, column=1)

# Dark purple rectangle - painted first therefore at the bottom.
x_start = 10
y_start = 30
x_width =100
y_height = 100
kula ="purple"
canvas_1.create_rectangle( x_start,  y_start,\
                    x_start + x_width, y_start + y_height,\
                    fill=kula, stipple = "gray12")

# Dark red rectangle - second therefore in the middle.
x_start = 60
y_start = 80
kula ="darkred"
canvas_1.create_rectangle( x_start,  y_start,\
                    x_start + x_width, y_start + y_height,\
                    fill=kula, stipple = "gray25")

# Dark green rectangle - painted last therefore on top of previous ones.
```

```
x_start = 110
y_start = 130
kula ="darkgreen"
canvas_1.create_rectangle( x_start,  y_start,\
                     x_start + x_width, y_start + y_height,\
                     fill=kula, stipple = "gray50")

# Dark blue  rectangle - painted last therefore on top of previous ones.
x_start = 160
y_start = 180

kula ="darkblue"
canvas_1.create_rectangle( x_start,  y_start,\
                     x_start + x_width, y_start + y_height,\
                     fill=kula, stipple = "gray75")
root.mainloop()
```

Discussion

Because the stipple fill patterns are made of precisely spaced dots the effect of overlapping stippled areas is not completely predictable. If one set of dots exactly covers the dots below then the shape underneath will be invisible but if it is shifted one pixel sideways or upwards then both will be visible and the resulting color will be a mixture of the two.

Points to note

The border or outline of any stipple filled shapes is not stippled.
The color of the background has a strong influence on the perceived color of the filled area.

What next?

As we will see in the next example, wide outline borders with contrasting colors dominate the impression of color of the stipple filled area. Unless we have good reasons for doing so it is best to minimize the effect of outlines by making them the same color as the fill area.

Draw Rectangles with Stipple Fill Variations

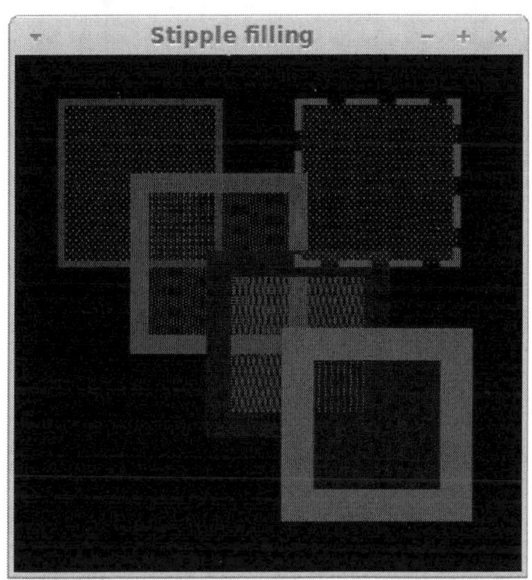


```
"""
Program name: stipple_fill_2.py
Objective: Stipple filled rectangles with distinctive borders.
Stipplebrush: stipple values: "gray12", "gray25", "gray50", or "gray75

Keywords: canvas, rectangles, overlap, stipple fill, dashed outline
=======================================================
Comments:Border color and width with stipple filling has a marked influence on
the final impression of color.

Tested on: Python 2.6,
Author:     Mike Ohlson de Fine
"""
#>>>>>>>>>>>>>>>>>>>>>>>>>>>>>>>>>>>>>>>>>>
from Tkinter import *
#from tkinter import *  # For Python 3.2.3 and higher.
root = Tk()
root.title('Stipple filling')
```

```
cw = 320                          # canvas width
ch = 320                          # canvas height
canvas_1 = Canvas(root, width=cw, height=ch, background="black")
canvas_1.grid(row=0, column=1)

# Dark purple rectangle - painted first therefore at the bottom
x_start = 30
y_start = 30
x_width =100
y_height = 100
kula ="purple"
canvas_1.create_rectangle( x_start,  y_start,
                    x_start + x_width, y_start + y_height,
                    fill=kula, outline= "darkred", width=4, stipple = "gray12")

# Dark red rectangle - second therefore in the middle.
x_start = 80
y_start = 80
kula ="darkred"
canvas_1.create_rectangle( x_start,  y_start,
                    x_start + x_width, y_start + y_height,
                    fill=kula, outline= "darkgreen", width=12, stipple = "gray25")

# Dark green rectangle - painted last therefore on top of previous ones.
x_start = 130
y_start = 130
kula ="darkgreen"
canvas_1.create_rectangle( x_start,  y_start,
                    x_start + x_width, y_start + y_height,
                    fill=kula, outline= "darkblue", width=16, stipple = "gray50")

# Dark blue  rectangle - painted last therefore on top of previous ones.
x_start = 180
y_start = 180

kula ="darkblue"
canvas_1.create_rectangle( x_start,  y_start,
                    x_start + x_width, y_start + y_height,
                    fill=kula, outline= "purple", width=20, stipple = "gray75")

# Dark purple rectangle - painted first therefore at the bottom.
x_start = 180
y_start = 30
x_width =100
y_height = 100
```

```
kula ="purple"
canvas_1.create_rectangle( x_start,  y_start,\
                x_start + x_width, y_start + y_height,\
                fill=kula, outline= "red", width=4, dash=16, stipple = "gray12")
root.mainloop()
```

Discussion

Although we have not focused on the influence of different background colors they are a major factor in the perceived impression of areas filled with stippled colors. Some pleasing and interesting effects arise when used in animated canvases.
In the next chapter we also see a simple demonstration of the influence of different background colors.

What next?

In this chapter we have explored in a fair amount of detail, all the major graphic variations that can be controlled by the programmer. Some of the examples can be criticized for being unnecessarily lengthy. They could have been made much more compact through 'cleverer' programming. But that would defeat the object of keeping things simple. Simple to understand, that is. Beware of clever if it means less clear. With well designed *for loops* and functions the programs would have been shorter but that would burden new would-be programmers with distractions of understanding. It is like trying to learn how to dance the tango and play the drums at the same time. One makes better progress doing one at a time.

2

Graphic Elements: Ovals

In this chapter we will cover how to draw:

- a circles
- an arc-circle
- a circle specified by radius and center positioned
- sets of concentric circles
- loop-generated concentric circles
- ellipses
- arrays of ellipses
- rounded rectangles

- rounded rectangles as a function

The basic elements of drawings are lines, ovals and rectangles. A circle is just a special case of an oval whose major and minor axes are the same length. Ovals are determined by the size of the rectangle that they will fit inside. This rectangle is called the "bounding box".
In this chapter we demonstrate some new and important programming ideas:

- Loops to control sequences of drawings
- Creation of our own functions where Tkinter does not provide what we need.

Draw a Circle

Here we draw a circle 100 pixels in diameter. We do something new here in the way we define the coordinates of the bounding box for the circle. We define a tuple list xy = 20, 20, 120, 120. The result is that **canvas_1.create_oval(xy)** has the same result as writing **canvas_1.create_oval[20, 20, 120,** 120], except that the first form is neater and actually easier to understand.
This is a better way to specify position coordinates because it provides a versatile and powerful way of manipulating long, complex shapes using the Python language. It also makes it easy to store and retrieve shapes as plain text files. In chapter 4 and 5 we use this extensively. It becomes possible to manipulate complicated shapes in two and three dimensions. They can be rotated, re-sized, shifted and skewed easily.

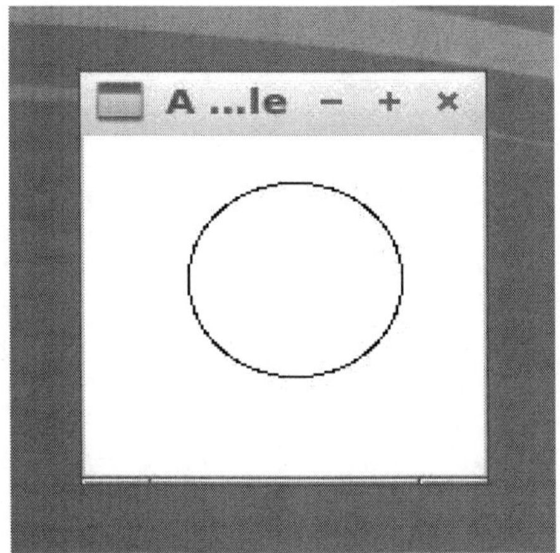


```
“”””
Program name: circle_1.py
Objective: A circle is a special case of an oval.

Keywords: canvas, oval, circle
===================================================
Comments: A circle is a special case of an oval and is defined by the box it fits
inside. This bounding box is specified in the same way as rectangles,
from bottom-left to top-right.

Tested on: Python 2.6, Python 2.7.3, Python 3.2.3
Author:        Mike Ohlson de Fine
"""
#>>>>>>>>>>>>>>>>>>>>>>>>>>>>>>>>>>>>>>>>>
from Tkinter import *
#from tkinter import *  # For Python 3.2.3 and higher.
root = Tk()
root.title('A circle')

cw = 150                              # canvas width
ch = 140                              # canvas height
canvas_1 = Canvas(root, width=cw, height=ch, background="white")
canvas_1.grid(row=0, column=1)

# specify bottom-left and top-right as a set of four numbers named 'xy'
xy = [20, 20, 120, 120]

canvas_1.create_oval(xy)
root.mainloop()
```

Discussion

This is very simple code. We have defined the oval we want drawn as the oval that will fit exactly inside a box starting at x_start = 20, y_start = 20 (bottom-left corner) and ending at x_end = 120, y_end -120. This is a perfectly square bounding box and the only oval shape that can fit exactly inside it is a perfect circle.

We make our code simple and neat by placing our start and end coordinates for the bounding box as the elements of a list named xy.

We will use this method of passing coordinates to a function more and more. It is undoubtedly the best way.

Points to note

There is another Tkinter canvas shape that is related to drawing circles and that is the *create_arc* function. However it is a bad way to draw circles because it never completes the circle because it is intended only to draw 'pie-slices' of a disk. The result of this is that there is always at least one line cutting the disc from the center to the diameter.

This is demonstrated in the next example.

Draw an Arc-Circle (Not a good choice)

Tkinter's create_arc function is definitely intended to draw pie slices of circles AND ovals. It is a poor method for drawing pure circles because it leaves a visible 'cut' in the drawing.

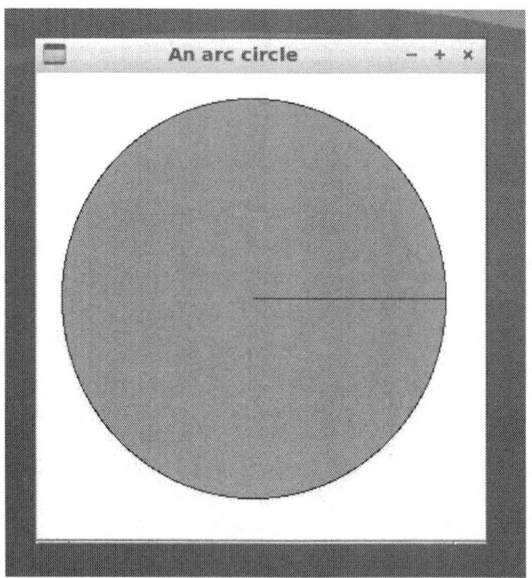

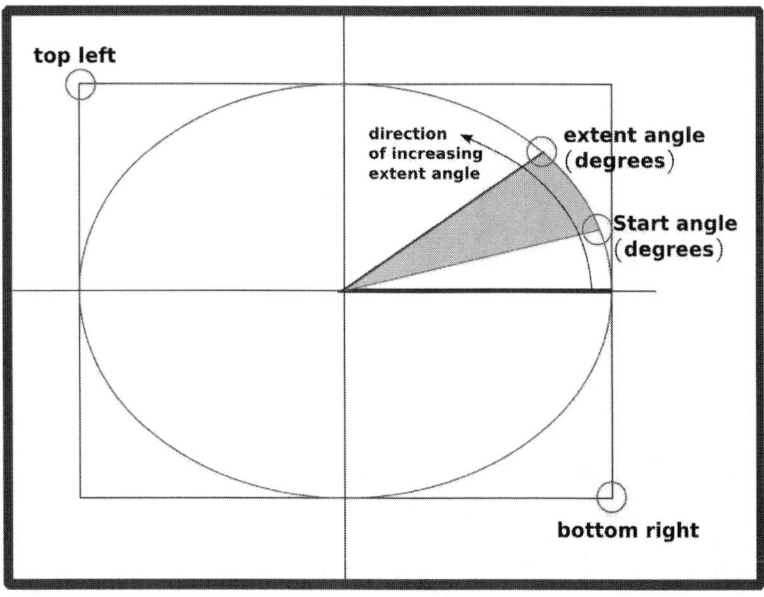

"""

Program name: arc_circle_1.py
Objective: Draw a circle as an almost complete circular arc

Keywords: circle, arc

```
=========================================================
Comments: The syntax of the instruction is:
create_arc(x_top_left, y_top_left, x_bottom_right, x_bottom_right,
start=degrees,extent=degrees,fill="cyan")

This is not a good way to make circles because they are never complete.
You cannot close the circle by asking for a 360 degree extent - you end up
with a line. 359.99999999 etc. is a close as you can get. But you are always
left with the radial line.
If you try to make an entire disk you end up with the excluded portion - merely a
line. Rather use the 'create_oval' function.

Tested on: Python 2.6, Python 2.7.3, Python 3.2.3
Author:        Mike Ohlson de Fine
"""
#>>>>>>>>>>>>>>>>>>>>>>>>>>>>>>>>>>>>>>>>>>>
from Tkinter import *
#from tkinter import *  # For Python 3.2.3 and higher.
root = Tk()
root.title('An arc circle')
cw = 350                          # canvas width
ch = 350                          # canvas height
canvas_1 = Canvas(root, width=cw, height=ch, background="white")
canvas_1.grid(row=0, column=1)

xy = 20, 20, 320, 320         # bounding box from x0,y0 to x1, y1
                              # arc from start_angle, in degrees to finish_angle
canvas_1.create_arc(xy, start=0, extent=359.999999999, fill="cyan")

root.mainloop()
#>>>>>>>>>>>>>>>>>>>>>>>>>>>>>>>>>>>>>>>>>>>
```

Discussion

The reason the create_arc is not good for drawing circles is that a key argument passed to the function is the *extent=number_of_degrees* and Tkinter does not allow it to be a complete circle at 360 degrees. It always has to be a fraction less, hence there is always a visible cut to mar the perfectness of the disk.

Points to note

The *create_arc* function is tailor made for pie charts used in business presentations. We can imagine a kind of sales, market-share, revenue, blah-blah type pre-formatted presentation where all the pie-charts are ready and waiting for the latest figures to be entered and shown within seconds to the management team. Fun and exciting? Okaaay.
It could also be used to make a pacman apple gobbler. More exciting? Oh Yeah!
However (there is often a *however* lurking behind a corner) these *create_arcs* are just the right thing for making rectangles with round corners as we will see in a few example's times.

What next?

This way of drawing circles by specifying the bottom left corner as the start and the top right as the end is inconvenient. Circles are more logically specified by stating the location of their center and their radius. When we draw a circle on a piece of paper using a compass we place the sharp tip of the compass where the center is to be and set the divider part to the radius of the circle and then rotate the pencil holder around and lo-and-behold a circle appears. This is the thinking behind the next example.

Draw a Circle, Specifying Radius and Center

Most of the time when we draw circles we would like to define it simply by stating where the center must be placed and how big it should be (the radius or the diameter). In this example we achieve this by using the expression
canvas_1.create_oval(center_x - Radius/2, center_y - Radius/2,   center_x + Radius/2, center_y + Radius/2,)
to define our circle.

This shows us that we can place complex algebraic expressions inside Tkinter functions where variables can be used.

```
"""
Program name: radius_center_circle_1.py
Objective: A circle specified in terms of its radius and center position.

Keywords: canvas, oval, circle, center, radius
============================================================
Comments:A circle is a special case of an oval and is defined by the
box it fits inside. The bounding box here is defined in terms of the radius
and position of the center. This is a more convenient and logical  way of drawing
a circle (geometrically speaking).

Tested on: Python 2.6, Python 2.7.3, Python 3.2.3
Author:         Mike Ohlson de Fine
"""
from Tkinter import *
#from tkinter import *  # For Python 3.2.3 and higher.
root = Tk()
root.title('Radius and center circle.')

cw = 150                                  # canvas width
ch = 140                                  # canvas height
canvas_1 = Canvas(root, width=cw, height=ch, background="white")
canvas_1.grid(row=0, column=1)

# specify bottom-left and top-right as a set of four numbers named 'xy'
center_x = 80
center_y = 60
Radius = 80

canvas_1.create_oval(center_x - Radius/2, center_y - Radius/2,\
                     center_x + Radius/2, center_y + Radius/2)
root.mainloop()
```

Discussion

In terms of a bounding box for our circle the bottom left position is $center\_x - Radius/2, center\_y - Radius/2$ and the top right is $center\_x + Radius/2, center\_y + Radius/2$

What next?

We demonstrate the value of defining circles using their center and radius in the next example where we want to create a family of circles on a common center.

Draw Concentric Circles

Here we show the usefulness of expressing circles in terms of radius and center by being able to draw concentric circles simply.

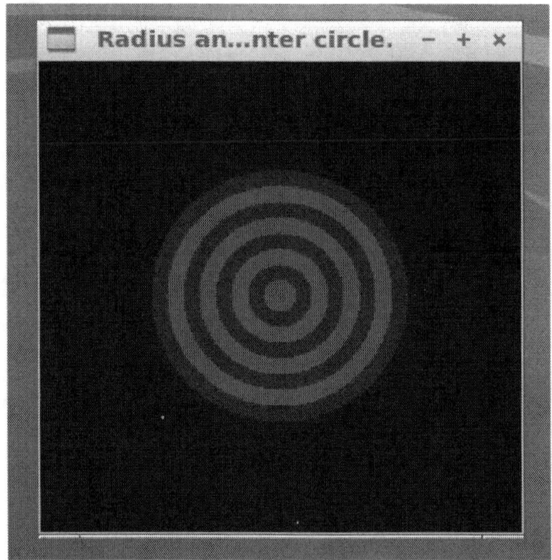

"""
Program name: concentric_circles_1.py
Objective: A set of circles specified in terms of their radius and center position.

Keywords: canvas, oval, circle, center, radius
==
Comments: A circle is a special case of an oval and is defined by the box it fits inside. The bounding box here is defined in terms of the radius and position of the center. This is a more convenient and logical way of drawing a circle (geometrically speaking).

```
Tested on: Python 2.6, Python 2.7.3, Python 3.2.3
Author:         Mike Ohlson de Fine
"""
from Tkinter import *
#from tkinter import *  # For Python 3.2.3 and higher.
root = Tk()
root.title('Radius and center circle.')

cw = 300                            # canvas width
ch = 300                            # canvas height
canvas_1 = Canvas(root, width=cw, height=ch, background="darkblue")
canvas_1.grid(row=0, column=1)

# specify bottom-left and top-right as a set of four numbers named 'xy'
center_x = 150
center_y = 150
Radius = 150

canvas_1.create_oval(center_x - Radius/2, center_y - Radius/2,\
              center_x + Radius/2, center_y + Radius/2,\
              fill= 'red', outline='blue', width= 10)
Radius = 110
canvas_1.create_oval(center_x - Radius/2, center_y - Radius/2,\
              center_x + Radius/2, center_y + Radius/2,\
              fill= 'red', outline='blue', width= 10)

Radius = 70
canvas_1.create_oval(center_x - Radius/2, center_y - Radius/2,\
              center_x + Radius/2, center_y + Radius/2,\
              fill= 'red', outline='blue', width= 10)

Radius = 30
canvas_1.create_oval(center_x - Radius/2, center_y - Radius/2,\
              center_x + Radius/2, center_y + Radius/2,\
              fill= 'red', outline='blue', width= 10)
root.mainloop()
```

Discussion

We leave the center constant and only need to alter the radius for each circle.

Points to note

We will see that the color combination of red and blue used in this example is a bit disturbing. Blue and red placed next to each other confuse the focusing optics of the eye because red is at the long wavelength end of the visible spectrum and blue is a the short wavelength end. This means that the two colors have slightly different distances to go through the eyeball and end up being focused at slightly different positions. Both will never be in perfect focus at the same time. Our brains do no approve.

What next?

When we want to draw many, many circles our code length will be long if we were just to extend the above program. To overcome this problem we use the power and beauty of the *for loop*.

Draw Loop controlled Concentric Circles

This program is similar in structure to the previous one except that it draws 32 more circles yet it is a shorter program. This is what makes loops so valuable.

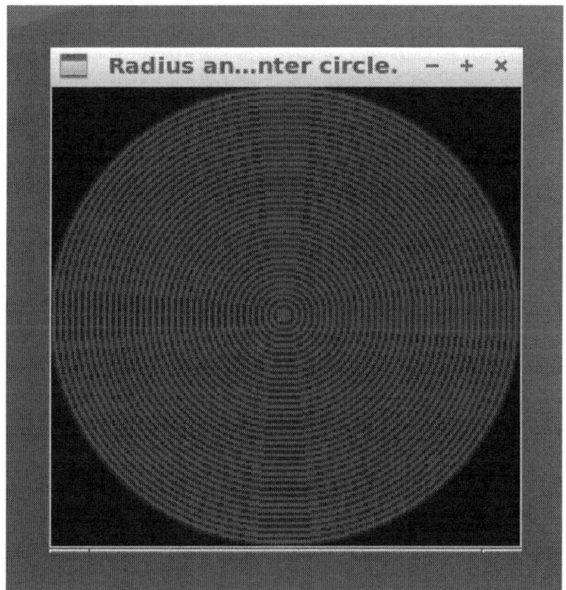


```
"""
Program name:loop_generated_concentric circles_3.py
Objective: Use a for loop to generate a large set of concentric circles .

Keywords: canvas, oval, circle, center, radius
==================================================
Comments: A circle is a special case of an oval and is defined by the
box it fits inside. The bounding box here is defined in terms of the radius
and position of the center. This is a more convenient and logical  way of drawing
a circle (geometrically speaking).

Tested on: Python 2.6, Python 2.7.3, Python 3.2.3
Author:        Mike Ohlson de Fine
"""
#>>>>>>>>>>>>>>>>>>>>>>>>>>>>>>>>>>>>>>>>
```

```
from Tkinter import *
#from tkinter import *  # For Python 3.2.3 and higher.
root = Tk()
root.title('Radius and center circle.')

cw = 300                              # canvas width
ch = 300                              # canvas height
canvas_1 = Canvas(root, width=cw, height=ch, background="darkblue")
canvas_1.grid(row=0, column=1)

# specify bottom-left and top-right as a set of four numbers named 'xy'
center_x = 150
center_y = 150
Radius = 150
number_of_rings = 40

for i in range(0, number_of_rings):

    canvas_1.create_oval(center_x - Radius, center_y - Radius,\
                    center_x + Radius, center_y + Radius,\
                    fill= 'red', outline='blue', width= 2)
    Radius -= 4

root.mainloop()
#>>>>>>>>>>>>>>>>>>>>>>>>>>>>>>>>>>>>>>>>
```

Draw an Ellipse

Now we will draw ovals as ovals and not as circles.

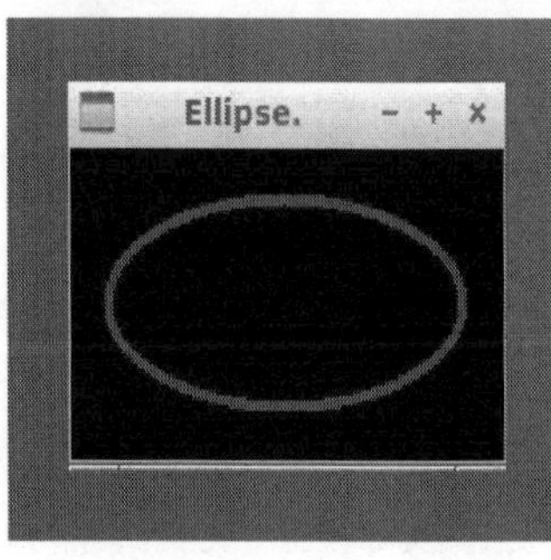


```
"""
Program name: ellipse_1.py
Objective: An ellipse is specified in terms of its bounding box,
```

```
in the same way as a rectangle.

Keywords: canvas, oval, ellipse
=================================================================
====================79
Comments: An ellipse is an oval. In Python/Tkinter it is defined by the
box it fits inside.

Tested on: Python 2.6, Python 2.7.3, Python 3.2.3
Author:         Mike Ohlson de Fine

"""
#>>>>>>>>>>>>>>>>>>>>>>>>>>>>>>>>>>>>>>>
from Tkinter import *
#from tkinter import *  # For Python 3.2.3 and higher.
root = Tk()
root.title('Ellipse.')

cw = 220                                # canvas width
ch = 120                                # canvas height
canvas_1 = Canvas(root, width=cw, height=ch, background="black")
canvas_1.grid(row=0, column=1)

# specify bottom-left and top-right as a set of four numbers named 'xy'
bottom_left_x = 20
bottom_left_y = 100
top_right_x = 200
top_right_y = 20

canvas_1.create_oval(bottom_left_x, bottom_left_y,\
                top_right_x, top_right_y,\
                 fill= 'black', outline='red', width= 4)

root.mainloop()
#>>>>>>>>>>>>>>>>>>>>>>>>>>>>>>>>>>>>>>>
```

Draw an Ellipse using Centre, Major and Minor axes

As we did when we defined circles in terms of radius and center, we now do the same sort of thing with an ellipse. And as before it allows to control large arrays of ovals through the use of loop instructions.

```
"""
Program name: ellipse_major_minor_1.py
Objective: An ellipse here is specified in terms of its center
and major and minor axis lengths.

Keywords: canvas, oval, ellipse, major axis, minor axis
=====================================================
Comments:  We modify the variables to read as center and
major and minor axis length

from tkinter import *  # For Python 3.2.3 and higher.
Author:        Mike Ohlson de Fine
"""
#>>>>>>>>>>>>>>>>>>>>>>>>>>>>>>>>>>>>>>>>
from Tkinter import *
#from tkinter import *  # For Python 3.2.3 and higher.
root = Tk()
root.title('Ellipse.')

cw = 300                              # canvas width
ch = 300                              # canvas height
canvas_1 = Canvas(root, width=cw, height=ch, background="black")
canvas_1.grid(row=0, column=1)

# specify bottom-left and top-right as a set of four numbers named 'xy'
center_x   = 150
center_y   = 150
major_axis = 280
minor_axis = 140

canvas_1.create_oval(center_x- major_axis/2, center_y- minor_axis/2,\
                center_x+ major_axis/2, center_y+ minor_axis/2,\
                   fill= 'black', outline='red', width= 4)

root.mainloop()
#>>>>>>>>>>>>>>>>>>>>>>>>>>>>>>>>>>>>>>>>
```

Draw an Array of Concentric Ellipses

Here we use a for loop to draw a sequence of ellipses on the same center. The size of the major axis is adjusted by the loop in 6 pixel decrements and minor axes is made to vary by small increments of the same amount.

```
""""
Program name: ellipse_array_1.py
Objective: An an array of ellipses are drawn controlling major and minor axis
lengths.

Keywords: canvas, oval, ellipse, major axis, minor axis
=====================================================
Comments:  We modify the variables to read as center and major and minor axis
length

Tested on: Python 2.6, Python 2.7.3, Python 3.2.3
Author:          Mike Ohlson de Fine

"""
#>>>>>>>>>>>>>>>>>>>>>>>>>>>>>>>>>>>>>>>>>>>>>>
from Tkinter import *
#from tkinter import *  # For Python 3.2.3 and higher.
root = Tk()
root.title('Ellipse array.')

cw = 300                                  # canvas width
ch = 400                                  # canvas height
```

```
canvas_1 = Canvas(root, width=cw, height=ch, background="black")
canvas_1.grid(row=0, column=1)

# specify bottom-left and top-right as a set of four numbers named 'xy'
center_x   = 150
center_y   = 200
major_axis = 280
minor_axis = 140
number_ellipses = 40

for i in range(0, number_ellipses):

    canvas_1.create_oval(center_x- major_axis/2, center_y- minor_axis/2,\
                    center_x+ major_axis/2,
 center_y+ minor_axis/2,\
                    outline='red', width= 1)
    major_axis -= 6
    minor_axis += 6

root.mainloop()
```

Draw a Rectangle with Round Corners

Tkinter does not offer a function for drawing rectangles with rounded corners. However with the experience we have gained thus far we can just fashion the Python code to do so for ourselves
With this example we demonstrate how we can create our own code procedures using the existing primitive drawing methods.

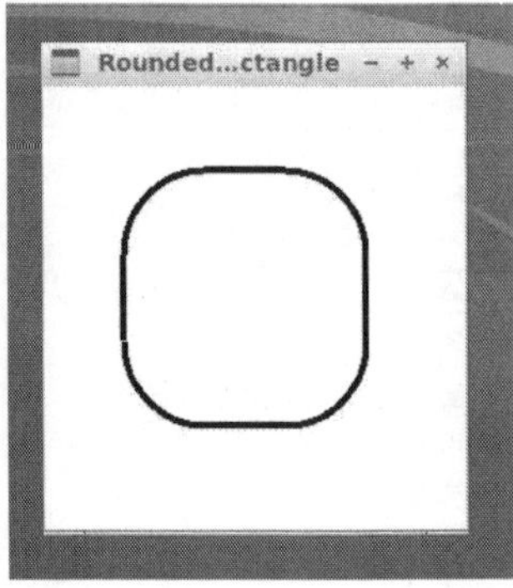

The Python code below was planned using the ideas and notation shown in the diagram shown below.

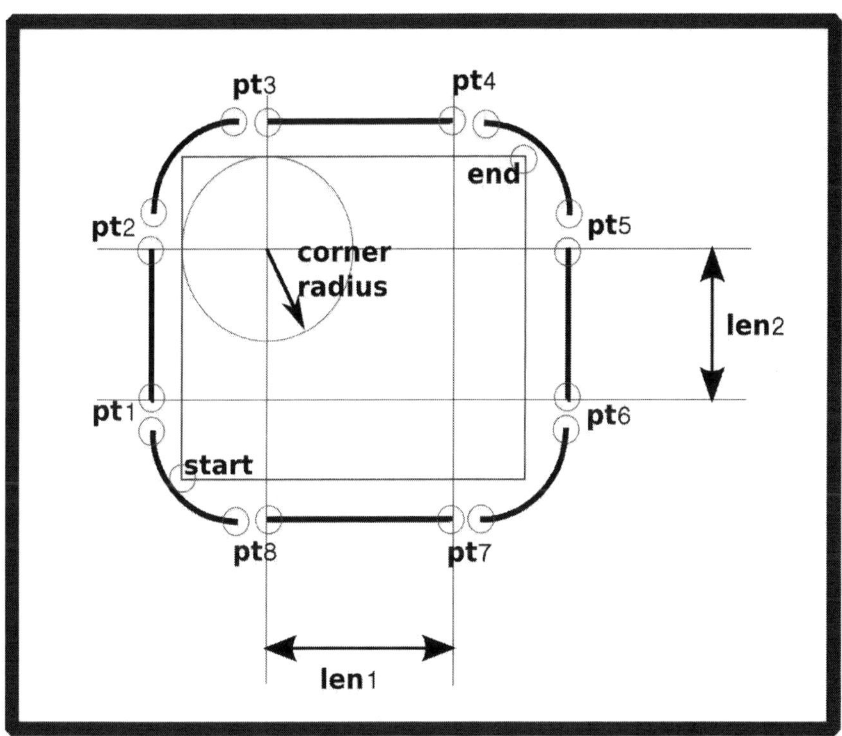


```
"""
Program name: rounded_rectangle_1.py
Objective: Draw a rounded rectangle using similar specifications to
a conventionl rectangle. The radius of the corners also needs to be stated.

Keywords: arc circle, rounded rectangle.
==========================================================
Comments: It is tricky to get each of the 34 coordinate values corrrect
and ways of progressive error correction should be part of the code
writing/testing process.

Tested on: Python 2.6, Python 2.7.3, Python 3.2.3
Author:        Mike Ohlson de Fine
"""

from Tkinter import *
```

```
#from tkinter import *  # For Python 3.2.3 and higher.
root = Tk()
root.title('Rounded rectangle')
cw = 260                              # canvas width
ch = 260                              # canvas height
canvas_1 = Canvas(root, width=cw, height=ch, background="white")
canvas_1.grid(row=0, column=1)

start_x = 50
start_y = 200
end_x = 200
end_y = 50
Radius =  40

len1 = end_x - start_x - 2*Radius
len2 = start_y - end_y - 2*Radius


pt1 = start_x, start_y - Radius
pt2 = start_x, start_y - Radius - len2
pt3 = start_x + Radius, end_y
pt4 = start_x + Radius + len1, end_y
pt5 = end_x,  end_y + Radius
pt6 = end_x, start_y - Radius
pt7 = end_x - Radius, start_y
pt8 = start_x + Radius, start_y

arc2 = pt2[0], pt2[1] + Radius
arc3 = pt3[0] + Radius, pt3[1]
arc4 = pt4[0] - Radius, pt4[1] + 2 *Radius
arc5 = pt5[0] , pt5[1] - Radius
arc6 = pt6[0] , pt6[1] - Radius
arc7 = pt7[0]- Radius, pt7[1]
arc8 = pt8[0] + Radius, pt8[1]
arc1 = pt1[0] , pt1[1] - Radius

canvas_1.create_line(pt1, pt2, fill="darkblue", width = 4)
canvas_1.create_line(pt3, pt4, fill="darkblue", width = 4)
canvas_1.create_line(pt5, pt6, fill="darkblue", width = 4)
canvas_1.create_line(pt7, pt8, fill="darkblue", width = 4)

canvas_1.create_arc(arc2, arc3, start=90, extent=90, outline="darkblue",
width=4)
canvas_1.create_arc(arc4, arc5, start=0, extent=90, outline="darkblue", width=4)
canvas_1.create_arc(arc6, arc7, start=270, extent=90, outline="darkblue",
```

```
width=4)

canvas_1.create_arc(arc8, arc1, start=-90, extent=-90, outline="darkblue",
width=4)
canvas_1.create_rectangle(arc8, arc1,  outline="red")
root.mainloop()
```

Discussion

We can see a slight flaw in the rounded rectangle in the bottom-left corner where the round corner meets the upright. For some reason there there is a single pixel-width hairline gap. It is barely noticeable until we are aware of it and then it glares at us with insolence. But we fix it in the next example by adding one degree of arc_extent to that particular corner. Another small irritation is the general appearance of curved and slanted lines in Python – at high definition they have a slightly ragged appearance. This is called *aliasing.* This is because a pixel is either one color or another. The drawing methods do not do anything extra like making a transition pixel of an intermediate color. This techniqu is called, unsurprisingly, anti-aliasing. We could do this if we wanted to. We just need to place another rounded rectangle beneath the intended one and give it a color that is intermediate between the background and the foreground outline. It makes for very complicated code. In the interest of simplicity we will not do it at this stage. In chapter three we see how to calculate intermediate colors and in chapter 5 we obtain a function for altering the size of complex objects.

What next?

The rounded rectangle requires in excess of thirty lines of code. If we need to make several rounded rectangles the program would quickly become long and messy. We now have a strong incentive to reduce length and complexity by defining a python function to do the job. It also makes it easier to fix up flaws line the hairline crack in the bottom right. We do this in the next example.

Create a Function for Rounded Rectangles

Here we use the previous method to define a function that can be used in a similar way to existing drawing methods in the Tkinter module.

```
"""
Program name: rounded_rectangle_function_1.py
Objective: Draw a rounded rectangle using similar specifications to
a conventionl rectangle. The radius of the corners also needs to be stated.

Keywords: arc circle, rounded rectangle.
========================================================
Comments: It is tricky to get each of the 34 coordinate values corrrect
and ways of progressive error correction should be part of the code
writing/testing process.

Tested on: Python 2.6, Python 2.7.3, Python 3.2.3
Author:        Mike Ohlson de Fine

"""
from Tkinter import *
#from tkinter import *  # For Python 3.2.3 and higher.
root = Tk()
root.title('Rounded rectangle')
cw = 500                              # canvas width
ch = 500                              # canvas height
canvas_1 = Canvas(root, width=cw, height=ch, background="white")
canvas_1.grid(row=0, column=1)

def round_rectangle(x_start, y_start, x_end, y_end, corner_radius, line_width,
outline_kula):
    """ Draw a rounded rectangle with all parameters selectable.
    """
    len1 = x_end - x_start - 2*corner_radius
    len2 = y_start - y_end - 2*corner_radius
```

```
    pt1 = x_start, y_start - corner_radius
    pt2 = x_start, y_start - corner_radius - len2
    pt3 = x_start + corner_radius, y_end
    pt4 = x_start + corner_radius + len1, y_end
    pt5 = x_end,  y_end + corner_radius
    pt6 = x_end, y_start - corner_radius
    pt7 = x_end - corner_radius, y_start
    pt8 = x_start + corner_radius, y_start

    arc2 = pt2[0], pt2[1] + corner_radius
    arc3 = pt3[0] + corner_radius, pt3[1]
    arc4 = pt4[0] - corner_radius, pt4[1] + 2 *corner_radius
    arc5 = pt5[0] , pt5[1] - corner_radius
    arc6 = pt6[0] , pt6[1] - corner_radius
    arc7 = pt7[0]- corner_radius, pt7[1]
    arc8 = pt8[0] + corner_radius, pt8[1]
    arc1 = pt1[0] , pt1[1] - corner_radius

    canvas_1.create_line(pt1, pt2, fill=outline_kula, width = line_width)
    canvas_1.create_line(pt3, pt4, fill=outline_kula, width = line_width)
    canvas_1.create_line(pt5, pt6, fill=outline_kula, width = line_width)
    canvas_1.create_line(pt7, pt8, fill=outline_kula, width = line_width)

    canvas_1.create_arc(arc2, arc3, style=ARC, start=90,  extent=90,
outline=outline_kula, width=line_width)
    canvas_1.create_arc(arc4, arc5, style=ARC, start=0,   extent=90,
outline=outline_kula, width=line_width)
    canvas_1.create_arc(arc6, arc7, style=ARC, start=270, extent=90,
outline=outline_kula, width=line_width)
    canvas_1.create_arc(arc8, arc1, style=ARC, start=-90, extent=-91,
outline=outline_kula, width=line_width)

# Test and demonstrate
#=====================
x_start = 50
y_start = 400
x_end = 400
y_end = 50
corner_radius =  50
line_width = 4
outline_kula ="darkblue"

round_rectangle(x_start, y_start, x_end, y_end, corner_radius, line_width,
outline_kula)
```

```
root.mainloop()
```

Discussion

The code above differs from the previous program because line width and color are variable arguments supplied to the function. This makes it more flexible. The whole point of using functions is to have the flexibility to use the function under a wide set of circumstances. However functions that cover every imaginable condition are complicated and difficult to write and debug. More importantly they are more difficult to use because the user will probably also need to be aware of the multitude of possibilities. Of course the code writer should build in defaults that save the user the bother of dealing with the complexity. Programming defaults and options adds even more complexity and what started as a straight forward problem ends up as a complicated nightmare. So, where practical, keep things simple.

Points to note

Simple is better than complicated. Explicit is better than implicit. Respect to Mr. Peters.

What next?

Often we need a function that is made to use the location of the center rather than the start and end boundaries. This is what we do next. It requires re-writing the definitions of the series of points pt1, pt2 etcetera. We also take the opportunity of doing a better job of identifying our points by means of short comments.

A Centered Function for Rounded Rectangles

If we want to create softer borders in different colors to

create, for example, a neon light glow effect, we need a function that allows us to specify the position of the center rather that the outside corners.
Here is the altered function:

```
def round_rectangle_centered(x_center, y_center, x_width, y_height,
corner_radius, line_width, outline_kula):
    """ Draw a rounded rectangle with all parameters selectable.
        The center, width and height are the primary choices.
    """

    pt1 = x_center - x_width/2, y_center + y_height/2 - corner_radius # Left
lower.
    pt2 = x_center - x_width/2, y_center - y_height/2 + corner_radius # Left
upper.
    pt3 = x_center - x_width/2 + corner_radius, y_center - y_height/2 # Top left.
    pt4 = x_center + x_width/2 - corner_radius, y_center - y_height/2 # Top right.
    pt5 = x_center + x_width/2 , y_center - y_height/2 +corner_radius # Right
upper.
    pt6 = x_center + x_width/2, y_center + y_height/2 - corner_radius # Right
lower.
    pt7 = x_center + x_width/2 - corner_radius, y_center + y_height/2 # Bottom
right.
    pt8 = x_center - x_width/2 + corner_radius, y_center + y_height/2 # Bottom
left.

    arc2 = pt2[0], pt2[1] + corner_radius
    arc3 = pt3[0] + corner_radius , pt3[1]
    arc4 = pt4[0] - corner_radius, pt4[1] + 2 *corner_radius
    arc5 = pt5[0] , pt5[1] - corner_radius
    arc6 = pt6[0] , pt6[1] - corner_radius
    arc7 = pt7[0]- corner_radius , pt7[1]
    arc8 = pt8[0] + corner_radius , pt8[1]
    arc1 = pt1[0] , pt1[1] - corner_radius

    canvas_1.create_line(pt1, pt2, fill=outline_kula, width = line_width)
    canvas_1.create_line(pt3, pt4, fill=outline_kula, width = line_width)
    canvas_1.create_line(pt5, pt6, fill=outline_kula, width = line_width)
    canvas_1.create_line(pt7, pt8, fill=outline_kula, width = line_width)

    canvas_1.create_arc(arc2, arc3, style=ARC, start=89,  extent=92,
outline=outline_kula, width=line_width) # Top left.
    canvas_1.create_arc(arc4, arc5, style=ARC, start=0,   extent=91,
outline=outline_kula, width=line_width) # Top right.
```

canvas_1.create_arc(arc6, arc7, style=ARC, start=269, extent=91, outline=outline_kula, width=line_width) # Bottom right.
canvas_1.create_arc(arc8, arc1, style=ARC, start=-90, extent=-91, outline=outline_kula, width=line_width) # Bottom left.

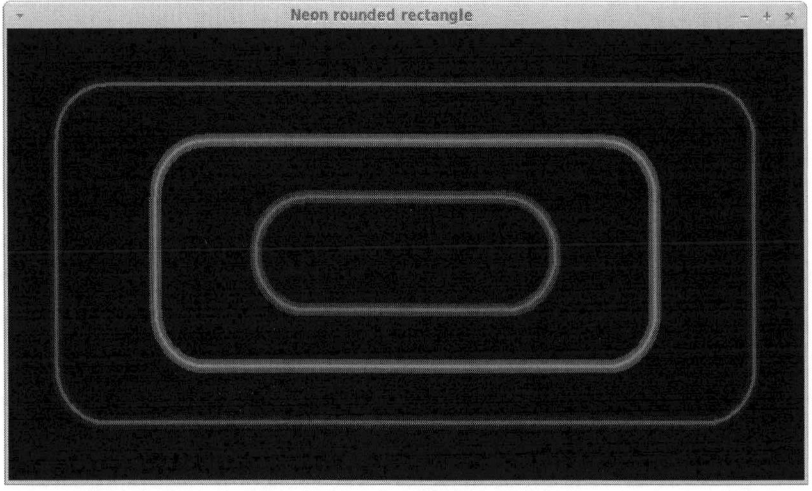

3

Graphic Elements: Color Control

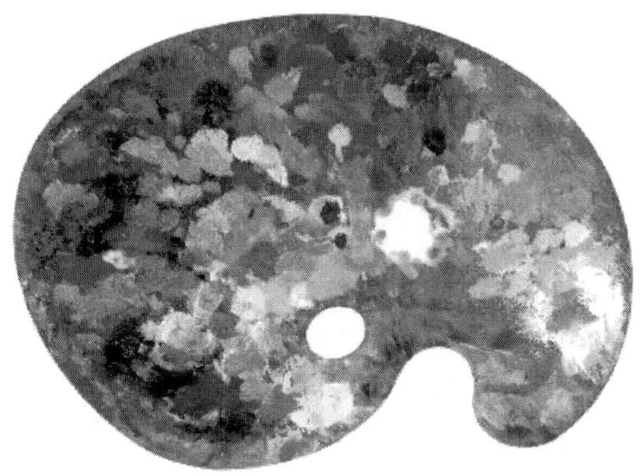

"A poplar tree is not green. It is a mix of blue green, lime green, silver green, light brown, cool grey and white." Thou Shall Not Use Comic Sans, by four anonymous design professionals.

In this chapter we will cover:

- how to paint swatches of primary color
- swatches of named web colors

- a minimal palette of named colors
- a complete palette of named colors
- construction of a color wedge
- construction of a discrete color wheel
- color scheme design using web tools
- using the Tkinter color selector-mixer
- construction of a continuous color disc
- construction of smoothly mixed color swatches
- the making of a rainbow
- creating Python lists of discrete color mixtures.

Controlling Color

Color is complicated. There are too many choices. Three primary colors, each divided into 256 levels of intensity give us 1.65 million choices. In addition we humans have thought up semi-arbitrary rules about which colors may be placed near each other to produce a pleasant mood or an unpleasant one if the scenario demands it. Artists and paint manufacturers have narrowed the choices down to a few hundred by giving them names and packing them in tubes and cans. It is all a bit daunting. Our task of controlling color digitally has apparently been simplified by confining our options to 256 levels of three primary colors of red, green and blue. Controlling color is difficult when they are expressed purely as numbers. Color is a vocabulary of visual communication. Colors evoke an emotional response in us and this introduces an extra dimension in how colors are used. For drawings to be effective and valued, color should be handled with the same thought and sensitivity as choice of words in spoken communication.

Artists refer to colors by names like vermillion, burnt umber, burnt sienna. Vendors of house paints give them romantic names like hot pink, lavender blush or misty rose.
Using colors by name in Python gives rise to the following difficulties:

- we have difficulty remembering which names are valid and recognized in the Tkinter library. Is the first letter upper-case for example?
- There are often several valid names for the same color. There is

a huge array of 'whites'.

- There is nothing in the name that indicates that color's relationship to other colors.

If colors are expressed purely as numbers then it becomes possible to control, combine and manipulate colors in systematic, programmable ways. Not easy but possible.

In this chapter we deal with both named colors and numerically defined colors.
We also briefly discuss how to combine colors in ways that should be appealing. A desirable tool that we want is the equivalent of an artist's mixing palette where we can place two end-colors and then mix various intermediate colors to create transitional colors. We create such a tool for ourselves.

Show Color Swatches

In the picture below we see yellow and the three primary colors used on computer monitors and television screens. Yellow is not primary in this computer world. We obtain it by mixing red with green. In the painter's world of brushes, tubes of pigment and canvas, yellow is primary and green is not. With pigments you achieve green by mixing blue and yellow.

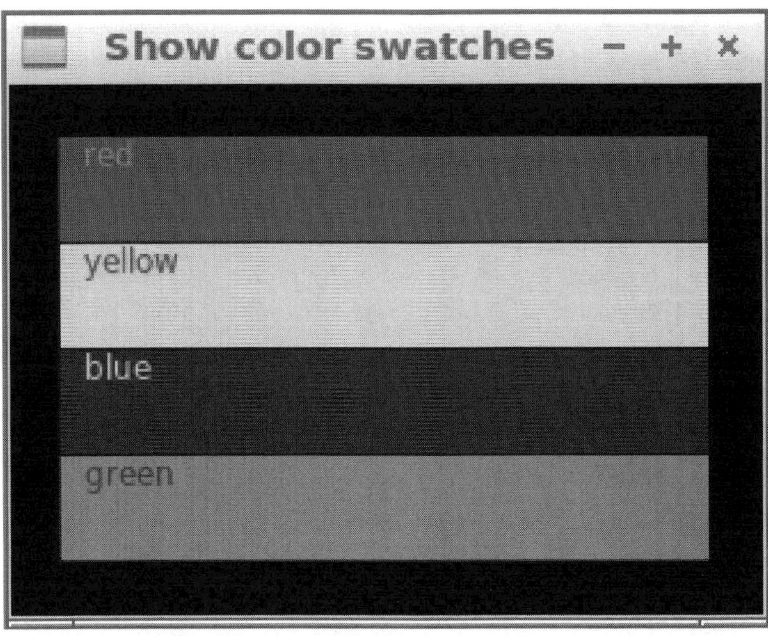


```
"""
Program name: show_swatches_1.py
Objective: Show swatches of web colours.

Keywords: canvas, rectangle, color web color, swatch
=================================================================
Explanation: We  show some named colors.

Tested on: Python 2.6, Python 2.7.3, Python 3.2.3
Author: Mike Ohlson de Fine

"""
from Tkinter import *
#from tkinter import *  # For Python 3.2.3 and higher.
root = Tk()
root.title("Show color swatches")

cw = 290                          # canvas width
ch = 200                          # canvas height
canvas_1 = Canvas(root, width=cw, height=ch, background="black")
canvas_1.grid(row=0, column=1)

# Colors to be displayed. "red","yellow", "blue","green"
```

```
x_start = 20
y_start = 20

x_width = 250
y_height = 40

text_offset = 0
text_width = 90

blok = [x_start, y_start, x_start + x_width, y_start + y_height]

canvas_1.create_rectangle(blok, fill="red")
canvas_1.create_text(blok[0]+10,  blok[1] ,  text="red", width=text_width, fill
="green", anchor=NW)

blok[1] += y_height
blok[3] += y_height
canvas_1.create_rectangle(blok, fill="yellow")
canvas_1.create_text(blok[0]+10,  blok[1] ,  text="yellow", width=text_width,
fill ="red", anchor=NW)

blok[1] += y_height
blok[3] += y_height
canvas_1.create_rectangle(blok, fill="blue")
canvas_1.create_text(blok[0]+10,  blok[1] ,  text="blue", width=text_width, fill
="yellow", anchor=NW)

blok[1] += y_height
blok[3] += y_height
canvas_1.create_rectangle(blok, fill="green")
canvas_1.create_text(blok[0]+10,  blok[1] ,  text="green", width=text_width, fill
="blue", anchor=NW)

root.mainloop()
```

Discussion

We have used the same form of the *create_rectangle* instruction that was used in chapter 2 to display our color swatches. We have made it easier to alter the size of all the swatches together through the way we have used the x_width and y_height variables to simultaneously change both size and spacing. This strategy of making whole groups of shapes

scaleable (re-sizeable) is a very important concept in computer graphics.
The other new thing done here is to use text labeling on a canvas through the *create_text* instruction.

Points to note

The topic of scaleability (shrinking and expanding) and shape transformation is very, very important in vector graphics and game creation. In this book we create functions for shrinking, expanding, distorting and translating (shifting) drawn objects. If we work with three dimensional graphics we also want to transform shapes by rotating them in any combination of three dimensions as well as applying perspective distortion. This is dealt with in book 7 of this series.

What next?

We delve into controlling text color on canvas in chapter 6. It is another rich topic with an interesting confusion of choices.

Show Color Groups as Named Lists of Named Colors

The example below shows us a few of the color names that Tkinter recognizes. The most important message here is that the names are not in any way uniform or consistent. There are not systematic rules governing their use.
In this example we use Python functions for the first time.

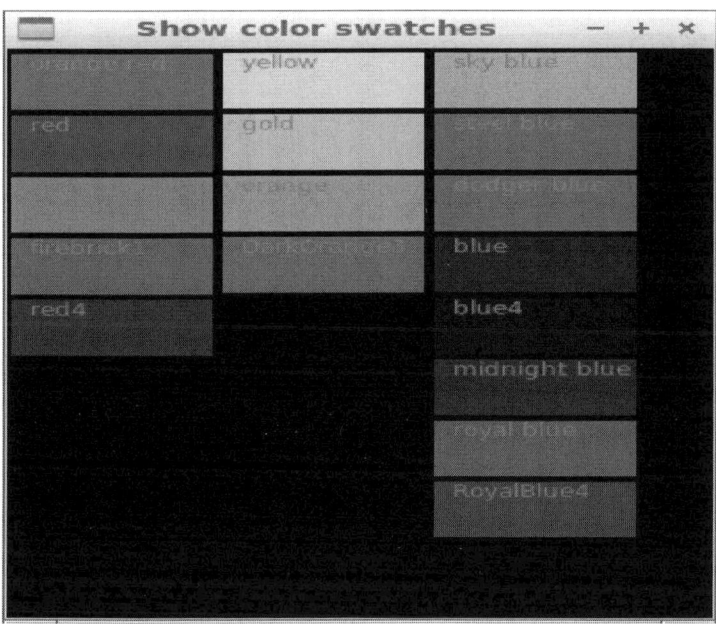


```
"""
Program name: show_named_colors_1.py
Objective: Show swatches of named web named colors.

Keywords: canvas, rectangle, color, web color, swatch
=================================================================
Explanation: We need a method of showing colors from lists of color names
The code should handle lists of variable length.

Tested on: Python 2.6,
Author: Mike Ohlson de Fine

"""
from Tkinter import *
#from tkinter import *  # For Python 3.2.3 and higher.
root = Tk()
root.title("Show color swatches")

cw = 340                              # canvas width
ch = 400                              # canvas height
canvas_1 = Canvas(root, width=cw, height=ch, background="black")
canvas_1.grid(row=0, column=1)
```

```
redColors = "orange red","red","IndianRed1","firebrick1","red4"

yellowColors= "yellow","gold","orange","DarkOrange3"

blue1Colors = "sky blue","steel blue", "dodger blue",\
"blue","blue4","midnight blue","royal blue",  "RoyalBlue4"

x_start = 2
y_start = 4

x_width = 98
x_offset = 2

y_height = 40
y_offset = 3

text_offset = 0
text_width = 90
blok = [x_start, y_start, x_start + x_width, y_start + y_height]

def showColors(selectedColor):
    """A columnar color swatch display. All colors laid down in a vertical stripe.
        The colors are grouped as named tuples.
    """
    for i in range (0, len(selectedColor)):
        kula = selectedColor[i]
        canvas_1.create_rectangle(blok, fill=kula)
        canvas_1.create_text(blok[0]+10,  blok[1] ,  text=kula, width=text_width,
fill ="green", anchor=NW)
        blok[1] += y_offset + y_height
        y0 = blok[1]
        blok[3] += y_offset + y_height
        y1 = blok[3]
    blok[1] = y_offset
    blok[3] = y_offset +  y_height
    blok[0] += x_width + 2 * x_offset
    blok[2] += x_width + 2 * x_offset
    # It is not necessary to return x0, y0 as they have global scope (note to self).

# Call the function for each list of colors.
showColors(redColors)
showColors(yellowColors)
showColors(blue1Colors)

root.mainloop()
```

Discussion

The key ideas in this example are to:

- economize on coding effort by using a Python function to avoid brute force repetition of sections of code.
- The ability to handle lists of variables with unspecified length.

From this point on we HAVE TO use functions because we are dealing with so many repetitions of actions that the programs would become ridiculously long otherwise. Once we use functions we must become aware of the concept of *name space.* The key idea is that if a variable is used inside a function then it's name only exists *while* function is being executed. So the namespace of a variable is the collection of execution areas where the variable name is visible and can be used in calculations and manipulations.

Points to note

Near the end of the Python code above there is a private programmers note: "# It is not necessary to return x0, y0 as they have global scope (note to self). ". When we are developing code everything is not clear to us. There are techniques we are uncertain about. To develop effective strategies and discover new possibilities we try ideas that are tentative. We explore and experiment. Part of the exploratory journey is to make rough sketches and notes. It may sound crazy but it is also very fruitful to have arguments and debates with ourselves – it effectively shines light into dark corners. Writing notes to ourselves as code comments is part of this process. Later on, before we publicly exhibit our final program, we clean it up and make it look neat and workmanlike by removing our working comments.

Namespace

Namespace: The frontier where we can lose our marbles if we don't have our wits about us.

This book is specifically about graphics. It is not explicitly about how to program in Python – that aspect is incidental. There are many excellent books about Python programming. However once we use functions we simply *must* have a basic understanding of how the names of objects work inside functions. Here is the thing.

1. An object given a name outside a function gets a global name and can be used and seen anywhere including inside functions anywhere in the code for that program. Inside the function we can *use it* but not *change it* .
2. An object given a name inside a function cannot be used or seen outside that function.
3. We pass values of variables outward from inside functions via the *return* statement.
4. There is a way to to operate on and change the values of global variables from inside a function. It is frowned upon by competent programmers as being untidy and perhaps badly thought out. But it is perfectly legal. What we do is label the global variable inside the function with the word **global.** This is regarded as unsavory because it leads to messy code and messy understanding of what is happening. Uncool.

We need to conduct some experiments to get the hang of namespace in Python.

Try the following short programs.

Version 1 where no attempt is made to re-assign the value of cat (a global).

```
''' Program name: namespace_1.py “””
cat = 'fuzzy people charming bird assassin.'
```

```
def walled_city():
    """Demonstrate that 'cat' is visible and useable inside function 'walled_city'.
    """
    elephant =  cat
    print 'From within the walled city: cat = ', cat
    print 'elephant = ', elephant
    #cat = ' seeker of the door to summer '

# Execute
walled_city()
print 'Outside the walls: cat = ', cat
''' Result:
mikeodf@mikeodf-HP-500B-Microtower ~ $ python2.7
/home/mikeodf/constr/namespace_1.py
From within the walled city: cat =  fuzzy people charming bird assasin
elephant =  fuzzy people charming bird assassin
Outside the walls: cat =  fuzzy people charming bird assassin.
'''
```

Version 2 where we try to re-assign the value of cat (a global) inside walled_city.

```
''' Program name: namespace_2.py “””
cat = 'fuzzy people charming bird assassin.'

def walled_city():
    """ Disastrous attempt to re-assign a value to cat.
    """

    elephant =  cat
    print 'From within the walled city: cat = ', cat
    print 'elephant = ', elephant
    #global cat
    cat = ' seeker of the door to summer ' # not allowed to change global variables.
    # Results in "UnboundLocalError: local variable 'cat' referenced before
assignment.

# Execute function walled_city.
walled_city()
print 'Outside the walls: cat = ', cat
```

This program crashes with the UnboundLocalError message during the attempted execution of the walled_city function.

This can be cured if we insert “global cat” just ahead of cat = ' seeker of the door to summer . What this achieves is to inform the Python interpreter that the name *cat* we are about to use is the global one that was first defined outside the function. This is nasty because inside the function we started to use cat just as a local variable and then halfway through we changed our minds and made it the global one.
Confusion reigns. Avoid.

What next?

This example was too limited to provide a meaningful palette of useful colors.
The next example provides something actually useful. The example after that is comprehensive and just too cumbersome to be useful but is included as a cross reference of valid color names.

A Minimised Palette of Named Colors

Her we have whittled the huge list of color names down to a fairly minimal but still useful set.

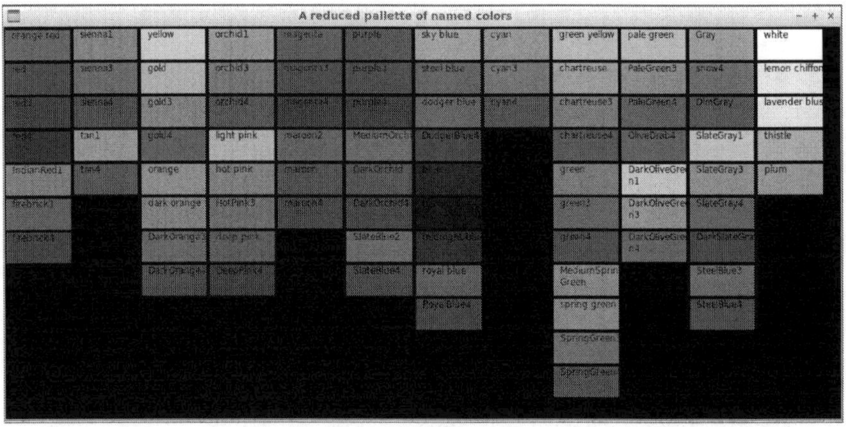

```
"""
Program name: minimized_palette_1.py
Objective: Show a reduced palette of web colours that are recognized by python.

Keywords: canvas, rectangle, color web color, reduced set, pallette
=================================================================
Comment:
Python/Tkinter has a large collection of colors with known names.
Many are similar and therefore redundant
A selection offering a broad choice is shown here.

Tested on: Python 2.6, Python 2.7.3, Python 3.2.3
Author: Mike Ohlson de Fine
"""
from Tkinter import *
#from tkinter import *  # For Python 3.2.3 and higher.
root = Tk()
root.title("A reduced pallette of named colors")

cw = 1150                          # canvas width
ch = 500                           # canvas height
canvas_1 = Canvas(root, width=cw, height=ch, background="black")
canvas_1.grid(row=0, column=1)


# Reds - reduced set
#=====================
red1Colors = "orange red",\
"red","red3","red4",\
"IndianRed1",\
"firebrick1","firebrick4"

# Browns  - reduced set
#======================
brown1Colors = "sienna1","sienna3","sienna4","tan1","tan4"

# Yellows  - reduced set
#=========================
yellowColors= "yellow","gold", "gold3","gold4",\
"orange","dark orange","DarkOrange3","DarkOrange4"

# Pink - reduced set
# ===================
pinkColors =  "orchid1","orchid3","orchid4",\
"light pink","hot pink","HotPink3",\
```

```
"deep pink","DeepPink4"

# Magenta - Maroon - reduced set
# ================================
magenta1Colors = "magenta","magenta3","magenta4",\
"maroon2","maroon","maroon4",\

# Purple - Maroon - reduced set
# ================================
magenta2Colors = "purple", "purple3","purple4",\
"MediumOrchid","DarkOrchid","DarkOrchid4",\
"SlateBlue2", "SlateBlue4",\

# Blues  - reduced set
#========================
blue1Colors = "sky blue","steel blue", "dodger blue",\
"DodgerBlue4","blue","blue4","midnight blue",\
"royal blue",  "RoyalBlue4",\

# Cyan -  reduced set
#========================
cyanColors = "cyan", "cyan3", "cyan4"

# Greens reduced set
#=======================
green1Colors = "green yellow","chartreuse","chartreuse3", "chartreuse4",\
"green", "green3", "green4",\
"MediumSpringGreen","spring green",  "SpringGreen3","SpringGreen4"

green2Colors = "pale green", "PaleGreen3", "PaleGreen4",\
"OliveDrab4","DarkOliveGreen1",\
"DarkOliveGreen3","DarkOliveGreen4"

# Grey -  reduced set
#========================
greyColors = "Gray","snow4","DimGray",\
"SlateGray1",  "SlateGray3", "SlateGray4",\
"DarkSlateGray", "SteelBlue3",  "SteelBlue4",\

#   WHITES
#========================
white1Colors = "white", \
"lemon chiffon", "lavender blush","thistle","plum",\

x_start = 2
```

```
y_start = 4

x_width = 90
x_offset = 2

y_height = 40
y_offset = 3

text_offset = 0
text_width = 90
blok = [x_start, y_start, x_start + x_width, y_start + y_height]

def showColors(selectedColor):
   """Basic columnar color swatch display. All colors are laid down in a vertical
stripe.
      The colors are grouped as a  named tuple.
   """
   for i in range (0 ,len(selectedColor)):
      kula = selectedColor[i]
      canvas_1.create_rectangle(blok, fill=kula)
      canvas_1.create_text(blok[0]+10,  blok[1] ,  text=kula, width=text_width,
fill ="black", anchor=NW)
      blok[1] += y_offset + y_height
      y0 = blok[1]
      blok[3] += y_offset + y_height
      y1 = blok[3]
   blok[1] = y_offset
   blok[3] = y_offset +  y_height
   blok[0] += x_width + 2 * x_offset
   blok[2] += x_width + 2 * x_offset
   return y0,y1

showColors(red1Colors)
showColors(brown1Colors)
showColors(yellowColors)
showColors(pinkColors)
showColors(magenta1Colors)
showColors(magenta2Colors)
showColors(blue1Colors)
showColors(cyanColors)
showColors(green1Colors)
showColors(green2Colors)
showColors(greyColors)
showColors(white1Colors)
```

```
root.mainloop()
```

Discussion

As we did in the previous two examples We have used the form of the *create_rectangle* instruction from chapter 2 where all our variable arguments are included in a list whose elements or members are named variables. As before we use the *create_text* instruction to label our swatches so that we could use the program output as a color chart for reference purposes..

Executing loops of unknown length.

How exactly do we execute loops when we do not know beforehand how many executions to perform? The answer lies with the *len(selectedColor)* function. This function puts an numerical integer in the place of len(selectedColor). The value of the integer doing the replacing is the number of elements in the object *selectedColor.* So the *for loop* executes once for each element inside *selectedColor.* Simple, neat and used a lot in Python code.

An Expanded Palette

Thousands of web programs use thousands more of named colors. New color names are invented daily. For example there is one called "wrong lipstick" which is a shave of purple..Only a sanely limited number are recognizable to Tkinter. This next program is an attempt to verify most of the Tkinter recognized color names. Clearly it is not simple or logical to use named colors if we intend to control color using calculations in Python code.

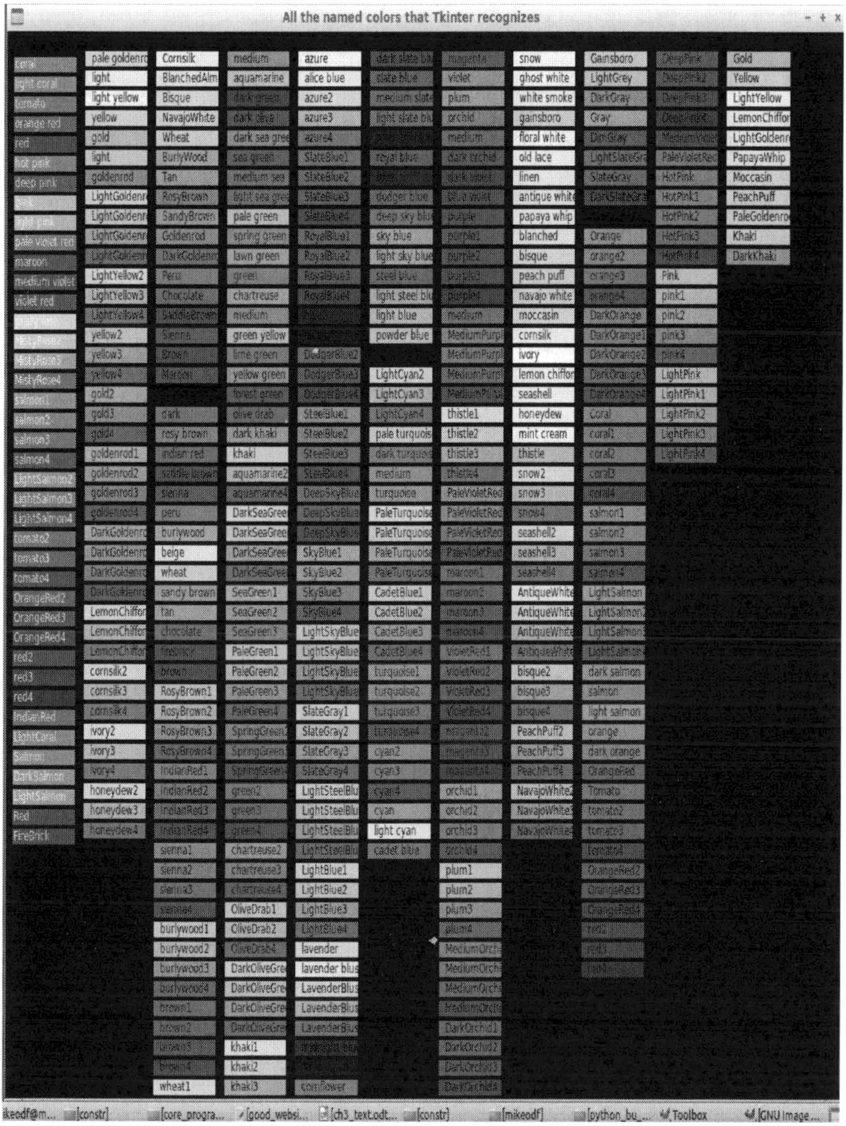

"""

Program name: all_color_names_1.py
Objective: Show palette using web colors that are known to Tkinter/Python.

Keywords: canvas, rectangle, color web color, redundant colors.
===

```
Comment: Python or Tkinter has a large collection of colors with known names.
A selection is shown here. There is no systematic way of way of linking names to
hue.
A reduced list is more useful.

Author:       Mike Ohlson de Fine
"""
from Tkinter import *
#from tkinter import *  # For Python 3.2.3 and higher.
root = Tk()
root.title("All the named colors that Tkinter recognizes")

cw = 1200                          # canvas width
ch = 1100                          # canvas height
canvas_1 = Canvas(root, width=cw, height=ch, background="black")
canvas_1.grid(row=0, column=1)

#  THE  WHITES
whiteColors = "snow", "ghost white", "white smoke", "gainsboro", "floral
white", "old lace", "linen",\
"antique white", "papaya whip", "blanched almond", "bisque", "peach puff",
"navajo white", "moccasin",\
"cornsilk", "ivory", "lemon chiffon", "seashell", "honeydew", "mint cream",
"thistle", "snow2", "snow3",\
"snow4", "seashell2", "seashell3", "seashell4", "AntiqueWhite1",
"AntiqueWhite2", "AntiqueWhite3",\
"AntiqueWhite4", "bisque2", "bisque3", "bisque4", "PeachPuff2", "PeachPuff3",
"PeachPuff4", "NavajoWhite2",\
"NavajoWhite3", "NavajoWhite4"

# THE BLUES
blue1Colors = "azure", "alice blue", "azure2", "azure3", "azure4", "SlateBlue1",
"SlateBlue2", "SlateBlue3",\
"SlateBlue4", "RoyalBlue1", "RoyalBlue2", "RoyalBlue3", "RoyalBlue4",
"blue2","blue4", "DodgerBlue2", "DodgerBlue3",\
"DodgerBlue4", "SteelBlue1", "SteelBlue2", "SteelBlue3", "SteelBlue4",
"DeepSkyBlue2", "DeepSkyBlue3", "DeepSkyBlue4",\
"SkyBlue1", "SkyBlue2", "SkyBlue3", "SkyBlue4", "LightSkyBlue1",
"LightSkyBlue2", "LightSkyBlue3", "LightSkyBlue4",\
"SlateGray1", "SlateGray2", "SlateGray3", "SlateGray4", "LightSteelBlue1",
"LightSteelBlue2", "LightSteelBlue3",\
"LightSteelBlue4", "LightBlue1", "LightBlue2", "LightBlue3", "LightBlue4",
"lavender", "lavender blush",\
"LavenderBlush2", "LavenderBlush3", "LavenderBlush4","midnight blue",
"navy", "cornflower blue"
```

blue2Colors = "dark slate blue","slate blue", "medium slate blue", "light slate blue", "medium blue",\
"royal blue", "blue", "dodger blue",\
"deep sky blue", "sky blue", "light sky blue", "steel blue", "light steel blue", "light blue", "powder blue"

turquoiseColors = "pale turquoise", "dark turquoise", "medium turquoise", "turquoise" - these are web colors but they do not work in Python/Tkinter.

# THE CYANS
cyanColors = "LightCyan2", "LightCyan3", "LightCyan4","pale turquoise", "dark turquoise", "medium turquoise",\
"turquoise", "PaleTurquoise1", "PaleTurquoise2", "PaleTurquoise3","PaleTurquoise4", "CadetBlue1", "CadetBlue2",\
"CadetBlue3", "CadetBlue4","turquoise1", "turquoise2", "turquoise3","turquoise4", "cyan2", "cyan3", "cyan4",\
"cyan", "light cyan", "cadet blue"

# THE MAGENTAS
magentaColors = "magenta","violet","plum","orchid", "medium orchid", "dark orchid", "dark violet",\
"blue violet", "purple", "purple1","purple2","purple3","purple4","medium purple","MediumPurple1",\
"MediumPurple2","MediumPurple3", "MediumPurple4","thistle1","thistle2","thistle3","thistle4","PaleVioletRed1","PaleVioletRed2", "PaleVioletRed3","PaleVioletRed4",\
"maroon1","maroon2","maroon3","maroon4","VioletRed1","VioletRed2","VioletRed3","VioletRed4",\
"magenta2","magenta3","magenta4","orchid1","orchid2","orchid3","orchid4","plum1","plum2","plum3","plum4",\
"MediumOrchid1","MediumOrchid2","MediumOrchid3","MediumOrchid4","DarkOrchid1","DarkOrchid2","DarkOrchid3","DarkOrchid4"

# THE REDS
redColors = "coral", "light coral", "tomato", "orange red", "red", "hot pink", "deep pink", "pink", "light pink",\
"pale violet red", "maroon", "medium violet red", "violet red", "misty rose","MistyRose2","MistyRose3",\
"MistyRose4","salmon1","salmon2","salmon3","salmon4","LightSalmon2","LightSalmon3","LightSalmon4",\
"tomato2","tomato3","tomato4","OrangeRed2","OrangeRed3","OrangeRed4","red2","red3","red4",\
"IndianRed","LightCoral","Salmon","DarkSalmon","LightSalmon","Red","FireBrick"

```
# dud name : ,"crimson"

pinkColors =
"DeepPink","DeepPink2","DeepPink3","DeepPink4","MediumVioletRed","Pale
VioletRed","HotPink","HotPink1","HotPink2",\
"HotPink3","HotPink4","Pink","pink1","pink2","pink3","pink4","LightPink","Li
ghtPink1","LightPink2","LightPink3","LightPink4"

# THE YELLOWS
yellowColors = yellowcolor= "pale goldenrod",     "light goldenrod yellow",
"light yellow", "yellow", "gold",\
"light goldenrod", "goldenrod", "LightGoldenrod1", "LightGoldenrod2",
"LightGoldenrod3", "LightGoldenrod4",\
"LightYellow2", "LightYellow3",
        "LightYellow4","yellow2","yellow3","yellow4","gold2","gold3","gold4"
,\
"goldenrod1","goldenrod2","goldenrod3","goldenrod4","DarkGoldenrod1","Dar
kGoldenrod2","DarkGoldenrod3",\
"DarkGoldenrod4","LemonChiffon2","LemonChiffon3","LemonChiffon4","corn
silk2","cornsilk3","cornsilk4",\
"ivory2","ivory3","ivory4","honeydew2","honeydew3","honeydew4"

# THE ORANGES
orangeColors =
"Orange","orange2","orange3","orange4","DarkOrange","DarkOrange1","DarkO
range2","DarkOrange3","DarkOrange4",\
"Coral","coral1","coral2","coral3","coral4","salmon1","salmon2","salmon3","sal
mon4","LightSalmon","LightSalmon2","LightSalmon3",\
"LightSalmon4","dark salmon","salmon","light salmon","orange","dark
orange","OrangeRed","Tomato","tomato2","tomato3","tomato4",\
"OrangeRed2","OrangeRed3","OrangeRed4","red2","red3","red4"

# GOLDS
goldColors =
"Gold","Yellow","LightYellow","LemonChiffon","LightGoldenrodYellow","Pap
ayaWhip","Moccasin","PeachPuff","PaleGoldenrod",\
"Khaki","DarkKhaki"

# PURPLES
purpleColors =
"Lavender","Thistle","Plum","Violet","Orchid","Magenta","MediumOrchid","M
ediumPurple",\
"BlueViolet","DarkViolet","DarkOrchid","DarkMagenta","Purple","SlateBlue","
DarkSlateBlue","MediumSlateBlue"
# dud names:"Fuchsia","Amethyst","Indigo",
```

# THE GREENS
greenColors = "medium aquamarine", "aquamarine", "dark green", "dark olive green", "dark sea green", "sea green",\
"medium sea green", "light sea green", "pale green", "spring green", "lawn green", "green","chartreuse",\
"medium spring green", "green yellow", "lime green", "yellow green", "forest green", "olive drab", "dark khaki",\
"khaki", "aquamarine2", "aquamarine4", "DarkSeaGreen1", "DarkSeaGreen2", "DarkSeaGreen3", "DarkSeaGreen4",\
"SeaGreen1", "SeaGreen2", "SeaGreen3", "PaleGreen1", "PaleGreen2", "PaleGreen3", "PaleGreen4",\
"SpringGreen2", "SpringGreen3", "SpringGreen4", "green2", "green3", "green4",\
"chartreuse2", "chartreuse3", "chartreuse4", "OliveDrab1", "OliveDrab2", "OliveDrab4",\
"DarkOliveGreen1", "DarkOliveGreen2", "DarkOliveGreen3", "DarkOliveGreen4",\
"khaki1", "khaki2", "khaki3", "khaki4"

BROWNS
brown1Colors =
"Cornsilk","BlanchedAlmond","Bisque","NavajoWhite","Wheat","BurlyWood","Tan","RosyBrown","SandyBrown","Goldenrod",\
"DarkGoldenrod","Peru","Chocolate","SaddleBrown","Sienna","Brown","Maroon"
brown2Colors = "dark goldenrod", "rosy brown", "indian red", "saddle brown", "sienna",\
"peru","burlywood","beige","wheat","sandy brown", "tan","chocolate","firebrick","brown",\
"RosyBrown1","RosyBrown2","RosyBrown3","RosyBrown4","IndianRed1","IndianRed2","IndianRed3",\
"IndianRed4","sienna1","sienna2","sienna3","sienna4","burlywood1","burlywood2","burlywood3",\
"burlywood4","brown1","brown2","brown3","brown4","wheat1","wheat2","wheat3","wheat4","tan1",\
"tan2","tan4","chocolate1","chocolate2","chocolate3","firebrick1","firebrick2","firebrick3","firebrick4"

GREYS
greyColors =
"Gainsboro","LightGrey","DarkGray","Gray","DimGray","LightSlateGray","SlateGray","DarkSlateGray"
dud names:"Silver",

```
x_start = 10
y_start = 25
x_width = 90
x_offset = 6
y_height = 16
y_offset = 3
text_offset = 2
text_width = 90
kbk = [x_start, y_start, x_start + x_width, y_start + y_height]

#column 1
for i in range (0,len(redColors)):
   kula = redColors[i]
   canvas_1.create_rectangle(kbk, fill=kula)
   canvas_1.create_text(x_start+text_offset,  kbk[1] ,  text=kula,
width=text_width, fill ="white", anchor=NW)
   kbk[1] += y_offset + y_height
   kbk[3] += y_offset + y_height

#column 2
kbk[0] += x_width + 2*x_offset
kbk[2] += x_width + 2*x_offset

kbk[1] = y_offset + y_height
kbk[3] = y_offset + 2 * y_height

for i in range (0,len(yellowColors)):
   kula = yellowColors[i]
   canvas_1.create_rectangle(kbk, fill=kula)
   canvas_1.create_text(kbk[0]+10,  kbk[1] ,  text=kula, width=text_width, fill
="black", anchor=NW)
   kbk[1] += y_offset + y_height
   kbk[3] += y_offset +  y_height

# column 3
kbk[0] += x_width + 2*x_offset
kbk[2] += x_width + 2*x_offset

kbk[1] = y_offset + y_height
kbk[3] = y_offset + 2 * y_height

for i in range (0,len(brown1Colors)):
   kula = brown1Colors[i]
   canvas_1.create_rectangle(kbk, fill=kula)
   canvas_1.create_text(kbk[0]+10,  kbk[1] ,  text=kula, width=text_width, fill
```

```
="black", anchor=NW)
    kbk[1] += y_offset + y_height
    kbk[3] += y_offset + y_height

kbk[1] += y_offset  + y_height
kbk[3] += y_offset  + y_height
for i in range (0,len(brown2Colors)):
    kula = brown2Colors[i]
    canvas_1.create_rectangle(kbk, fill=kula)
    canvas_1.create_text(kbk[0]+10,  kbk[1] ,  text=kula, width=text_width, fill
="black", anchor=NW)
    kbk[1] += y_offset  + y_height
    kbk[3] += y_offset  + y_height

# column 4
kbk[0] += x_width + 2*x_offset
kbk[2] += x_width + 2*x_offset

kbk[1] = y_offset  + y_height
kbk[3] = y_offset  + 2 * y_height
for i in range (0,len(greenColors)):
    kula = greenColors[i]
    canvas_1.create_rectangle(kbk, fill=kula)
    canvas_1.create_text(kbk[0]+10,  kbk[1] ,  text=kula, width=text_width, fill
="black", anchor=NW)
    kbk[1] += y_offset  + y_height
    kbk[3] += y_offset  + y_height

# column 5
kbk[0] += x_width + 2*x_offset
kbk[2] += x_width+ 2*x_offset

kbk[1] = y_offset  + y_height
kbk[3] = y_offset  + 2 * y_height
for i in range (0,len(blue1Colors)):
    kula = blue1Colors[i]
    canvas_1.create_rectangle(kbk, fill=kula)
    canvas_1.create_text(kbk[0]+10,  kbk[1] ,  text=kula, width=text_width, fill
="black", anchor=NW)
    kbk[1] += y_offset  + y_height
    kbk[3] += y_offset  + y_height

# column 6
kbk[0] += x_width + 2*x_offset
kbk[2] += x_width + 2*x_offset
```

```
kbk[1] = y_offset  + y_height
kbk[3] = y_offset  + 2 * y_height
for i in range (0,len(blue2Colors)):
   kula = blue2Colors[i]
   canvas_1.create_rectangle(kbk, fill=kula)
   canvas_1.create_text(kbk[0]+10,  kbk[1] ,  text=kula, width=text_width, fill
="black", anchor=NW)
   kbk[1] += y_offset  + y_height
   kbk[3] += y_offset  + y_height

kbk[1] += y_offset  + y_height
kbk[3] += y_offset  + y_height
for i in range (0,len(cyanColors)):
   kula = cyanColors[i]
   canvas_1.create_rectangle(kbk, fill=kula)
   canvas_1.create_text(kbk[0]+10,  kbk[1] ,  text=kula, width=text_width, fill
="black", anchor=NW)
   kbk[1] += y_offset  + y_height
   kbk[3] += y_offset  + y_height

# column 7
kbk[0] += x_width + 2*x_offset
kbk[2] += x_width + 2*x_offset

kbk[1] = y_offset  + y_height
kbk[3] = y_offset  + 2 * y_height
for i in range (0,len(magentaColors)):
   kula = magentaColors[i]
   canvas_1.create_rectangle(kbk, fill=kula)
   canvas_1.create_text(kbk[0]+10,  kbk[1] ,  text=kula, width=text_width, fill
="black", anchor=NW)
   kbk[1] += y_offset  + y_height
   kbk[3] += y_offset  + y_height

# column 8
kbk[0] += x_width + 2*x_offset
kbk[2] += x_width + 2*x_offset

kbk[1] = y_offset  + y_height
kbk[3] = y_offset  + 2 * y_height
for i in range (0,len(whiteColors)):
   kula = whiteColors[i]
   canvas_1.create_rectangle(kbk, fill=kula)
   canvas_1.create_text(kbk[0]+10,  kbk[1] ,  text=kula, width=text_width, fill
```

```
="black", anchor=NW)
    kbk[1] += y_offset  + y_height
    kbk[3] += y_offset  + y_height

# column 9
kbk[0] += x_width + 2*x_offset
kbk[2] += x_width + 2*x_offset

kbk[1] = y_offset  + y_height
kbk[3] = y_offset  + 2 * y_height
for i in range (0,len(greyColors)):
    kula = greyColors[i]
    canvas_1.create_rectangle(kbk, fill=kula)
    canvas_1.create_text(kbk[0]+10,  kbk[1] ,  text=kula, width=text_width, fill
="black", anchor=NW)
    kbk[1] += y_offset  + y_height
    kbk[3] += y_offset  + y_height

kbk[1] += y_offset  + y_height
kbk[3] += y_offset  + y_height
for i in range (0,len(orangeColors)):
    kula = orangeColors[i]
    canvas_1.create_rectangle(kbk, fill=kula)
    canvas_1.create_text(kbk[0]+10,  kbk[1] ,  text=kula, width=text_width, fill
="black", anchor=NW)
    kbk[1] += y_offset  + y_height
    kbk[3] += y_offset  + y_height

# column 10
kbk[0] += x_width + 2*x_offset
kbk[2] += x_width + 2*x_offset

kbk[1] = y_offset  + y_height
kbk[3] = y_offset  + 2 * y_height
for i in range (0,len(pinkColors)):
    kula = pinkColors[i]
    canvas_1.create_rectangle(kbk, fill=kula)
    canvas_1.create_text(kbk[0]+10,  kbk[1] ,  text=kula, width=text_width, fill
="black", anchor=NW)
    kbk[1] += y_offset  + y_height
    kbk[3] += y_offset  + y_height

# column 11
kbk[0] += x_width + 2*x_offset
kbk[2] += x_width + 2*x_offset
```

```
kbk[1] = y_offset  + y_height
kbk[3] = y_offset  + 2 * y_height
for i in range (0,len(goldColors)):
   kula = goldColors[i]
   canvas_1.create_rectangle(kbk, fill=kula)
   canvas_1.create_text(kbk[0]+10,  kbk[1] ,  text=kula, width=text_width, fill
="black", anchor=NW)
   kbk[1] += y_offset  + y_height
   kbk[3] += y_offset  + y_height

root.mainloop()
```

Comment

It should be possible to reduce the length of this program. The simplest approach would be to simply append all the colors into one long list and make no attempt to organize it into columns by hue. This would defeat the object of having a nice organized list of available, tested, valid color names. This raises an important point in the philosophy of writing software. Anyone who has tried to read and understand code written by someone else knows that it is easier to write the software again from scratch for oneself rather than trying to understand 'cleverly' written, dense code. The real surprise comes when we know that it was ourself that wrote the code some months earlier but now we can neither understand exactly how the code worked did nor what was in our mind when we wrote it. This last discovery is both frightening and humbling.

So the fruit of this bitter lesson is that it is nearly always a good idea to:

- Use self-explanatory variable names.
- Use plenty of comments.
- Do not try to make code dense and compact at the expense of being easy to follow.

Now what?

Having seen some of the disadvantages of using named colors in Python code we now change direction toward complete and consistent control of color – the numerical way.
This is where we stop using romantic color names and just use numbers. In particular we use what has become one of the de facto international standards for web color specification, the hexadecimal red-green-blue color word of the form'#rrggbb' where rr is a hexadecimal number from 0 to 255 for how much red to use, gg the amount of green and bb the amount of blue. The other 'standard' is that used in JAVA programs which is a red,green,blue decimal triplet.

Numerically Specified Color

From here on we stop using names for colors. We use numbers instead. Tkinter provides a simple, consistent and practically universal convention for specifying color: the hexadecimal red-green-blue string.
Here is how it works. Each of the primary colors of red, green or blue can take on a numerical value from 0 (total absence of color) to 255 (fully saturated color). The color values for each primary color are converted to hexadecimal numbers and then placed adjacent to each other in a string preceded by the #' symbol. For example white is all the colors in full saturation, Each primary color 'channel' is thus 255 which when converted to hex is 'ff'. So the color number for total white is '#ffffff'. Pure red is '#ff0000', pure green is '#00ff00' while pure blue is '#0000ff'. Pure black would be '#000000'.

(A **hex triplet** is a six-digit, three-byte hexadecimal number used in HTML, CSS, SVG, and other computing applications, to represent colors. The bytes represent the red, green and blue components of the color. One byte represents a number in the range 00 to FF (in hexadecimal notation), or 0 to 255 in decimal notation.)

Controlling colors numerically introduces its own particular difficulties. The biggest problem is predicting how a specific mixture of primary colors is going to look on a computer screen or a printer. Controlling hue and saturation (the darkness or brightness) of a color adds a further complexity.

We start explore these problems by constructing a color wheel which is a colored diagram that illustrates the effect of mixing primary colors. It includes variations of hue as well as degree of saturation . The first stage in the creation of the color wheel is to construct one wedge-shaped segment of the wheel. In the example that follows this one we construct the

A Color Wedge of Varying Brightness

Here we construct a wedge that is one twelfth portion of a circular disk. The pure primary color is the larges disk inside the wedge. Increasingly darker colors are closer to the thin end and lighter colors toward the wide end.

```
"""
Program name: color_wedge_1 .py
Objective: Draw a single color wedge with varying brightness.

Keywords: canvas, canvas, color, wedge
================================================================
Comments:

Tested on: Python 2.6, Python 2.7.3, Python 3.2.3
Author: Mike Ohlson de Fine
"""
from Tkinter import *
#from tkinter import *  # For Python 3.2.3 and higher.
root = Tk()
root.title("Color wedge")

cw = 200                              # canvas width
ch = 300                              # canvas height
chart_1 = Canvas(root, width=cw, height=ch, background="white")
chart_1.grid(row=0, column=0)

x_tip = 100
y_tip = 250
width= 50      #standard disk diameter
hite = width*2  # median wedge height.
```

```
# Draw the background dark-red triangle.
kula = "#660000"
wedge =[ x_tip, y_tip, x_tip-width,y_tip-4.4*width, x_tip+width, y_tip-
4.4*width ]
chart_1.create_polygon(wedge,fill=kula)

hFac = [0.25,   0.45,  0.75,  1.2,  1.63,  1.87,  2.05] # Proportional height factors.
wFac = [0.2,   0.36,  0.6,   1.0,   0.5,   0.3,  0.25]     # Proportional width factors.

kulas = [ "#000000","#c80000", "#a00000", "#ff0000", "#ff5050", "#ff8c8c",
"#ffc8c8"]

for i in range(len(kulas)):
   x0 = x_tip-width*wFac[i]/2
   y0 = y_tip-hite*hFac[i]  +width*wFac[i]/2
   x1 = x_tip+width*wFac[i]/2
   y1 = y_tip-hite*hFac[i] - width*wFac[i]/2
   chart_1.create_oval(x0,y0 ,x1 ,y1 ,  fill=kulas[i], outline=kulas[i])

root.mainloop()
```

Discussion

The variables used to construct the wedge are designed to make it scalable (alter its size) and allow it to be positioned anywhere on the canvas. The position is determined by the position of the wedge tip at *x_tip, y_tip*. The size is determined by the variable *width*.

Points to note

With geometric shapes and other shapes like disks at specific positions within the outer geometric shape, all objects have to be maintained in proportion to each other. The code expressing these relationships can become difficult to follow. Designing such groups requires some trial and error to some extent. It is a great labor saving strategy to sit down before coding and first try to draw the layout with pencil and paper. Try to extract and write down the geometric relationships between the shapes. It is not imperative to do so but it can

save hours of trial and error.
An important thing to note about numerical color construction is that although our primary color is red, in order to lighten it and make appear to be mixed with white, we have to add increasing amounts of both green and blue simultaneously. On the other hand to make it progressively darker we simply lower the amount of red in the color.

A Color Wheel

Now we extend the previous example to create the segmented wheel that shows the result of mixing together the colors on each side. It is important to understand these mixing relationships in a general, intuitive way.

The Origin of the word Channel. In various discussions in the rest of this chapter we use the term **channel** when referring to the primary color components of red, green and blue. The concepts behind this come from from the way television cameras used to work. An image falling on the optics of the camera was separated into red, green and blue components by colored filters. Each of three filters would only allow one of the primary colors through and block the other two. Each separate color band would then be transmitted separately for viewing. Thus each color band is referred to as a color channel.

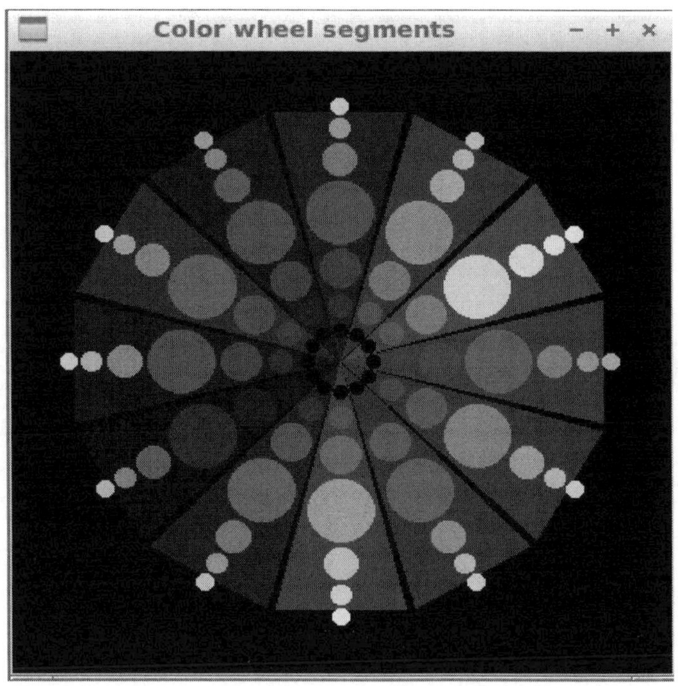


```
"""
Program name: primary_color_wheel_1 .py
Objective: Draw the primary red, green, blue color wheel framework.

Keywords: canvas, rotate, trigonometry, color wheel.
=====================================================
Comment: Draw the color wheel using trigonometric relations.

Tested on: Python 2.6, Python 2.7.3, Python 3.2.3
Author: Mike Ohlson de Fine
"""
from Tkinter import *
#from tkinter import *  # For Python 3.2.3 and higher.
import math
root = Tk()
root.title("Color wheel segments")

cw = 400                          # canvas width
ch = 400                          # canvas height
chart_1 = Canvas(root, width=cw, height=ch, background="black")
chart_1.grid(row=0, column=0)
```

```
theta_deg = 0.0
x_orig = 200
y_orig = 200
x_width = 40
y_hite = 160

xy0 = [x_orig,  y_orig]
xy1 = [x_orig - x_width, y_orig - y_hite]
xy2 = [x_orig + x_width, y_orig - y_hite ]
wedge =[ xy0, xy1 , xy2 ]

width= 40               #standard disk diameter
hite = width * 2        # median wedge height.

hFac = [0.25,   0.45,  0.75,  1.2,  1.63,  1.87,  2.05]    # Radial factors
wFac = [ 0.2,   0.36,   0.6,  1.0,   0.5,   0.3,  0.25]     # disk diameter factors

#RED
kulaRed         =  ["#000000", "#6e0000", "#a00000", "#ff0000",\
                "#ff5050", "#ff8c8c", "#ffc8c8", "#440000" ]
# Khaki
kulaRRedGreen   =  ["#000000", "#606000", "#8f9f00", "#b3b300",\
                "#d6d600", "#dbdb30", "#dbdb77", "#3e2700" ]
# Yellow
kulaRedGreen    =  ["#000000", "#6e6e00", "#a0a000", "#ffff00",\
                "#ffff50", "#ffff8c", "#ffffc8", "#444400" ]
# Orange
kulaRedGGreen   =  ["#000000", "#493100", "#692f00", "#a25d00",\
                "#ff8300", "#ffa55a", "#ffb681", "#303030" ]
# Green
kulaGreen       =  ["#000000", "#006e00", "#00a000", "#00ff00",\
                "#50ff50", "#8cff8c", "#c8ffc8", "#004400" ]
# Dark green
kulaGGreenBlue  =  ["#000000", "#003227", "#009358", "#00a141",\
                "#00ff76", "#72ff99", "#acffbf", "#003a1d" ]
# Cyan
kulaGreenBlue   =  ["#000000", "#006e6e", "#00a0a0", "#00ffff",\
                "#50ffff", "#8cffff", "#c8ffff", "#004444" ]
# Steel Blue
kulaGreenBBlue  =  ["#000000", "#002c46", "#00639c", "#008cc8",\
                "#00b6ff", "#7bb6ff", "#addfff", "#001a27" ]
# Blue
kulaBlue        =  ["#000000", "#00006e", "#0000a0", "#0000ff",\
                "#5050ff", "#8c8cff", "#c8c8ff", "#000044" ]
# Purple
```

```
kulaBBlueRed    =  ["#000000", "#470047", "#6c00a2", "#8f00ff",\
                "#b380ff", "#d8b3ff", "#f1deff", "#200031" ]
# Crimson
kulaBlueRed    =  ["#000000", "#6e006e", "#a000a0", "#ff00ff",\
                "#ff50ff", "#ff8cff", "#ffc8ff", "#440044" ]
# Magenta
kulaBlueRRed    =  ["#000000", "#380023", "#80005a", "#b8007b",\
                "#ff00a1", "#ff64c5", "#ff89ea", "#2e0018" ]

angle = [ 0.0, 30.0, 60.0, 90.0, 120.0, 150.0, 180.0, 210.0,\
          240.0, 270.0, 300.0, 330.0, 360.0 ]
kulas = [ kulaRed, kulaRRedGreen, kulaRedGreen, kulaGreen,
kulaGGreenBlue,\
       kulaGreenBlue, kulaGreenBBlue, kulaBlue, kulaBBlueRed, kulaBlueRed,\
       kulaBlueRRed, kulaBlueRRed ]

# ROTATE
def rotate(xya, xyb, theta_deg_incr):     #xya, xyb are 2 component points
  “””General purpose line rotation function
  “””
   theta_rad = math.radians(theta_deg_incr)
   a_radian  = math.atan2( (xyb[1] - xya[1]) , (xyb[0] - xya[0]) )
   a_length  = math.sqrt( (xyb[1] - xya[1])**2 + (xyb[0] - xya[0])**2)
   theta_rad +=  a_radian
   theta_deg = math.degrees(theta_rad)
   new_x = a_length * math.cos(theta_rad)
   new_y = a_length * math.sin(theta_rad)
   return   new_x,   new_y,  theta_deg     # theta_deg = post rotation angle

# GENL. SEGMENT BACKGROUND FUNCTION
def segmentBackground(kula, angle, xy1, xy2):
   xy_new1 = rotate(xy0, xy1,  angle) # rotate xy1
   xy1 =[ xy_new1[0] + xy0[0], xy_new1[1] + xy0[1] ]
   xy_new2 = rotate(xy0,  xy2,  angle) # rotate xy2
   xy2 =[ xy_new2[0] + xy0[0], xy_new2[1] + xy0[1] ]
   wedge =[ xy0, xy1 , xy2 ]
   chart_1.create_polygon(wedge,fill=kula[7])

# GENL. COLOR DISKS FUNCTION
def colorDisks( kula, angle):
   global hite, width, hFac, wFac
   for i in range(0, 7):  # green segment disks
      xya = [xy0[0], xy0[1] - hite * hFac[i] ]   # position of point for rotation
      xy_new1 = rotate(xy0,  xya,  angle) # rotate xya
      # NEW CIRCLE CENTERS AFTER ROTATION OF CENTERLINE
```

```
        x0_disk = xy_new1[0] + xy0[0]  - width*wFac[i]/2
        y0_disk = xy_new1[1] + xy0[1]  + width * wFac[i]/2
        xya = [x0_disk, y0_disk]    # BOTTOM LEFT
        x1_disk = xy_new1[0] + xy0[0]  + width*wFac[i]/2
        y1_disk = xy_new1[1] + xy0[1]  - width * wFac[i]/2
        xyb = [x1_disk, y1_disk]  #TOP RIGHT
        chart_1.create_oval(xya ,xyb ,  fill=kula[i], outline=kula[i])

for i in range(12):
    segmentBackground( kulas[i], angle[i], xy1, xy2)
    colorDisks( kulas[i], angle[i])

root.mainloop()
```

Discussion

Each segment of the disk places colored disks obtained from an array (a Python list) of eight colors. There are twelve segments so we make convenient use of a two dimensional array *kulas* to contain all the detailed color information.

Rotation

In order to conveniently rotate our color wedges to the appropriate position on the color wheel we use the function *rotate(center, outer point, angle)* which uses the trigonometric functions of sine, cosine and tangent. If you find math unattractive that is fine. Just understand that the arguments you put into the rotation function are the center point as x.y coordinates, the outer point which will be rotated about the center point and amount of rotation degrees. The function returns the new position of the rotated point and its angle relative to the center point.

Numerical Color Design

We noted previously that we humans cannot intuitively mix numbers in the same way we can mix pigments from a tube to synthesize exactly the color we need. What we desire is a readily available tool that allows colors to be mixed and matched. We also would benefit from some expert guidance on how totally different colors can be tastefully combined. There are such tools available for free on the web. One of the best is **Color Scheme Designer** at http://colorschemedesigner.com/. It is excellent for obtaining the numerical value of web colors that Tkinter uses.

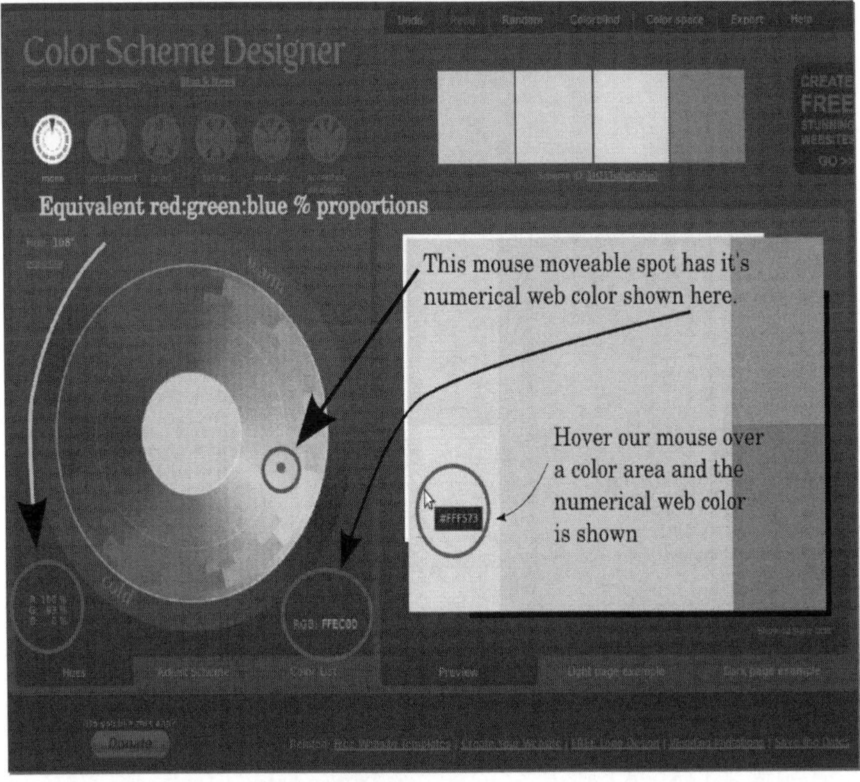

The light-to-dark adjustment page.

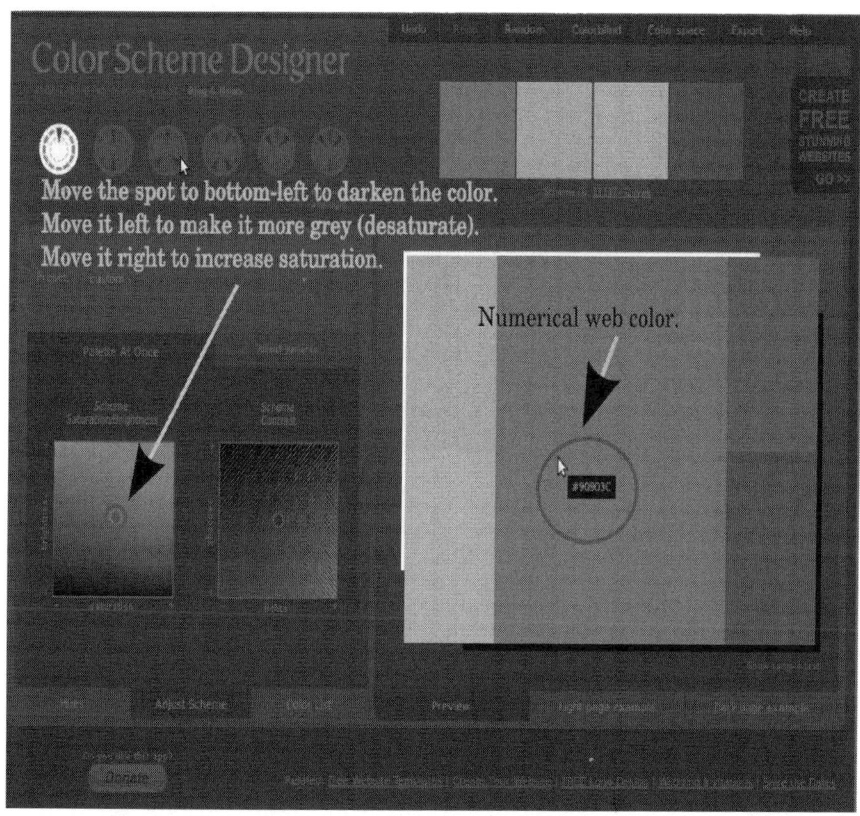

Points to note

Tasteful color combination varies from person to person and from culture to culture. The best guide to attractive color combinations is nature as shown in appealing color photographs. For example a photo of a sunset will have a combination dark blue, light blue, purple, pink, orange and yellow. Those same color combinations tend to go well together on a web page where they could be used for borders. Banners, logos and text.

What next?

Color Scheme Designer is a beautiful and sophisticated

graphic designer's tool. There are others out on the web but it is definitely one of the best. What if we are not connected to the internet when we want to create colors of any hue or brightness? Fortunately Tkinter has a very good built-in color mixer that provides all the information about colors we might need. It is called “askcolor”.

Tkinter's Color Mixer: askcolor

This wonderful little tool is something that we already have if we are using Python with Tkinter. Using it requires just two lines:

from tkColorChooser import askcolor
askcolor()

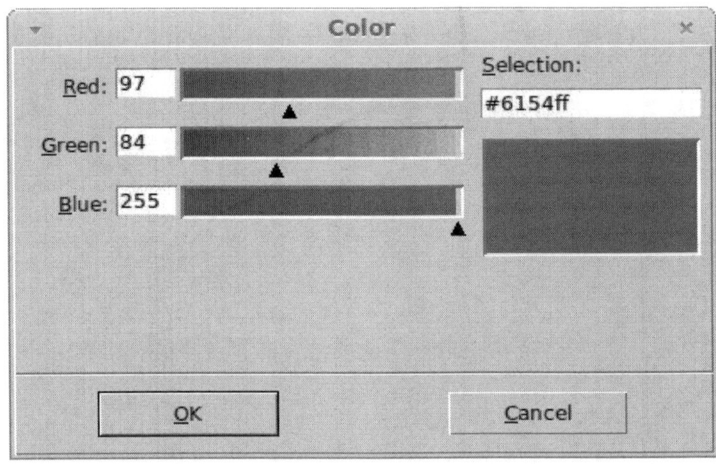

For the sake of consistency and future accessibility we write the code in the standard format we have been using.

```
"""
Program name: color_selector_mixer_1.py
Objective: Use the color selector that comes with Tkinter.

Keywords: color construction, selection, mixer.
==================================================
```

```
===================79
Comments: Remarkably simple.  However the Tkinter name is tkColorChoose
and the tkinter name is tkinter.colorchooser.

Tested on: Python 2.6,
Author: Mike Ohlson de Fine
"""
#from tkinter import *  # For Python 3.2.3 and higher.
from tkColorChooser import askcolor
#from tkinter.colorchooser import askcolor
askcolor()
```

Points to note

This "askcolor" tool is compact. It can be made even smaller by dragging a corner inward using the mouse. This means we can use it to match colors in the following way on a bitmap, jpeg, gif or png format image. We move the *askcolor* tool so that the mixed color panel is on top of the image area we want to match and adjust the color control sliders until we get the best match we can by eye. Then we take note of the hex color string below the "selection:" label. That hex color will give the color we can use in our code.

What next?

How can we construct a rainbow? It is not completely straightforward because it needs some trigonometry as well as carefully controlled color manipulation. The next two examples cover some of the color manipulation. After that we work out the trigonometry and produce the rainbow.

A Continuous Color Disk

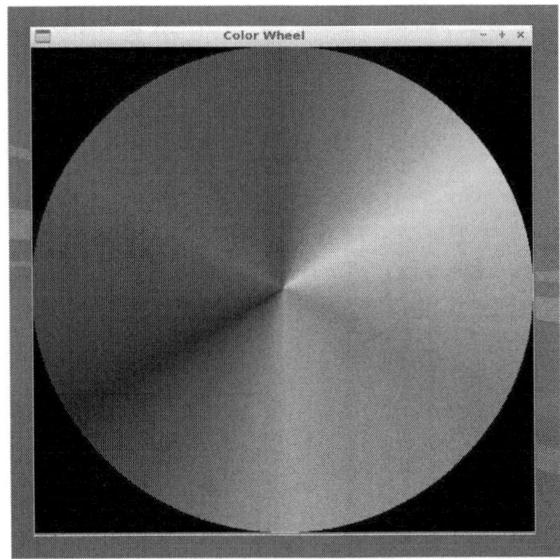


```
"""
Program name: color_wheel_1.py
Objective: Draw a progressive arc of a circle while mixing controlled
amounts of red, green and blue. Animate the display of corresponding
hex color value.

Keywords: circle, arc, progressive color wheel, hex color, animation
==================================================
 Comments: The periphery of the disk is divided into 60 degree sectors with
ramp-and-fall sections that govern the amount of pimary color that should
be present.

Tested on: Python 2.6, Python 2.7.3, Python 3.2.3
Author: Mike Ohlson de Fine
"""
from Tkinter import *
#from tkinter import *  # For Python 3.2.3 and higher.
root = Tk()
root.title("Color Wheel")

cw = 600                                  # canvas width
ch = 600                                  # canvas height
canvas_1 = Canvas(root, width=cw, height=ch, background="black")
canvas_1.grid(row=0, column=1)
#cycle_period = 200
```

```
redFl = 255.0
greenFl = 0
blueFl = 0
kula = "#000000"

arcStart = 89
arcEnd = 90

xCentr = 300
yCentr = 300
radius = 300
circ = xCentr - radius, yCentr + radius, xCentr + radius, yCentr - radius

# angular position markers, degrees
A_ANG = 0
B_ANG = 60
C_ANG = 120
D_ANG = 180
E_ANG = 240
F_ANG = 300
#G_ANG = 1
G_ANG = 359
intervals = 60 # degrees

# Percent color at each position marker
# index       0   1    2  3    4    5    6  7
redShift   = 100, 100,   0,   0,   0, 100, 100   # percent of red
greenShift =  0,  100, 100, 100,   0,   0,   0   # percent of green
blueShift  =  0,    0,   0, 100, 100, 100,   0   # percent of blue

# Rate of change of color per degree, rgb integer counts per degree.
red_rate = [0,1,2,3,4,5,6,7]
green_rate = [0,1,2,3,4,5,6,7]
blue_rate = [0,1,2,3,4,5,6,7]

# Calibrate counts-per-degree in each interval, place in xrate list
for i in range(0,6):
   red_rate[i] = 256.0 * (redShift[i+1]   - redShift[i])/(100 * intervals)
   green_rate[i] = 256.0 * (greenShift[i+1] - greenShift[i])/(100 * intervals)
   blue_rate[i] = 256.0 * (blueShift[i+1]  - blueShift[i])/(100 * intervals)

def rgb2hex(redFl, greenFl, blueFl):
    # Convert integer to hex color.
   red = int(redFl)
   green = int(greenFl)
```

```
    blue = int(blueFl)
    rgb = red, green, blue
    return '#%02x%02x%02x' % rgb

for i in range (0, 362):
    canvas_1.create_arc(circ, start=arcStart, extent=arcStart - arcEnd,\
                    fill= kula, outline= kula)
    arcStart = arcEnd
    arcEnd -=1

    # Color component transitions in 60 degree sectors
    if  i>A_ANG and i<B_ANG:
        redFl   +=  red_rate[0]
        greenFl +=  green_rate[0]
        blueFl  += blue_rate[0]
        kula = rgb2hex(redFl, greenFl, blueFl)

    if  i>B_ANG and i<C_ANG:
        redFl   +=  red_rate[1]
        greenFl +=  green_rate[1]
        blueFl  +=  blue_rate[1]
        kula = rgb2hex(redFl, greenFl, blueFl)

    if  i>C_ANG and i<D_ANG:
        redFl   +=  red_rate[2]
        greenFl +=  green_rate[2]
        blueFl  +=  blue_rate[2]
        kula = rgb2hex(redFl, greenFl, blueFl)

    if  i>D_ANG and i<E_ANG:
        redFl   +=  red_rate[3]
        greenFl +=  green_rate[3]
        blueFl  +=  blue_rate[3]
        kula = rgb2hex(redFl, greenFl, blueFl)

    if  i>E_ANG and i<F_ANG:
        redFl   +=  red_rate[4]
        greenFl +=  green_rate[4]
        blueFl  +=  blue_rate[4]
        kula = rgb2hex(redFl, greenFl, blueFl)

    if  i>F_ANG and i<G_ANG:
        redFl   +=  red_rate[5]
        greenFl +=  green_rate[5]
        blueFl  +=  blue_rate[5]
```

```
    kula = rgb2hex(redFl, greenFl, blueFl)

root.mainloop()
```

Discussion

Us humans are schooled in the use of decimal arithmetic. Hexadecimal numbers are convenient for arithmetic based on binary which is a foreign language to most of us. In the above program we mix colors numerically as decimal percentages for conceptual convenience. We need to scale up our percentage figures by 255/100 to cover the range 0 – 255 that corresponds to the hexadecimal range 0 – ff.
To covert these scaled up numbers to the hexadecimal string that Tkinter will recognise we use the function

```
def rgb2hex(redFl, greenFl, blueFl):
    # Convert integer to hex color.
   red = int(redFl)
   green = int(greenFl)
   blue = int(blueFl)
   rgb = red, green, blue
    return '#%02x%02x%02x' % rgb
```

There is a warning that goes with the use of this function and it it this. Numbers which are greater than 255 for any color or numbers which are negative will attempt produce color strings that do not exist and the program will terminate with an error message. Bullet proof code should have conditional statements that force the numbers to stay inside the 0 – 255 range if any Python command tries to do otherwise. In examples later in this chapter we incorporate these precautions.

Points to note

The statement *return '#%02x%02x%02x' % rgb* is the key to the conversions of numbers in the 0-255 decimal range into hexadecimal strings. A brief form of the instruction would be '%02x' rr which means "take the decimal value rr and convert it to a hexadecimal string.

What next?

Ultimately we would like to be able to fill any shape with any mixture of colors. This introduces an overwhelming numbers variations in how the colors should vary. Should the color change radially starting at some defined point inside the shape? Should it follow the contours of the shape? Should it form diagonal bands? And so on. I chapter 5 on Textured color we demonstrate a small selection from the limitless choices conceivable.

Continuous Controlled Variation of Color

The previous example is specifically designed to fill a circular disk with a controlled combination of the primary colors of red, green and blue. This works out because we have carefully divided a circle into tightly controlled segments. If we want a more general and versatile way to fill rectangles we must craft our coloring functions in more general terms to allow them to be positioned anywhere on the screen and made to be any size.
This is done below. Note that the three 'mesa' shaped red, green and blue polygons are not produced by the Python program but were inserted afterward to show the amount of the three primary color components present in the smoothly mixed combination resulting in the top rainbow spectrum.

```
"""
Program name: color_mix_swatches_1.py
Objective: Draw a colored ractangle composed of vertical lines only.
Vary the colors according to three controlled RGB
percentage numbers (0% = 0 , 100% = 255)

Keywords: rectangle, lines, progressive, color spectrum, color mixing, function
=============================================================
Comments: Draw a smooth linear spectrum of color.

Tested on: Python 2.6, Python 2.7.3, Python 3.2.3
Author: Mike Ohlson de Fine
"""
from Tkinter import *
#from tkinter import *  # For Python 3.2.3 and higher.
root = Tk()
root.title("Red-Green-Blue Color Transition Spectrum")
cw = 1580                             # canvas width
ch = 200                              # canvas height
canvas = Canvas(root, width=cw, height=ch, background="black")
canvas.grid(row=0, column=1)

# Color variation lists: Transition ramps or tapers.
Red_ramp1, Red_ramp2, Red_ramp3        = [100.0,   0.0 ], [0.0,   0.0 ],     [0.0,
100.0 ]
Green_ramp1, Green_ramp2 , Green_ramp3  = [ 0.0,  100.0 ], [ 100.0,  0.0 ],
[ 0.0,  00.0  ]
Blue_ramp1, Blue_ramp2 , Blue_ramp3    = [ 0.0,    0.0 ], [ 0.0,    100.0 ],
[ 100.0,    0.0 ]

Red_ramp4, Red_ramp5, Red_ramp6  = [100.0, 100.0], [100.0, 0.0 ],  [0.0,
0.0 ]
Red_ramp7, Red_ramp8, Red_ramp9  = [0.0,    0.0 ], [0.0,  100.0],  [100.0,
100.0]
```

```
Green_ramp4, Green_ramp5 , Green_ramp6  = [ 0.0, 100.0 ], [ 100.0,  100.0 ],  [
100.0,  100.0  ]
Green_ramp7, Green_ramp8 , Green_ramp9  = [ 100.0,  0.0 ], [ 0.0,  0.0 ],  [ 0.0,
00.0  ]

Blue_ramp4, Blue_ramp5 , Blue_ramp6     = [ 0.0,  0.0 ], [ 0.0,  0.0 ], [ 0.0, 100.0
]
Blue_ramp7, Blue_ramp8 , Blue_ramp9     = [ 100.0, 100.0 ], [ 100.0, 100.0 ],
[ 100.0,  0.0 ]

xy_start  = [ 20, 20 ]         # Bottom left.
swatch_height = 60             # Swatch height.
y_gap = 20                     # Gap between swatches

num_steps = 255

def rgb2hex(redFl, greenFl, blueFl):
    """ Convert Red %, Green %, Blue % to numerical hex web color.
        Return: the hex web color.
    """
    red = int(redFl)
    green = int(greenFl)
    blue = int(blueFl)
    rgb = red, green, blue
    return '#%02x%02x%02x' % rgb


def kula_ramp( xy_start, Red_ramp, Green_ramp, Blue_ramp, num_steps, ):
    """ Paint a rectangular color mixture swatch with primary colors expressed.
        Each transitional color is one pixel wide.
        as % percent values (ie. from 0 to 100.
    """
    redShift   =  (Red_ramp[1]-Red_ramp[0])/num_steps
    greenShift =  (Green_ramp[1]-Green_ramp[0])/num_steps
    blueShift  =  (Blue_ramp[1]-Blue_ramp[0])/num_steps

    for m in range(num_steps):
        # Red channel.
        redValue   = (Red_ramp[0] + redShift* m)* 2.55  # Current red amount in
0-255 range.
        if redValue >= 255.0:            # Ensure redValue remains less than FF
hexadecimal.
            redValue = 255.0
        if redValue <= 0.0:              # Ensure redValue remains greater than 0.
```

```
        redValue = 0.0

    # Green channel.
    greenValue   = (Green_ramp[0] + greenShift* m)* 2.55  # Current green
amount in 0-255 range.
    if greenValue >= 255.0:
        greendValue = 255.0
    if greenValue <= 0.0:
        greendValue = 0.0

    # Blue channel.
    blueValue   = (Blue_ramp[0] + blueShift* m)* 2.55  # Current blue amount
in 0-255 range.
    if blueValue >= 255.0:
        blueValue = 255.0
    if blueValue <= 0.0:
        blueValue = 0.0
    kula = rgb2hex(redValue, greenValue, blueValue)    # Convert to web hex
color.
    canvas.create_line(xy_start[0]+m, xy_start[1], xy_start[0]+m,
xy_start[1]+swatch_height, fill= kula, width = 1)
  return xy_start[0]+num_steps

# Rainbow Spectrum.
#
>>>>>>>>>>>>>>>>>>>>>>>>>>>>>>>>>>>>>>>>>>>>>>>>>>>>>>>>>>>>
>>>>>
xy_start[0] = kula_ramp(xy_start, Red_ramp4, Green_ramp4, Blue_ramp4,
num_steps)
xy_start[0] = kula_ramp(xy_start, Red_ramp5, Green_ramp5, Blue_ramp5,
num_steps)
xy_start[0] = kula_ramp(xy_start, Red_ramp6, Green_ramp6, Blue_ramp6,
num_steps)
xy_start[0] = kula_ramp(xy_start, Red_ramp7, Green_ramp7, Blue_ramp7,
num_steps)
xy_start[0] = kula_ramp(xy_start, Red_ramp8, Green_ramp8, Blue_ramp8,
num_steps)
xy_start[0] = kula_ramp(xy_start, Red_ramp9, Green_ramp9, Blue_ramp9,
num_steps)
#>>>>>>>>>>>>>>>>>>>>>>>>>>>>>>>>>>>>>>>>>>>>>>>>>>>>>>>>>>>>
>>>>>
root.mainloop()
```

Discussion

This uses the same strategy as the previous example where we specify ramp variables like
Red_ramp1, Red_ramp2, Red_ramp3 = [100.0, 0.0], [0.0, 0.0], [0.0, 100.0]
which regulate start and end values for the three zones of color mixture that we have divided the colored strip into.
The dimensions of the colored strip are determined by

```
xy_start = [ 20, 20 ]        # Bottom left.
swatch_height = 60           # Swatch height.
y_gap = 20                   # Gap between swatches
```

The last line is not needed here but will be needed in the next example where we create multiple color mixture strips.

Points to note

To avoid the catastrophes that would be caused by trying to make meaningful hexadecimal color strings out of negative numbers or numbers greater than 255 we clamp the allowable range of numbers with code sequences like the following:

```
if greenValue >= 255.0:
        greendValue = 255.0
if greenValue <= 0.0:
        greendValue = 0.0
```

What next?

Next we explore how to mix any two arbitrary colors.

Complex Color Mixing

What colors will we get if we mix complex mixtures of colors together?
The results turn out to be difficult to predict. In this example we look at some examples where we have mixed varying

percentages of each of the primary colors in systematic ways to try and develop a way of getting a reference set of mixtures.
Ultimately we would like to answer the following type of question. If we start with greenish mixture and end with orange what colors would we get in between? A similar version of the same question would be: If we start with the greenish mixture how do we transform it smoothly into an orange? This would be the kind of thing we would want to do to change the color of the sky from night to dawn to bright morning in an animated picture scene.

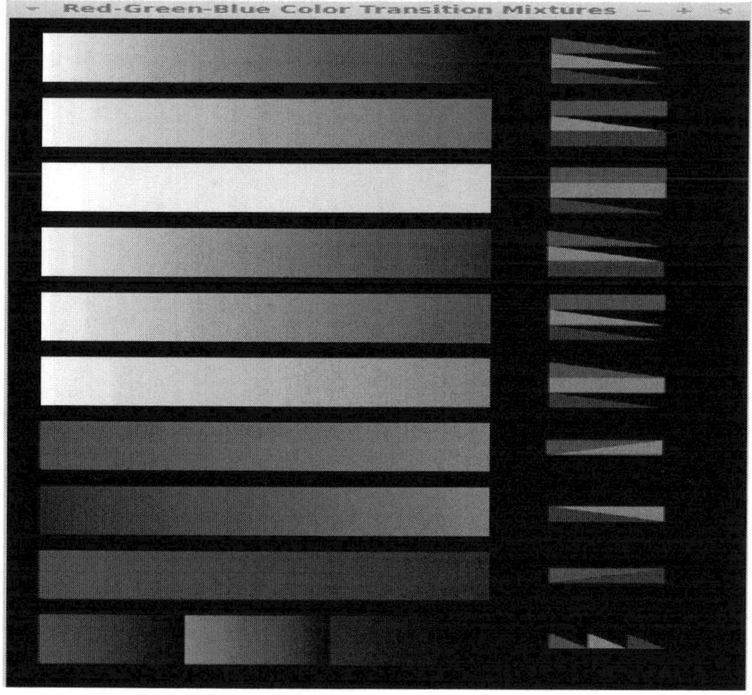

For this example we use exactly the same program as the one above except that we substitute the code below for the six lines between the herring-bone separators “#>>>>>>>>>...”
In the diagram, on the right of each rectangular mixed color

swatch we have inserted an explanatory diagram illustrating the relative amounts of the three primary colors in the mix as a colored wedge. For example in the first grey swatch at the top we start with the maximum amount of red, green and blue and gradually reduce all three at the same rate as the color changes through darker grays toward black.

```
#>>>>>>>>>>>>>>>>>>>>>>>>>>>>>>>>>>>>>>>>>>>>>>>>>>>>>>>>>>
>>>>>
# White → Grey → Black
xy_start = [ 20, xy_start[1] ]
Red_ramp1, Green_ramp1, Blue_ramp1      = [100.0,   0.0 ], [ 100.0,  0.0 ],
[ 100.0, 0.0 ]
xy_start[0] = kula_ramp(xy_start, Red_ramp1, Green_ramp1, Blue_ramp1,
num_steps)
# White → Violet.
xy_start = [ 20, xy_start[1] + y_gap + swatch_height ]
Red_ramp1, Green_ramp1, Blue_ramp1      = [100.0,   100.0 ], [ 100.0,  0.0 ],
[ 100.0, 100.0 ]
xy_start[0] = kula_ramp(xy_start, Red_ramp1, Green_ramp1, Blue_ramp1,
num_steps)
# White → Yellow
xy_start = [ 20, xy_start[1] + y_gap + swatch_height]
Red_ramp1, Green_ramp1, Blue_ramp1      = [100.0,   100.0 ], [ 100.0,  100.0 ],
[ 100.0, 0.0 ]
xy_start[0] = kula_ramp(xy_start, Red_ramp1, Green_ramp1, Blue_ramp1,
num_steps)
# White → Blue
xy_start = [ 20, xy_start[1] + y_gap + swatch_height]
Red_ramp1, Green_ramp1, Blue_ramp1      = [100.0,   00.0 ], [ 100.0,  0.0 ],
[ 100.0, 100.0 ]
xy_start[0] = kula_ramp(xy_start, Red_ramp1, Green_ramp1, Blue_ramp1,
num_steps)
# White → Red
xy_start = [ 20, xy_start[1] + y_gap + swatch_height]
Red_ramp1, Green_ramp1, Blue_ramp1      = [100.0,   100.0 ], [ 100.0,  0.0 ],
[ 100.0, 0.0 ]
xy_start[0] = kula_ramp(xy_start, Red_ramp1, Green_ramp1, Blue_ramp1,
num_steps)
# White → Green
xy_start = [ 20, xy_start[1] + y_gap + swatch_height]
Red_ramp1, Green_ramp1, Blue_ramp1      = [100.0,   0.0 ], [ 100.0,  100.0 ],
[ 100.0, 0.0 ]
xy_start[0] = kula_ramp(xy_start, Red_ramp1, Green_ramp1, Blue_ramp1,
```

```
num_steps)
# Red → Green
xy_start = [ 20, xy_start[1] + y_gap + swatch_height]
Red_ramp1, Green_ramp1, Blue_ramp1      = [100.0,   0.0 ], [ 0.0,  100.0 ], [ 0.0,
00.0 ]
xy_start[0] = kula_ramp(xy_start, Red_ramp1, Green_ramp1, Blue_ramp1,
num_steps)
# Blue → Green
xy_start = [ 20, xy_start[1] + y_gap + swatch_height]
Red_ramp1, Green_ramp1, Blue_ramp1      = [0.0,   0.0 ], [ 0.0,  100.0 ], [ 100.0,
00.0 ]
xy_start[0] = kula_ramp(xy_start, Red_ramp1, Green_ramp1, Blue_ramp1,
num_steps)
# Red - > Blue
xy_start = [ 20, xy_start[1] + y_gap + swatch_height]
Red_ramp1, Green_ramp1, Blue_ramp1      = [100.0,   0.0 ], [ 0.0,  0.0 ], [ 0.0,
100.0 ]
xy_start[0] = kula_ramp(xy_start, Red_ramp1, Green_ramp1, Blue_ramp1,
num_steps)
# Red
num_steps = 83
xy_start = [ 20, xy_start[1] + y_gap + swatch_height]
Red_ramp1, Green_ramp1, Blue_ramp1      = [100.0,   0.0 ], [ 0.0,  0.0 ], [ 0.0,
0.0 ]
xy_start[0] = kula_ramp(xy_start, Red_ramp1, Green_ramp1, Blue_ramp1,
num_steps)
# Green
xy_start = [ 103, xy_start[1] ]
Red_ramp1, Green_ramp1, Blue_ramp1      = [0.0,   0.0 ], [ 100.0,  0.0 ], [ 0.0,
0.0 ]
xy_start[0] = kula_ramp(xy_start, Red_ramp1, Green_ramp1, Blue_ramp1,
num_steps)
# Blue
xy_start = [ 186, xy_start[1] ]
Red_ramp1, Green_ramp1, Blue_ramp1      = [0.0,   0.0 ], [ 0.0,  0.0 ], [ 100.0,
0.0 ]
xy_start[0] = kula_ramp(xy_start, Red_ramp1, Green_ramp1, Blue_ramp1,
num_steps)
#>>>>>>>>>>>>>>>>>>>>>>>>>>>>>>>>>>>>>>>>>>>>>>>>>
```

A Rainbow by Rotation

How can we create a rainbow? The program below creates the kind double rainbow that we sometimes see when there is a bright rainbow against a dark grey sky. The inner rainbow is much fainter.

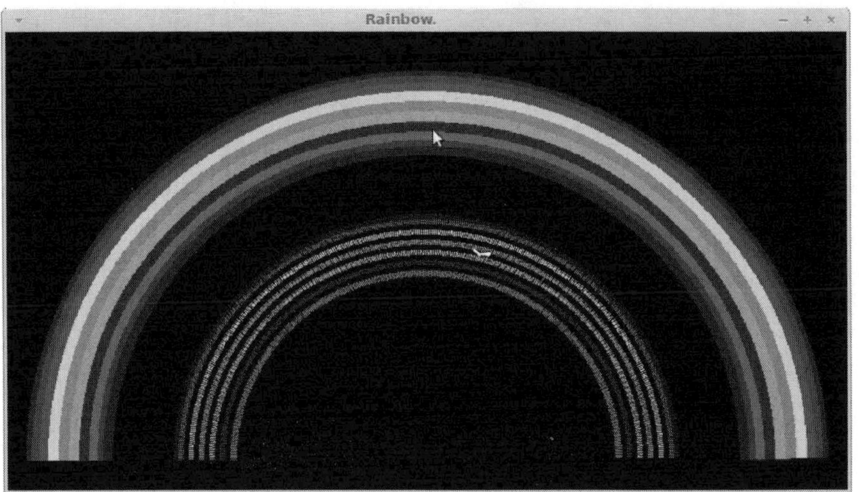


```
"""
Program name: rainbow_1.py
Objective: Draw a rainbow.

Keywords: canvas, rainbow, color, rotation.
=================================================================
Comments: A general purpose shape rotation function is used. The shape in
this case is a straight line segment.

Tested on: Python 2.6, Python 2.7.3, Python 3.2.3
Author: Mike Ohlson de Fine
"""
from Tkinter import *
#from tkinter import *  # For Python 3.2.3 and higher.
from copy import *
from copy import *
```

```
import math
root = Tk()
root.title("Rainbow.")
canvas_1 = Canvas(root, width=800, height=450, background="#000000")
canvas_1.grid(row=0, column=1)

def rotate_shape(shape, xy_center, angle_degrees):
    """ Rotate any shape about a center point xy_center.
    """
    angle_rad = math.radians(angle_degrees)
    x_cen = xy_center[0]
    y_cen = xy_center[1]
    new_shape = []
     for i in range(int(len(shape)/2) ):
        x_temp = shape[2*i]  - x_cen
        y_temp = shape[2*i+1] - y_cen
        radian_temp  = math.atan2(y_temp, x_temp )
        length_temp = math.sqrt( y_temp**2 + x_temp**2)
        new_angle = angle_rad + radian_temp
        new_x = length_temp * math.cos(new_angle) + x_cen
        new_y = length_temp * math.sin(new_angle) + y_cen
        new_shape.append(new_x)
        new_shape.append(new_y)
    return   new_shape   # angle_deg = post rotation angle

kulas_1 = ['#550000', '#aa0000', '#ff0000','#ffff00', '#00ff00', '#00ffff', '#0000ff',
'#ff00ff','#660066', '#330044']
kulas_2 = ['#440000', '#ff0000','#000000','#ffff00','#000000', '#00ff00','#000000',
'#00ffff','#000000', '#0000ff','#000000', '#ff00ff','#440044']

line_1 = [20,420,   25,420,    32,420, 40,420,   50,420,    60,420,  70,420,  80,420,
88,420, 94,420,   100,420,    104,420]
line_2 = [160,420,  165,420,  170,420, 175,420,  180,420, 185,420,   190,420,
195,420, 200,420, 205,420, 210,420, 215,420, 220,420, 225,420, 230,420  ,
235,420 ]

xy_center = 400.0, 420.0
for j in range(10):
   line_a = line_1[2*j], line_1[2*j+1], line_1[2*j+2], line_1[2*j+3]
   for i in range(720):
      new_shape = rotate_shape(line_a, xy_center, 0.25*i )
      canvas_1.create_line(new_shape, fill=kulas_1[j], width=3 )

for j in range(12):
   line_b = line_2[2*j], line_2[2*j+1], line_2[2*j+2], line_2[2*j+3]
```

```
    for i in range(360):
        new_shape = rotate_shape(line_b, xy_center, 0.5*i )
        canvas_1.create_line(new_shape, fill=kulas_2[j], width=1 )


root.mainloop()
```

Discussion

Essentially the curved bands of color are made of short straight lines of different colors.
There are two versions of these multicolored lines, line_1 and line_2. Line_1 has an extra segment at the start and end to accommodate darker outer transition colors to represent a muted (darker) transition band between the bright inner color and the black background. The inner small rainbow appears darker because the colored segmented lines are interspersed with black lines as you can see by looking as the color list kulas_2 – every second color is '#000000' which is black.

Points to note

To rotate each multi-segmented line we use a function *rotate_shape(shape, xy_center,* angle_degrees) which takes a list (the *shape* argument) of x,y position coordinate pairs of any length and complexity and rotates it by an amount *angle_degrees* round a center position given by *xy_center.* The function is borrowed from the next chapter.

What next?

Often we want a nice series of colors that change in gradual steps from one given color to another. That is we want a list of colors that goes in discrete steps from one color to another. The next example does this.

Controlled color transition be

Now we develop a technique for obtaining a discrete number of intermediate steps in color mixtures going from a chosen start color and ending with a different chosen color. Our program should perform the arithmetic for the mixing process and display the results so that we can select numerical hex web colors to use.
The program below produces only a single series of discrete colors between red and yellow. To get the eight sets shown below insert the code below the heading “color transitions” underneath the **Discussion** paragraph below.

Color transition from a start to an end color

#ff0000 255 0 0	#00ffff 0 255 255	#000000 0 0 0	#0088ff 0 136 255	#00ff00 0 255 0	#fff700 255 247 0	#e339a4 227 57 164	#890043 137 0 67
#ff2400 255 36 0	#00daff 0 218 255	#242424 36 36 36	#0074e1 0 116 225	#24da00 36 218 0	#dad324 218 211 36	#d33aab 211 58 171	#7b0049 123 0 73
#ff4800 255 72 0	#00b5ff 0 181 255	#484848 72 72 72	#0060c3 0 96 195	#48b500 72 181 0	#b5af48 181 175 72	#c33bb2 195 59 178	#6d004f 109 0 79
#ff6c00 255 108 0	#0090ff 0 144 255	#6c6c6c 108 108 108	#004ca5 0 76 165	#6c9000 108 144 0	#908b6c 144 139 108	#b33cb9 179 60 185	#5f0055 95 0 85
#ff9000 255 144 0	#006bff 0 107 255	#909090 144 144 144	#003887 0 56 135	#906b00 144 107 0	#6b6790 107 103 144	#a33dc0 163 61 192	#51005b 81 0 91
#ffb400 255 180 0	#0046ff 0 70 255	#b4b4b4 180 180 180	#002469 0 36 105	#b44600 180 70 0	#4643b4 70 67 180	#933ec7 147 62 199	#430061 67 0 97
#ffd800 255 216 0	#0021ff 0 33 255	#d8d8d8 216 216 216	#00104b 0 16 75	#d82100 216 33 0	#211fd8 33 31 216	#833fce 131 63 206	#350067 53 0 103
#fffc00 255 252 0	#0000ff 0 0 255	#fcfcfc 252 252 252	#00002d 0 0 45	#fc0000 252 0 0	#0000fc 0 0 252	#7340d5 115 64 213	#27006d 39 0 109

"""
Program name: color_8_discrete_transitions_1.py
Objective:Creates 8 sets of discrete transition sequences between two end colors. The start and end colors can be either in R:G:B lists or as a single hex color value.

Keywords: canvas, color transition, sequence, color blending, discrete

```
===========================================================
Comments: The start and end colors are given as as pairs of hex color value
'#rrggbb'.
The user specifies how transition steps there will be.
 The colors are labelled with their hex web designations.

Tested on: Python 2.6, Python 2.7.3, Python 3.2.3
Author: Mike Ohlson de Fine

"""
from Tkinter import *
#from tkinter import *  # For Python 3.2.3 and higher.
root = Tk()
root.title("Color transition from a start to an end color")
canvas_1 = Canvas(root, width=1250, height=400, background="black")
canvas_1.grid(row=0, column=1)

fnt = 'Bookantiqua 12 bold'
fnt_2 = 'Bookantiqua 10 bold'

def hex2rgb(hex_color):
    """ Convert a hex color of the from '#rrggbb'
        to three element tuple of base 10 integers corresponging to (red, green,
blue).
    """
    start_kula = 0,0,0
    end_kula = 0,0,0
    n1 = [1,  3, 5]
    n2 = [3,  5, 7]
    rgb_color = []
    for i in range(0,3):
        a = n1[i]
        b = n2[i]
        kula_slice = hex_color[a:b]
        #print ' kula_slice: ', kula_slice
        c = int(kula_slice, 16)

        rgb_color.append(c)  # '16' is the base from which to convert.
    rgb_color = tuple(rgb_color)
    return rgb_color

 # hex rgb inputs.
 def discrete_kula_series(start_color, end_color, num_steps):
     """ Create the color transition list between a start and an end color (hex rgb).
         Generate Color Transition Series as hex RGB inputs
```

```
    """
    start_color_int = hex2rgb(start_color)
    end_color_int = hex2rgb( end_color)
    delt_red = (end_color_int[0] - start_color_int[0])/(num_steps - 1)
    delt_green = (end_color_int[1] - start_color_int[1])/(num_steps - 1)
    delt_blue = (end_color_int[2] - start_color_int[2])/(num_steps - 1)
    color_series_int = []
    color_series_hex = []
    for i in range(num_steps+1):
        next_red = start_color_int[0]+i*delt_red
        if next_red <=0.0:
            next_red = 0.0
        next_green = start_color_int[1]+i*delt_green
        if next_green <=0.0:
            next_green = 0.0
        next_blue = start_color_int[2]+i*delt_blue
        if next_blue <=0.0:
            next_blue = 0.0
        next_color_int = next_red, next_green, next_blue
        color_series_int.append(next_color_int)
        if i < num_steps:
            next_color_hex = '#%02x%02x%02x' % next_color_int
            color_series_hex.append(next_color_hex)
            color_series_int.append(next_color_int)
        else:
            next_color_hex =  '#%02x%02x%02x' % end_color_int
            color_series_hex.append(next_color_hex)
            color_series_int.append(next_color_int)
    return color_series_hex

def show_swatch(color_hex, x_start, y_start, width, height, gap):
    """  Paint a swatch specified by the xy position, width and height.
         'gap' the separation between the swatch and the label.
    """
    panel = x_start, y_start, x_start+width, y_start+height
    canvas_1.create_rectangle(panel, fill = color_hex)
    y_start = y_start + height + gap
    canvas_1.create_text(x_start + width+10, y_start-height-10, text= color_hex,
fill='grey', width=200,\
                        anchor=NW, font=fnt) #font='Bookantiqua 16 bold'
    color_int =  hex2rgb(color_hex)
    canvas_1.create_text(x_start + width+10, y_start-height+10, text= color_int,
fill='grey', width=200,\
                        anchor=NW, font=fnt_2) #font='Bookantiqua 16 bold'
```

```
# color transitions
#=====================================================
# Colors specified as Hex rrggbb (full scale = ff)
start_color_hex_1 = '#ff0000'
end_color_hex_1   = '#ffff00'

#=====================================================
# Swatch geometry
#=================
x_start = 20
y_start = 10
width = 40
height = 40
gap = 8
num_steps = 8
#=====================================================
# Generate the color series and display them.
#==================================
kulas = discrete_kula_series(start_color_hex_1, end_color_hex_1, num_steps )
for i in range(num_steps):
   show_swatch(kulas[i], x_start, y_start, width, height, gap)
   y_start += height+gap
#=====================================================

root.mainloop()
```

Discussion

This program uses two key functions to achieve it purpose. Firstly we need to slice up the numerical color distance between the given start and end colors. The numerical size of this transition slice is progressively added to the starting color in each red, green and blue color channel so that it transforms by discrete intervals toward the end color. The arithmetic to achieve this is performed using the traditional decimal system we are comfortable with. The *hex2rgb(hex_color)* function does the conversion from a hexadecimal color string to separate red, green and blue decimal channels.

The *discrete_kula_series(start_color, end_color, num_steps)* function takes the hexadecimal *start_color* and *end_color* and splits the color distance between the two into a desired number of steps (argument *num_steps).* From inside this function another function *hex2rgb(hex_color)* is called to perform the conversion from a hexadecimal color string to separate red, green and blue decimal channels.

```
# color transitions
#===================================================
# Colors specified as Hex rrggbb (full scale = ff)
start_color_hex_1 = '#ff0000'
end_color_hex_1   = '#ffff00'

start_color_hex_2 = '#00ffff'
end_color_hex_2  =  '#0000ff'

start_color_hex_3 = '#000000'
end_color_hex_3 =  '#ffffff'

start_color_hex_4 = '#0088ff'
end_color_hex_4 =  '#000033'

start_color_hex_5 = '#00ff00'
end_color_hex_5 =  '#ff0000'

start_color_hex_6 = '#fff700'
end_color_hex_6 =  '#0000ff'

start_color_hex_7 = '#e339a4'
end_color_hex_7   = '#7746d7'

start_color_hex_8 = '#890043'
end_color_hex_8   = '#2a0671'

#==================================================
# Swatch geometry
#================
x_start = 20
y_start = 10
width = 40
height = 40
gap = 8
num_steps = 8
#=================================================
```

```
# Generate the color series and display them.
#==================================
kulas = discrete_kula_series(start_color_hex_1, end_color_hex_1, num_steps )
for i in range(num_steps):
    show_swatch(kulas[i], x_start, y_start, width, height, gap)
    y_start += height+gap

x_start += width + 110
y_start = 10
kulas = discrete_kula_series(start_color_hex_2, end_color_hex_2, num_steps )
for i in range(num_steps):
    show_swatch(kulas[i], x_start, y_start, width, height, gap)
    y_start += height+gap

x_start += width + 110
y_start = 10
kulas = discrete_kula_series(start_color_hex_3, end_color_hex_3, num_steps )
for i in range(num_steps):
    show_swatch(kulas[i], x_start, y_start, width, height, gap)
    y_start += height+gap

x_start += width + 110
y_start = 10
kulas = discrete_kula_series(start_color_hex_4, end_color_hex_4, num_steps )
for i in range(num_steps):
    show_swatch(kulas[i], x_start, y_start, width, height, gap)
    y_start += height+gap

x_start += width + 110
y_start = 10
kulas = discrete_kula_series(start_color_hex_5, end_color_hex_5, num_steps )
for i in range(num_steps):
    show_swatch(kulas[i], x_start, y_start, width, height, gap)
    y_start += height+gap

x_start += width + 110
y_start = 10
kulas = discrete_kula_series(start_color_hex_6, end_color_hex_6, num_steps )
for i in range(num_steps):
    show_swatch(kulas[i], x_start, y_start, width, height, gap)
    y_start += height+gap

x_start += width + 110
y_start = 10
kulas = discrete_kula_series(start_color_hex_7, end_color_hex_7, num_steps )
```

```
for i in range(num_steps):
    show_swatch(kulas[i], x_start, y_start, width, height, gap)
    y_start += height+gap

x_start += width + 110
y_start = 10
kulas = discrete_kula_series(start_color_hex_8, end_color_hex_8, num_steps )
for i in range(num_steps):
    show_swatch(kulas[i], x_start, y_start, width, height, gap)
    y_start += height+gap
```

What next?

In chapter 4 and 5 we extend techniques of combining colors that enhance the textures of vector graphic images.

4

Graphic Elements: Polygons

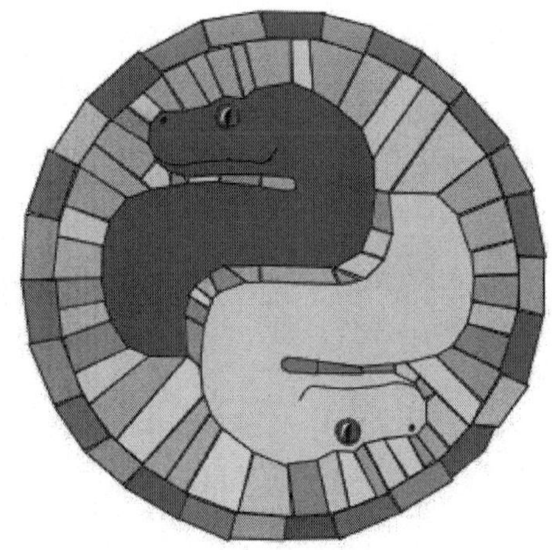

In this chapter we will cover:

- how to draw the simplest polygon
- how to draw a polygon star
- how to repositioning of polygons
- how to alter the size of polygons
- a practical approach to debugging code
- understanding the color fill rules of polygons
- understanding the color filling of complex polygons

- transformation of polygons by shifting, amplifying and rotating
- filling polygon shapes with graded shades of color

Polygons

Polygons are spaces enclosed by multi-sided lines. The segmented lines making a polygon can be smoothed into curves. Polygons are a very versatile drawing primitives.

Draw a Triangular Polygon

This is the simplest polygon that can be drawn.

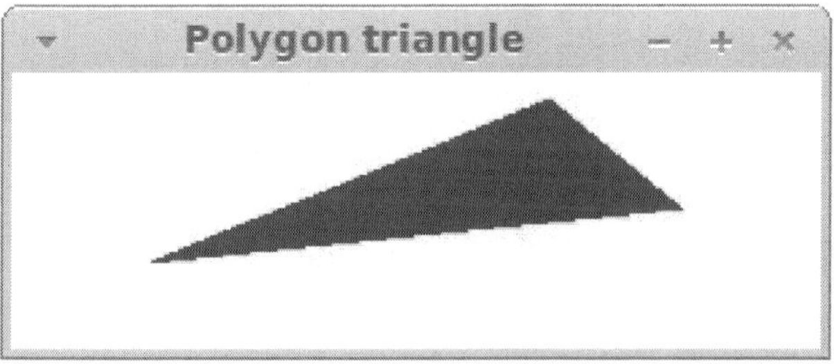

.   .

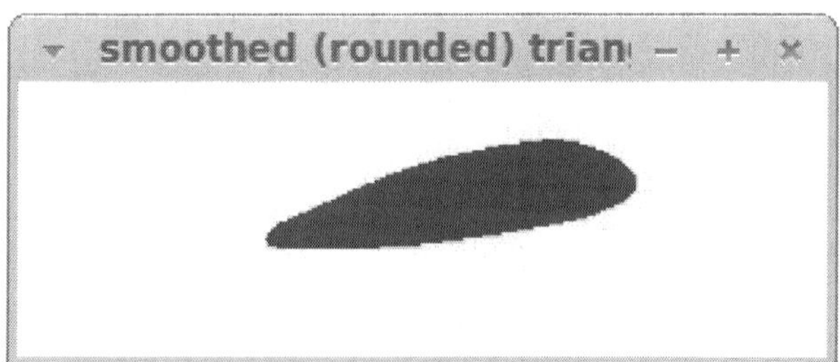


```
"""
Program name: poly_triangle_1.py
Objective: Draw a triangle - the simplest polygon.

Keywords: polygon. triangle
```

```
===========================================================
Comments:
a polygon is made by joining a sequence of x-y points,
with the last point automatically joined to the first by a line to close
the polygon.

Tested on: Python 2.6, Python 2.7, Python 3.2.3
Author: Mike Ohlson de Fine
"""
from Tkinter import *
#from tkinter import *  # For Python 3.2.3 and higher.
root = Tk()

cw = 300                                # canvas width
ch = 100                                # canvas height
canvas_1 = Canvas(root, width=cw, height=ch, background="white")
canvas_1.grid(row=0, column=1)

#                           point 1   point 2   point 3
canvas_1.create_polygon(200,10,  250,50,   50,70,     fill="red")

root.mainloop()
```

Discussion

The create_polygon function in Tkinter always joins the the last point in it's list of x,y coordinates to the first point by a line. This creates an enclosed area inside the line segments that can be filled with any color. Later on we will see that if any of the lines enclosing a polygon cross each other then somehow some of the interior of the polygon ends up on the outside. The result is that that some of the enclosed space s are not filled with color. Interesting effects can be created this way.

Points to note

A long complicated shape is composed of many points in a list. The same list will work equally well in a *create_polygon* function or in a *create_line* function. The main difference in the end is that the polygon can be filled with a color while the line cannot.

What next?

Using techniques from the previous chapter we can create pleasing shading effects inside polygons. These require us to develop functions that attempt to control shades of color in a systematic way. These issues are tackled toward the end of this chapter.

Draw a Star Polygon

Here we encounter the phenomenon of negative and positive spaces which occur when the sides of a polygon cross each other. When one edge of a polygon crosses over another of it's edges this will create a twist in the surface of the polygon. The twist results in a loop of the polygon covering another part of the surface then the fill color is cancelled out in the area of overlap. This is effectively happening in the case of the star shown below. This is why there is an unfilled area in the center. This phenomenon is more simply demonstrated in the example headed “Polygon Fill Rules”.

```
"""
Program name: star_polygon_1.py
Objective: Draw a 5-point star.

Keywords: polygon. star
============================================
```

```
Comments: A polygon is made by joining a sequence of x-y points,
with the last point automatically joined to the first by a line to close
the polygon.

Tested on: Python 2.6, Python 2.7.3, Python 3.2.3
Author: Mike Ohlson de Fine
"""
from Tkinter import *
#from tkinter import *  # For Python 3.2.3 and higher.
root = Tk()
root.title('Star polygon')

cw = 200                                   # canvas width
ch = 100                                   # canvas height
canvas_1 = Canvas(root, width=cw, height=ch, background="white")
canvas_1.grid(row=0, column=1)

# blue star, anchored to an anchor point.
x_anchor = 15
y_anchor = 50

canvas_1.create_polygon(x_anchor,      y_anchor,\
                  x_anchor + 20,  y_anchor - 40,\
                  x_anchor + 30,  y_anchor + 10,\
                  x_anchor,       y_anchor - 30,\
                  x_anchor + 40,  y_anchor - 20,\
                  fill="blue")
root.mainloop()
```

Discussion

In this code we have used the variable names x_anchor, y_anchor. This is to emphasize the idea that any drawn object might be made up of fixed and variable parameters. In this instance we want to determine the position of our drawn shape by specifying a particular point on the canvas. This point is defined as a pair of names variables. The values of these variables x_anchor, y_anchor can be re-assigned any time ans the shape will be repeated but in a different position. This is done in the next example.

What next?

Polygons are general purpose shapes which can be made as complex as we wish. If we develop the techniques for shifting, rotating, size changing we have a very versatile way of drawing and controlling shapes. The rest of this chapter is devoted to developing these techniques.

A Series of Shifted Polygons

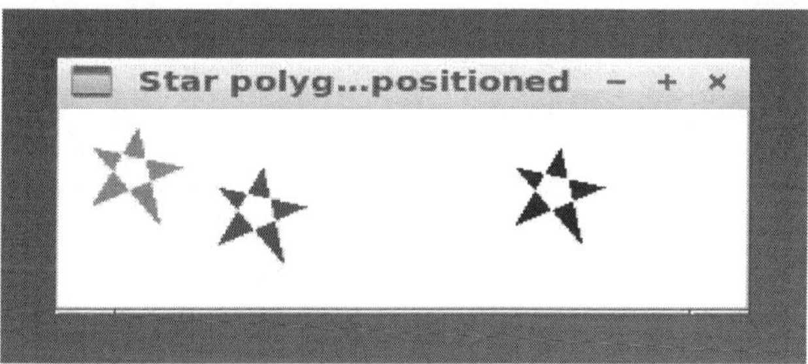

As mentioned above we are now going to separate the shape of our polygon, which is a star, from the position it is drawn. The advantage of this is that establishing the shape is somewhat tricky, requiring us to use creativity and may take a fair amount of trial and error before we are satisfied. We only want to ever go through this process once. Where we want to place our star on the canvas is simpler and should not require us to go through the whole process of re-creating the star shape. We have achieved this by reusing the identical *create_polygon* instruction three times. All we change each time are the values of the anchor coordinates x_anchor and y_anchor.

```
"""
Program name: repositioned_star_polygon_1.py
Objective: Draw a series of stars each with their own start position.

Keywords: polygon, anchor point, star
```

```
===========================================================
Comments:Each separate star is drawn relative to a pair variables,
x_anchor and y_anchor It simple to re-position different stars just
by reassigning the values of the anchor position.

Little warning: Beware of a quirk of line continuation indicators'\'. If there
are spaces
or other invisible characters on the same line, after them, these  mess up the
interpretation and cause errors. When you copy paste from a work processor
this occurs.

Tested on: Python 2.6, Python 2.7,Python 3.2.3
Author: Mike Ohlson de Fine
"""
from Tkinter import *
#from tkinter import *  # For Python 3.2.3 and higher.
root = Tk()
root.title('Star polygon repositioned')
cw = 300                              # canvas width
ch = 100                              # canvas height
canvas_1 = Canvas(root, width=cw, height=ch, background="white")
canvas_1.grid(row=0, column=1)

# Green star, fixed to an anchor point.
x_anchor = 15
y_anchor = 50
canvas_1.create_polygon(x_anchor,       y_anchor,\
                    x_anchor + 20,   y_anchor - 40,\
                    x_anchor + 30,   y_anchor + 10,\
                    x_anchor,        y_anchor - 30,\
                    x_anchor + 40,   y_anchor - 20,\
                      fill="green")

# Red star, fixed to an anchor point.
x_anchor = 70
y_anchor = 70
canvas_1.create_polygon(x_anchor,       y_anchor,\
                    x_anchor + 20,   y_anchor - 40,\
                    x_anchor + 30,   y_anchor + 10,\
                    x_anchor,        y_anchor - 30,\
                    x_anchor + 40,   y_anchor - 20,\
                      fill="red")
```

```
# Blue star, fixed to an anchor point.
x_anchor = 200
y_anchor = 60
canvas_1.create_polygon(x_anchor,        y_anchor,\
                        x_anchor + 20,   y_anchor - 40,\
                        x_anchor + 30,   y_anchor + 10,\
                        x_anchor,        y_anchor - 30,\
                        x_anchor + 40,   y_anchor - 20,\
                           fill="blue")

root.mainloop()
```

Discussion

Now we have an pattern for repeatedly drawing a shape in any chosen position. Naturally we want to be able to change the size as well.

Points to note

We can see from the code shown above that there is the code pattern that we use repeatedly:

```
x_anchor = 200
y_anchor = 60
canvas_1.create_polygon(x_anchor,        y_anchor,\
                        x_anchor + 20,   y_anchor - 40,\
                        x_anchor + 30,   y_anchor + 10,\
                        x_anchor,        y_anchor - 30,\
                        x_anchor + 40,   y_anchor - 20,\
                              fill="blue")
```

This is a little bit messy. It can be re-written as a Python function as:

```
def draw_star(x_anchor, y_anchor, color):
    canvas_1.create_polygon(x_anchor,        y_anchor,\
                        x_anchor + 20,   y_anchor - 40,\
                        x_anchor + 30,   y_anchor + 10,\
                        x_anchor,        y_anchor - 30,\
                        x_anchor + 40,   y_anchor - 20,\
                              fill="blue")
```

Each time we wished to draw another star we would just

write
draw_star(xx, yy, new_color). We have not used this technique yet because we need to focus on the working of the Tkinter graphic functions rather than the features of Python which may be slightly distracting at this stage. Do not worry we will use functions to good effect later in this chapter.

A Series of Re-sized Polygons

Now we introduce an "amplification factor" to the previous code pattern so that we are able to both re-position the stars as well as alter their size.

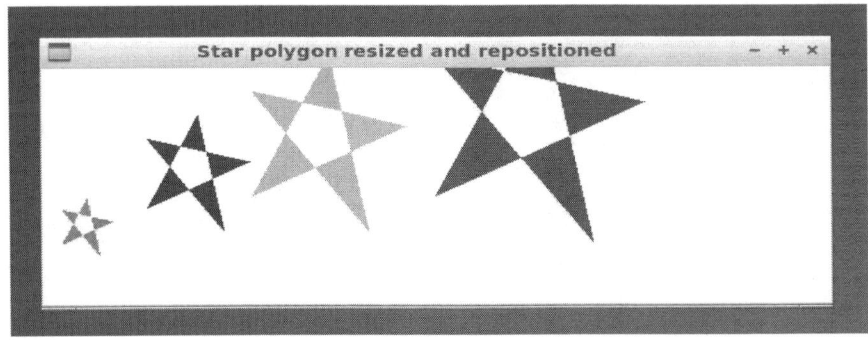


```
"""
Program name: positioned_sized_star_1.py
Objective: Draw a series of stars each with their own start position
           and size (scaled larger or smaller from a prototype).

Keywords: polygon, anchor point, scaled size, star
==============================================================
Comments:
A scale factor "size_scaling" is used to change the size of the stars
By having each separate star draw itself relative to a pair variables,
x_anchor and y_anchor as well as the size_scaling, it simple to re-position
and re-size different stars just by reassigning the values of the anchor
position.
```

```
Tested on: Python 2.6, Python 2.7, Python 3.2.3
Author: Mike Ohlson de Fine
"""
from Tkinter import *
#from tkinter import *  # For Python 3.2.3 and higher.
root = Tk()
root.title('Star polygon resized and repositioned')
cw = 600                            # canvas width
ch = 200                            # canvas height
canvas_1 = Canvas(root, width=cw, height=ch, background="white")
canvas_1.grid(row=0, column=1)

# Small green star, anchored to an anchor point.
size_scaling = 1
x_anchor = 15
y_anchor = 150


canvas_1.create_polygon(x_anchor,       y_anchor,\
              x_anchor + 20 * size_scaling,   y_anchor - 40* size_scaling,\
              x_anchor + 30 * size_scaling,   y_anchor + 10* size_scaling,\
              x_anchor,       y_anchor - 30* size_scaling,\
              x_anchor + 40 * size_scaling,   y_anchor - 20* size_scaling,\
                fill="green")
# Green star, size 2, anchored to an anchor point.
size_scaling = 2
x_anchor = 80
y_anchor = 120
canvas_1.create_polygon(x_anchor,       y_anchor,\
              x_anchor + 20 * size_scaling,   y_anchor - 40* size_scaling,\
              x_anchor + 30 * size_scaling,   y_anchor + 10* size_scaling,\
              x_anchor,       y_anchor - 30* size_scaling,\
              x_anchor + 40 * size_scaling,   y_anchor - 20* size_scaling,\
                fill="darkgreen")
# Green star, size 3, anchored to an anchor point.
size_scaling = 3
x_anchor = 160
y_anchor = 110
canvas_1.create_polygon(x_anchor,       y_anchor,\
              x_anchor + 20 * size_scaling,   y_anchor - 40* size_scaling,\
              x_anchor + 30 * size_scaling,   y_anchor + 10* size_scaling,\
              x_anchor,       y_anchor - 30* size_scaling,\
              x_anchor + 40 * size_scaling,   y_anchor - 20* size_scaling,\
```

```
                    fill="lightgreen")
# Green star, size 4, anchored to an anchor point.
size_scaling = 4
x_anchor = 300
y_anchor = 110
canvas_1.create_polygon(x_anchor,       y_anchor,\
                x_anchor + 20 * size_scaling,   y_anchor - 40* size_scaling,\
                x_anchor + 30 * size_scaling,   y_anchor + 10* size_scaling,\
                x_anchor,       y_anchor - 30* size_scaling,\
                x_anchor + 40 * size_scaling,   y_anchor - 20* size_scaling,\
                    fill="forestgreen")
root.mainloop()
```

The Labor of Debugging and Survival

Debugging complex code can easily take more time than writing it in the first place. This is why it is clever, smart, cunning and wonderful to write your code in a way that is going to make the debugging process *part of the code* right from the start, even if it seems to make it longer than need be. We do this particularly when we first begin a coding task. We can always strip out the extra lines of code later if we want to show other people what neat and pretty code we can write. We may want to show examples of our code at a job interview! Then we want to make it look slick and professional.

Here are some things we can do to assist debugging during code development.

1. Create check points at various points in the developing code to examine the values of variables. Use the print statement for this:

print 'variable-to-be-examined = ', variable-to-be-examined

Where 'variable-to-be-examined' is the name of the variable we are interested in at the time.

2. Switch these check points on and off by adding and removing the '#' character at the beginning of the line. The # converts an executable statement into a comment that is ignored for execution purposes.
3. Write notes to yourself, as comments, while writing code. Ask yourself questions. Note things that you have still to do. Often we start writing a section of program without having a clear idea of EXACTLY what we intend to do. The action of writing such experimental code is to try and nail down precisely what problem we need to solve. It is also a good way to clear up patchy understanding of language rules and syntax.
4. Write auxiliary test code that checks if our main code works as expected. For example we might write a function that should rotate a shape. Our test code would be a set of points making up an easily interpreted shape, like a triangle. If our rotation code is flawed it would be easy to spot a distortion in the triangle. In fact the smart thing to do would be to draw the triangle before and after rotation. Any mistakes will be fairly apparent.
5. Arrange large groups of input data like shape lists into neat rows and columns to ease the task of hunting for bad values, missing commas and other typos.
6. Test you code on edge cases. Use values that are very small, very large, both negative and positive. Also test the particular case where a value is exactly zero. An edge case is a set of variable values that forces our code to try and complete it's task outside the area where it works easily. A common example occurs when one expression is divided by another. If the the divisor (the part doing the dividing) is close to zero then the result can become astronomically large - too large to fit in the computer's memory. Avoiding such divide-by-zero errors requires us to incorporate test conditions in our code. If a divisor is tested and found to be zero, then a disaster prone division can be sidestepped by an

if else instruction pair. This is a common problem when we transform shapes by attempting to rotate them.

7. Change only one thing at a time and test the code between each change. If the program fails we know exactly what the cause was and can back up to the good version.

8. Preserve a consistent series of independent copies of your code while it is being changed and developed. In particular you should save a unique copy of your code when it has worked successfully. The next step after some success is inevitably to extend the code toward a further goal and very often there is failure along the road. When this happens we want to be able to go back one or more steps to code that worked successfully. Adding incremental revision numbers to program names that are saved successes is a convenient and traceable way to handle this backup process. For example if we are developing code to eventually simulate the flying action of a bird we might name our initial attempt "birdy_fly_1.py". The next version would be "birdy_fly_2.py" and the one after that "birdy_fly_3.py".

9. Keep real physical backup copies in a two different places from your original. You may be burgled and your computer stolen. Your dwelling may burn down or get flooded. You do not want to lose one day of work let alone a few months. If your building burned down the copy on the hard drive of your working machine in your study and the backup on a memory stick in the cupboard in your bedroom would both be destroyed by the same fire. A couple of copies kept at different companies in the internet cloud would survive the local fire.

To summarize our basic rules of programming pain and injury avoidance:

1. Create checkpoints.
2. Write notes to yourself.
4. Arrange input data neatly to aid inspection for rogue

values.
5. Make test routines.
6. Test edge cases.
7. Change only one thing at a time.
8. Preserve successive revisions.
9. Make regular independent physical backups.

What next?

The next two examples explore how polygon fill rules create transparent regions when the edges of polygons cross over each other.

Polygon Fill Rules

Here we demonstrate the color-fill and no-fill attribute of polygons whose edges cut across each other multiple times. As mentioned previously this effect will not occur if the polygon shape has a simple twist in it. However if the twist results in an internal loop in the polygon covering another portion of the polygon surface then the overlapped section becomes transparent and the background shows through the overlapped region.

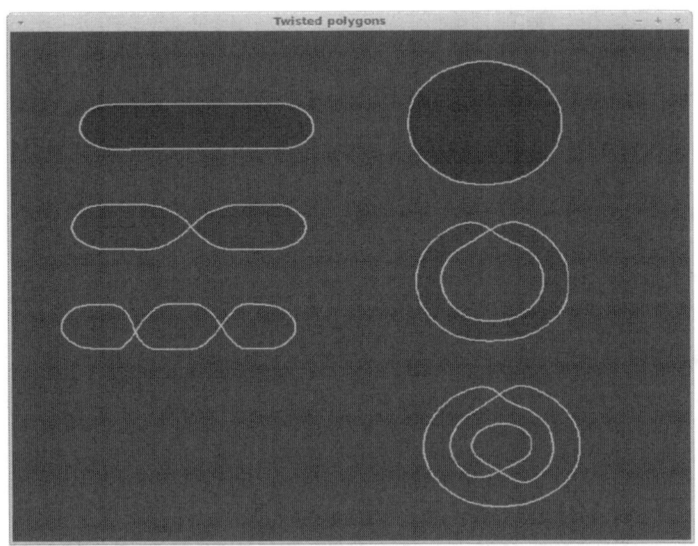


```
"""
Program name: poly_twists_1.py
Objective: Demonstrate the fill rules for polygons with external and
internal odd-even color areas.

Keywords: canvas,  polygon, internal, external, spaces, odd-even fill
=============================================================
Comments: Only internal twisted loops result in fill cancellation

Tested on: Python 2.6, Python 2.7, Python 3.2
Author: Mike Ohlson de Fine
"""
from Tkinter import *
#from tkinter import *  # For Python 3.2.3 and higher.
root = Tk()
root.title('Twisted polygons')
cw = 800                              # canvas width.
ch = 650                              # canvas height.
canvas_1 = Canvas(root, width=cw, height=ch, background="#664444")
canvas_1.grid(row=0, column=1)

twist_1 = [ 204.6,93.7 , 116.0,93.7 , 100.3,97.3 , 90.3,103.4 , 83.9,113.7 ,\
 82.5,129.5 , 90.3,140.9 , 103.9,148.0 , 120,152.3 , 135.7,151.2 ,\
 312.8,151.2 , 328.2,151.2 , 341.4,147.0 , 351.0,139.8 , 358.2,131.2 ,\
 357.8,115.9 , 350.7,105.2 , 337.8,97.7 , 324.6,93.7 , 306.7,93.4 , 237.1,94.1 ]
canvas_1.create_polygon(twist_1, width = 2, fill='#6a0aab',
outline='#d2f700',smooth = 1)
```

```
twist_2 = [  191.7,222.3 , 120,222.0 , 107.8,222.3 , 95.3,224.1 , 84.2,228.4 ,
74.2,241.6 , 72.5,255.2 , 80.3,268.0 , 92.8,275.2 , 108.2,279.5 , 128.2,279.1 ,
185.7,280.2 , 236.7,222.7 , 309.6,222.7 , 320,222.3 , 332.1,227.0 , 343.5,236.2 ,
348.9,245.2 , 348.2,259.5 , 340.3,269.5 , 326.7,277.0 , 315,279.8 , 294.6,279.8 ,
235,280.2  ]
canvas_1.create_polygon(twist_2, width = 2, fill='#9c02a7', outline='#d2f700',
smooth = 1)

twist_3 = [  136.4,349.8 , 103.9,349.8 , 89.6,349.8 , 76.0,353.4 , 65.7,361.6 ,
60.7,371.6 , 60.3,384.5 , 68.5,395.2 , 83.2,404.5 , 98.9,405.9 , 119.2,406.2 ,
133.2,406.6 , 169.6,349.5 , 199.2,349.1 , 232.8,349.8 , 265.3,406.6 ,
294.2,406.2 , 313.9,405.9 , 325.7,398.0 , 336.4,386.2 , 336.0,372.0 ,
328.2,360.9 , 315.7,353.0 , 303.5,350.5 , 281.7,349.1 , 265.71429,350.2 ,
227.8,406.6 , 194.6,406.6 , 154.2,407.3 ]
canvas_1.create_polygon(twist_3, width = 2, fill='#cb0077',  outline='#d2f700',
smooth = 1)

loop_1 = [  541.0,40.9 , 502.5,54.5 , 470,89.1 , 468.2,146.2 , 503.9,185.2 ,
538.9,198.4 , 586.0,197.0 , 625,176.6 , 649.6,139.5 , 649.2,95.9 , 617.8,56.6 ,
573.9,40.2 ]
canvas_1.create_polygon(loop_1, width = 2, fill='#6a0aab' , outline='#d2f700',
smooth = 1 )

loop_2 = [ 546.7,241.6 , 508.9,256.2 , 478.5,291.6 , 477.1,345.5 , 507.5,383.7 ,
543.2,398.7 , 601.7,395.9 , 642.8,369.1 , 657.1,339.5 , 655.3,293.0 , 620,253.7 ,
584.2,242.00504 , 544.6,269.5 , 520.7,284.1 , 506.7,304.5 , 507.8,338.0 ,
526.0,360.5 , 550,372.7 , 586.0,371.6 , 615.3,354.1 , 629.2,327.3 , 624.2,299.1 ,
606.7,278.4 , 578.2,267.0 ]
canvas_1.create_polygon(loop_2, width = 2, fill='#9c02a7', outline= '#d2f700',
smooth = 1)

loop_3 = [ 561.0,452.0 , 523.2,464.1 , 492.1,495.2 , 482.8,537.0 , 497.5,574.1 ,
537.1,604.8 , 590,609.8 , 637.5,592.0 , 665,561.6 , 671.7,522.0 , 654.6,484.8 ,
622.8,459.8 , 592.5,451.2 , 555.3,479.8 , 528.2,496.6 , 515.3,523.0 , 520,550.9 ,
545.7,576. , 591.4,554.1 , 611.0,541.6 , 613.5,520.5 , 598.9,506.2 , 576.7,500.9 ,
552.1,508.75 , 540,527.0 , 545.7,544.5 , 566.0,556.6 , 599.6,580.2 , 618.5,570.9 ,
635.3,551.6 , 639.2,528.4 , 631.0,502.3 , 609.2,484.1 , 585.3,475.9 ]

canvas_1.create_polygon(loop_3, width = 2, fill='#cb0077', outline='#d2f700',
smooth = 1)

root.mainloop()
```

Discussion

The yellow line demonstrates the continuous series of position points that are in the list of points applied to the create_polygon function.

Polygon of Many Loops

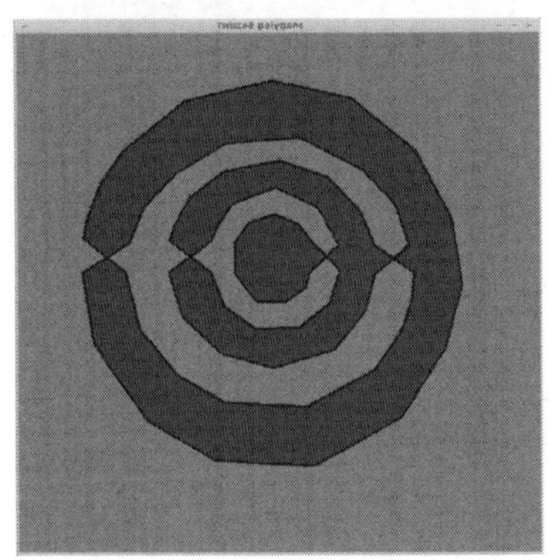

```
"""
Program name: poly_loopy_1.py
Objective: Demonstrate smooth polygons with odd-even color spaces.

Keywords: canvas, bent line, polygon, odd-even fill
==================================================================
Comments:

Tested on: Python 2.6, Python 2.7, Python 3.2.3
Author: Mike Ohlson de Fine
"""
from Tkinter import *
#from tkinter import *  # For Python 3.2.3 and higher.
root = Tk()
root.title('Loopy polygon')
cw = 600                        # canvas width.
ch = 600                        # canvas height.
canvas_1 = Canvas(root, width=cw, height=ch, background= "#8888ff")
canvas_1.grid(row=0, column=1)

multi_twist = [109.1, 286.7, 103.0, 315.0, 167.7, 368.5, 189.9, 457.4, 246.5,
```

```
528.1, 319.2, 568.5, 444.5, 575.6, 550.5, 519.0, 593.0, 455.4, 607.1, 409.9,
611.1, 369.5, 549.5, 327.1, 529.3, 274.5, 478.8, 223.0, 406.1, 196.8, 321.2,
213.9, 265.7, 254.3, 243.4, 295.8, 235.4, 319.0, 300.0, 369.5, 320.2, 421.0,
367.7, 456.4, 435.4, 454.4, 479.8, 417.0, 497.0, 365.5, 454.6, 323.0, 434.4,
294.7, 398.0, 278.6, 358.6, 291.7, 337.4, 322.0, 338.4, 371.5, 370.7, 413.9,
413.2, 415.0, 443.5, 392.7, 450.5, 368.5, 495.0, 326.1, 463.7, 268.5, 400.0,
238.2, 334.4, 263.4, 309.1, 299.8, 301.0, 319.0, 234.4, 368.5, 253.5, 437.2,
315.2, 493.7, 396.0, 516.0, 487.9, 487.7, 536.4, 428.1, 550.5, 371.5, 603.1,
328.1, 582.9, 264.4, 533.4, 210.9, 438.4, 162.4, 325.3, 169.5, 245.5, 216.0,
196.0, 268.5, 174.8, 322.0, 101.0, 369.5, 119.2, 478.6, 200.0, 596.8, 305.1,
659.4, 454.6, 667.5, 590.9, 591.7, 656.6, 485.7, 681.9, 388.7, 666.7, 286.7,
613.2, 180.6, 516.2, 100.8, 396.0, 73.5, 259.6, 104.8, 165.7, 181.6, 130.3, 232.6]

canvas_1.create_polygon(multi_twist, width = 4, fill='#6a0aab',
outline='#440000')

root.mainloop()
```

Discussion

In this example we used a photographic image as the background because it helps to emphasize how twisted-over regions of the polygon become transparent.

What next?

Polygons are the basis of the wonderful artificial worlds created in video games. Creating and controlling the virtual world of a computer game requires the manipulation of colored polygons in three dimensions. The basic methods used are surprisingly simple and elegant because they use a neat body of mathematics called Linear Algebra. We will not be using these in this book but we will be working out how to rotate, resize, skew and shift polygons in two dimensions. We used a bit of rotation in the previous chapter.

Polygon Transformation

We now work with shapes that can be as complicated as we

please. A line that turns and meanders in complicated knots gets manipulated in exactly the same way as a simple polygon. The only thing that that distinguishes them are the Tkinter functions used to draw them.
A line is drawn with *create_line(...)* and a polygon is drawn with *create_polygon(...)*. The actual list of values inside them can be identical. In the case of the polygon the inside of the shape gets filled with a color.

Because we are going to be altering the shape and position of an object we need to make up some rules about what we mean by position, size and orientation. And we must try to keep things simple if possible – not always easy.
In this book we use the bounding box to describe the position and size of any object. This idea is widespread on software. The bounding box is the horizontal rectangle into which the object will fit exactly. The top left is denoted by the pair of position coordinates x_org, y_org, short for x_origin and y_origin.
The exact center of the bounding box is *x_cen, y_cen,* which is short for x_center, y_center.

Polygon Location

The diagram below summarises our definitions of position, size and orientation that we will be using. The program code shown below takes a complex shape, the silhouette of a python, and draws it together with the box that contains it as well as the geometric center of that box. There is also a reference position *x_org, y_org* that is sometimes used.
The list of coordinates for the shape is the object named *python_1*. We will use this same object in the next three programs.

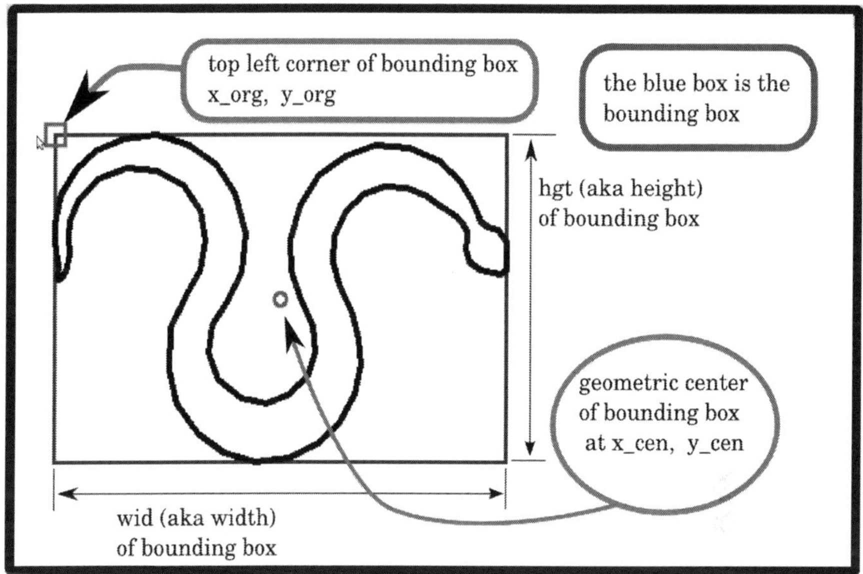

The code to produce the picture of the python and it's bounding box follows.

```
"""
Program name: poly_python_1.py
Objective: Illustrate polygon shape parameters.

Keywords: canvas, shapedemonstration, center, bounding box.
=====================================================
Comments: Take note of the instruction  "for i in range(int(len(shape)/2)):" in the
function "locate_shape(shape)". It has to have the "int(...) in order to work under
Python 3.xx.
Without it we get and error as follows:
  for i in range(len(shape)/2):    # Separate out the x and components.
TypeError: 'float' object cannot be interpreted as an integer

Under Python 2.xx the form "for i in range(len(shape)/2):" works fine.

Tested on: Python 2.6, Python 2.7, Python 3.2.3
Author: Mike Ohlson de Fine
"""
from Tkinter import *
#from tkinter import *  # For Python 3.2.3 and higher.
```

```
root = Tk()
root.title("Show a Python.")
canvas_1 = Canvas(root, width=500, height=400, background="white")
canvas_1.grid(row=0, column=1)

python_1 = [ 75.2,186.9 , 76.26,177.8 , 73.9,167.9 , 72.5,160.3, 72.6,147.2\
 , 78.2,125.0 , 90.4,106.8 , 106.0,93.4 , 129.0,83.8 , 155.3,81.1\
 , 182.3,88.6 , 203.5,103.5 , 218.9,124.5 , 227.7,155.0 , 224.7,183.1\
 , 213.3,205.8 , 200.7,222.5 , 197.7,244.2 , 205.8,263.9 , 225.2,278.3\
 , 246.2,281.6 , 265.4,275.0 , 279.8,260.9 , 286.1,243.7 , 283.8,224.2\
 , 273.7,204.0 , 266.1,182.6 , 264.9,159.6 , 272.7,134.1 , 288.3,112.4\
 , 309.6,97.0 , 333.8,89.1 , 362.1,90.6 , 387.3,101.3 , 404.0,116.7\
 , 413.1,131.3 , 416.9,138.9 , 420.3,145.8 , 425.7,150.2 , 433.6,151.5\
 , 440.6,161.4 , 441.4,171.0 , 440.9,176.3 , 440.9,181.6 , 435.6,184.6\
 , 430.3,184.3 , 425.0,182.8 , 419.7,182.1 , 411.3,175.8 , 408.2,165.8\
 , 409.1,159.3 , 408.8,153.3 , 405.4,147.2 , 399.7,141.9 , 389.9,136.4\
 , 382.8,132.1 , 376.2,127.3 , 360.3,120.7 , 341.4,119.7 , 324.2,126.0\
 , 310.3,138.6 , 301.0,156.8 , 299.7,175.8 , 304.5,192.9 , 316.1,214.9\
 , 321.4,233.8 , 322.9,252.8 , 317.6,274.5 , 305.8,295.5 , 288.6,311.6\
 , 265.4,323.2 , 237.1,326.0, 211.1,318.79 , 190.1,304.8 , 172.4,282.1\
 , 165.6,257.3 , 167.4,225.2 , 179.5,199.5 , 190.6,182.3 , 195.4,160.38\
 , 190.9,138.4 , 177.0,119.4 , 155.3,108.3 , 131.0,106.1 , 108.0,114.4\
 , 92.4,130.3 , 85.1,144.7 , 84.0,157.3 , 84.6,170.4 , 82.3,183.1\
 , 78.2,188.1 , 76.1,188.8 ]


def locate_shape(shape):
    """ Calculate the bounding box location, center and dimensions.
        x_org, y_org is the bottom-left corner, the origin.
        wid is the width of the bounding box, hgt is the height.
        and x_cen, y_cen is the center of the bounding box.
    """
    x_list = []
    y_list = []
    for i in range(int(len(shape)/2)):    # Separate out the x and components.
        x_list.append(shape[2*i])
        y_list.append(shape[2*i+1])
    x_org = min(x_list)
    y_org = min(y_list)
    wid = max(x_list) - x_org
    hgt = max(y_list) - y_org
    x_cen = x_org + wid/2.0
    y_cen = y_org + hgt/2.0
    xy_cen = [x_cen, y_cen]
    xy_size = [ wid, hgt]
```

```
    return xy_cen, xy_size

def show_shape_metrics(shape):
    """ Draw the shape, its bounding box, the center and graphical origin.
    """
    xy_bunch = locate_shape(shape) #return xy_cen, xy_size
    x_cen = xy_bunch[0][0]
    y_cen = xy_bunch[0][1]
    wid = xy_bunch[1][0]
    hgt = xy_bunch[1][1]
    x_org = x_cen - wid/2
    y_org = y_cen - hgt/2
    canvas_1.create_oval(x_cen-5, y_cen-5,  x_cen+5, y_cen+5, outline= 'red',
fill='', width=1 )
    canvas_1.create_rectangle(x_cen- wid/2, y_cen-hgt/2,  x_cen+wid/2,
y_cen+hgt/2, outline= 'black', fill='', width=1 )
    canvas_1.create_rectangle(x_org -8, y_org -8, x_org +8, y_org +8, outline=
'red', fill='', width=1 )

show_shape_metrics(python_1)
canvas_1.create_polygon(python_1, outline='black', fill='', width= 4 )

root.mainloop()
```

What next?

We need robust and simple-to-use methods of changing the shape, size and orientation of drawn objects. The next three examples cover this.

Polygon Shifting and Relocation

In the next three examples we have three key functions for changing the position of a shape, changing it's size and finally rotating it around some chosen point. These functions have been written to be generally useful for any two dimensional shape. The general term for the process of translation (moving position), changing size and rotating is *transform*.

The most elegant for achieving such transformations belong

to the branch of mathematics called linear algebra and they deal with two dimensions as a special case of three dimensions. However we avoid using these techniques in this book because it would be a digression from the main purpose of discovering code techniques that enable us to be creative without high level mathematics.

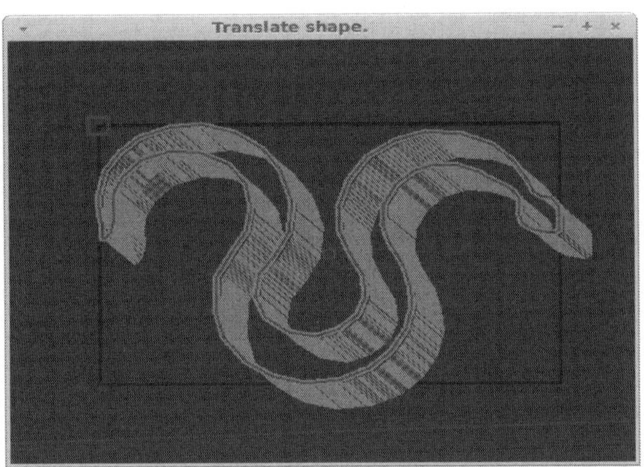


```
def translate_shape(shape, x_shift, y_shift):
    """ Expand or contract a shape about a given point x_center, y_center.
       An enhancement could be to expand it about the mean of the coordinates.
    """
    new_shape = []
    for i in range(int(len(shape)/2 )):
        x_new = shape[2*i]  + x_shift
        y_new = shape[2*i+1] + y_shift
        new_shape.append(x_new)
        new_shape.append(y_new)
    return new_shape

shift_python = translate_shape(python_1, x_shift, y_shift)
canvas_1.create_polygon(shift_python, outline= 'green', fill='', width=2,
smooth=1 )
```

Discussion

If we insert the above *translate_shape(...)* funtion into code of the “demo_python_1.py” code and execute it via the two lines:

shift_python = translate_shape(python_1, x_shift, y_shift)
canvas_1.create_polygon(shift_python, outline= 'green', fill='', width=2,

smooth=1) ,
then the above image will appear on your monitor screen.

Polygon Amplification (Re-sizing)

As we did before, if we now add the function
amplify_2d_shape(...)
to the "demo_python_1.py" code and execute it using

```
amplified_python = amplify_2d_shape(python_1, 1.6, 1.6 )
show_shape_metrics(amp_python)
canvas_1.create_polygon(show_python, outline= 'blue', fill='', width=2, smooth=1 )
```

The amplify_2d_shape() function has two amplification arguments. Tthe first *x_amplify* applies to the horizontal direction and the second y_amplify applies to the vertical direction. So we can amplify the directions independently. For example x_amplify = 0.5 and y_amplify = 1.0 would make the shape narrower by half but leave the height unchanged. We will see the sequence of larger and larger python silhouettes shown below

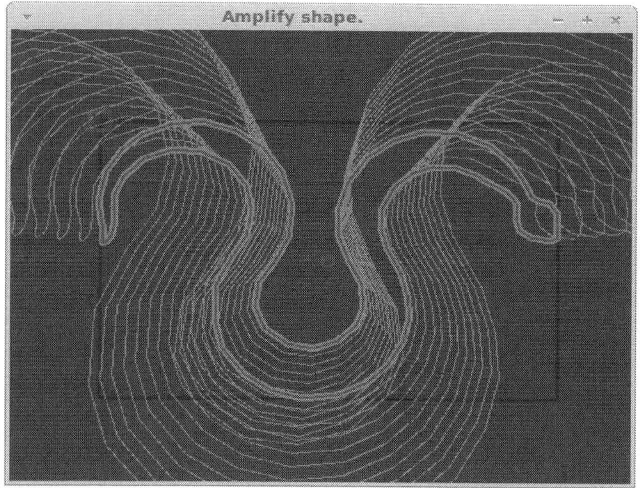

The Amplification function

```
def amplify_2d_shape(shape, x_amplify, y_amplify):
    """ Expand or contract a shape about the center of its bounding box.
    """
    new_shape = []
    xy_bunch = locate_shape(python_1)
    x_cen = xy_bunch[0][0]
    y_cen = xy_bunch[0][1]
    wid = xy_bunch[1][0]
    hgt = xy_bunch[1][1]
    x_org = x_cen - wid/2
    y_org = y_cen - hgt/2
    for i in range(int(len(shape)/2 )):
        x_ampd = (shape[2*i]   - x_org)*x_amplify + x_org - wid*(x_amplify - 1)/2
        y_ampd = (shape[2*i+1] - y_org)*y_amplify + y_org - hgt*(y_amplify -
1)/2
        new_shape.append(x_ampd)
        new_shape.append(y_ampd)
    return new_shape
```

Execution and display of amplification code

Insert the following code into the "demo_python_1.py" program and execute it.

```
amplified_python = amplify_2d_shape(python_1, 1.6, 1.6 )
show_shape_metrics(amp_python)
canvas_1.create_polygon(show_python, outline= 'blue', fill='', width=2,
smooth=1 )

canvas_1.create_polygon(python_1, outline='green',fill ='', width = 6 )
canvas_1.create_polygon(python_1, outline='#008800',fill ='', width = 2 )
```

Discussion

We have added two new functions to our original "demo_python_1.py". In the next example we add a third function for rotation. Using these three functions we can now acquire shapes from many different sources and it no longer matters if their size, location and orientation are incorrect or inconvenient. By means of these functions we can make the size, location and rotation anything we choose. For this reason we must try to keep the code both simple as well as applicable to the widest variety of situations.

Points to note

We have written our functions such that we only need the list of shape coordinates. We do not even have to know where it is. The function locate_shape(shape) will discover and return the position of the center as well as the size. The size is the width and height of the bounding box. This *locate_shape* function can be used inside the other functions when we need to find the center or size of an object.

Polygon Rotation

Again, as we did before, if we now add the function
rotate_shape(shape, xy_center, angle_degrees)
to the *"demo_python_1.py"* code and execute it.

However we need to notice a difference in thinking when we use rotation. An important argument supplied to the rotate_shape function is the position *xy_center*, given as a pair of x and y coordinates. The *xy_center* is the position of the point about which the python shape will be rotated. The result of choosing different centers is shown in the images below.

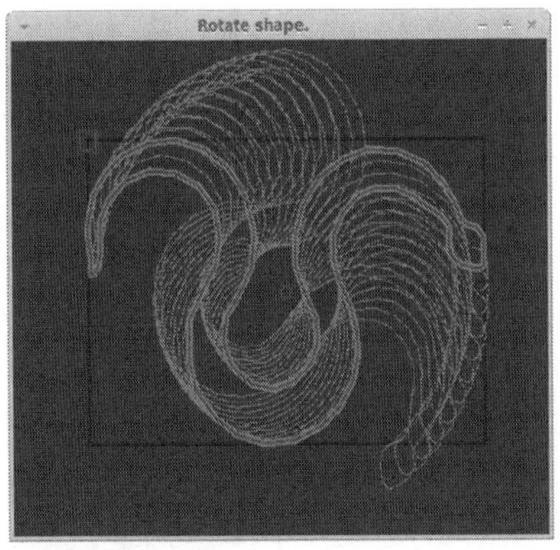

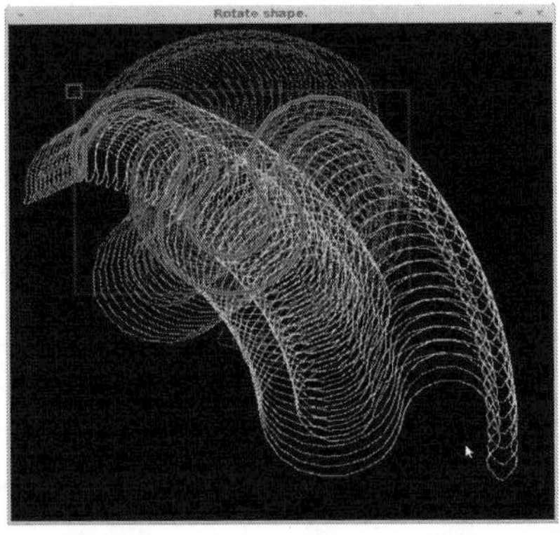

The rotation function

```
def rotate_shape(shape, xy_center, angle_degrees):
    """ Rotate any shape about a cetner point xy_center.
    """
    angle_rad = math.radians(angle_degrees)
    x_cen = xy_center[0]
    y_cen = xy_center[1]
    new_shape = []
    for i in range(int(len(shape)/2) ):
        x_temp = shape[2*i]  - x_cen
        y_temp = shape[2*i+1] - y_cen
        radian_temp  = math.atan2(y_temp, x_temp )
        length_temp = math.sqrt( y_temp**2 + x_temp**2)
        new_angle = angle_rad + radian_temp
        new_x = length_temp * math.cos(new_angle) + x_cen
        new_y = length_temp * math.sin(new_angle) + y_cen
        new_shape.append(new_x)
        new_shape.append(new_y)
    return   new_shape   # angle_deg = post rotation angle
```

Execution and display of rotation code

```
xy_center = show_shape_metrics(python_1)
for i in range(22):
    rotate_python = rotate_shape(python_1, xy_center, i*5)
    canvas_1.create_polygon(rotate_python, outline='red', fill='' )

xy_center = -100, -100
```

```
for i in range(12):
    rotate_python = rotate_shape(python_1, xy_center, i*1)
    canvas_1.create_polygon(rotate_python, outline='green', fill='' )

xy_center = 10, 500
for i in range(22):
    rotate_python = rotate_shape(python_1, xy_center, i*2)
    canvas_1.create_polygon(rotate_python, outline='yellow', fill='' )

canvas_1.create_polygon(python_1, outline='green',fill ='', width = 6 )
canvas_1.create_polygon(python_1, outline='#008800',fill ='', width = 2 )
```

Discussion

An abbreviated version of our final program that includes our collection of geometric transformation functions would look like:

Points to note

We have built up the following set of useful functions for manipulating complex lines and polygon shapes:

1. locate_shape(shape)
2. amplify_2d_shape(shape, x_amplify, y_amplify)
3. show_shape_metrics(shape)
4. translate_shape(shape, x_shift, y_shift)
5. rotate_shape(shape, xy_center, angle_degrees)

The common argument in each function is *shape*. It is a good idea to makes related families to functions have a similar look and layout where practical. We are likely to want to use some or all these functions again and again. It is also likely that we will want to add new functions that do new things but make use of the older functions. Consequently it is helpful to establish some rules to conform to when writing these functions. The rules are designed to make it easy and intuitive to use any of the functions.
Looking at the five functions shown above we can extract the following rules:

1. Use explicit and self explanatory function names.
2. Use use self-explanatory names for arguments passed to functions.
3. Place the arguments in a consistent sequence. For example we always place 'shape' as the first argument.

Should we make a module?

Good question. If we are going to be using shifting, expanding, contracting and rotating of 2D shapes in the future it will probably be a great saving of effort and result in more compact code if we group all the useful functions together under a common name and make it into a Python module. Then we would just call particular functions from the module as we needed them. This makes a lot of sense but we will not do it yet because at this stage time we keep the focus on graphic manipulation and not global module design. We also want to honour the promise that readers should be able to copy and paste the examples straight out of the book without extra baggage. In this last example we have have been forced to compromise on that undertaking in order to avoid pages and pages of long programs with only small differences between them.

What next?

Having developed some handy shape manipulation tools as well a basic understanding of how to control color from the previous chapter it is now natural to want to control the visual appearance of shapes using color. What is involved in changing texture? Can we shade shapes with different degrees of color? Color texture and shading add a new level of complexity to the code but it is well worth the effort. The next section is the beginning of this new exploration.

Polygon Shading

We know how to fill a polygon with a single color and we know how to create a sequence of colors that start with one given color and end with another. We have also got methods of shifting, shrinking and rotating shapes. Why not combine all these to try and make visually interesting objects?

So the first task is to combine color sequences inside a shape while altering its size.

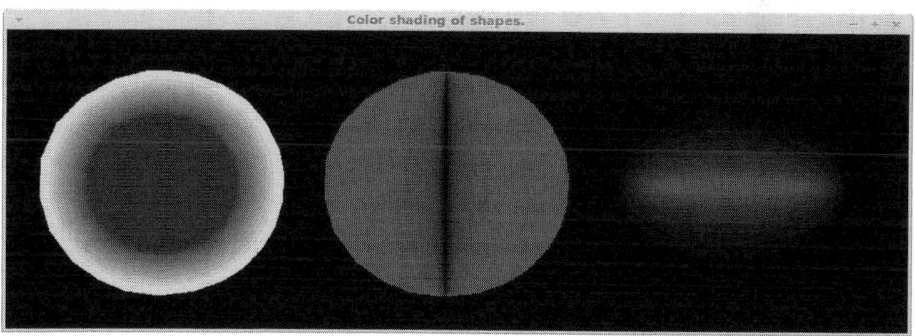


```
"""
Program name: poly_shader_1.py
Objective: Color a polygon shape using a transition sequence between two end colors.

Keywords: canvas, color transition, sequence, polygon, shape.
=============================================================
Comments: The polygon shape is re-drawn repeatedly on the same center,
 decreasing the size each time. This effectively creates layers within
 the shape. Each shape layer is filled with a slightly different color.
The start and end colors are given as as pairs of hex color value '#rrggbb'.
"discrete_kula_series(...) returns the color sequence used.

Tested on: Python 2.6, Python 2.7, Python 3.2.3
Author: Mike Ohlson de Fine
"""
from Tkinter import *
```

```
#from tkinter import *  # For Python 3.2.3 and higher.
root = Tk()
root.title("Color shading of shapes.")
canvas_1 = Canvas(root, width=950, height=350, background="#000000")
canvas_1.grid(row=0, column=1)

sun = [375.7,49.5 , 456.4,62.3 , 525,93.0 , 587.8,138.0\
 , 637.8,202.3 , 675,283.7 , 687.1,356.6 , 684.2,438.0\
 , 662.8,509.5 , 630.7,569.5 , 582.8,625.9 , 530,665.2\
 , 454.2,698.0 , 360.7,710.9 , 270.7,696.6 , 200,665.9\
 , 130.7,610.9 , 70.7,518.7 , 42.1,416.6 , 48.5,307.3\
 , 89.2,205.9 , 152.1,129.5 , 243.5,73.7 , 324.2,52.3 ]

def hex2rgb(hex_color):
    """ Convert a hex color of the from '#rrggbb'
        to three element tuple of base 10 integers corresponging to (red, green,
blue).
    """
    start_kula = 0,0,0
    end_kula = 0,0,0
    n1 = [1,  3, 5]
    n2 = [3,  5, 7]
    rgb_color = []
    for i in range(0,3):
        a = n1[i]
        b = n2[i]
        kula_slice = hex_color[a:b]
        #print ' kula_slice: ', kula_slice
        c = int(kula_slice, 16)

        rgb_color.append(c)  # '16' is the base from which to convert.
    rgb_color = tuple(rgb_color)
    return rgb_color

# RGB inputs
def discrete_kula_series(start_color, end_color, num_steps):
    """ Create the color transion list between a start and an end color (hex rgb).
        Generate Color Transition Series as hex RGB inputs
    """
    start_color_int = hex2rgb(start_color)
    end_color_int = hex2rgb( end_color)
    delt_red = (end_color_int[0] - start_color_int[0])/(num_steps - 1)
    delt_green = (end_color_int[1] - start_color_int[1])/(num_steps - 1)
    delt_blue = (end_color_int[2] - start_color_int[2])/(num_steps - 1)
    color_series_int = []
```

```
    color_series_hex = []
    for i in range(num_steps+1):
        next_red = start_color_int[0]+i*delt_red
        if next_red <=0.0:
            next_red = 0.0
        next_green = start_color_int[1]+i*delt_green
        if next_green <=0.0:
            next_green = 0.0
        next_blue = start_color_int[2]+i*delt_blue
        if next_blue <=0.0:
            next_blue = 0.0
        next_color_int = next_red, next_green, next_blue
        color_series_int.append(next_color_int)
        if i < num_steps:
            next_color_hex = '#%02x%02x%02x' % next_color_int
            color_series_hex.append(next_color_hex)
            color_series_int.append(next_color_int)
        else:
            next_color_hex =  '#%02x%02x%02x' % end_color_int
            color_series_hex.append(next_color_hex)
            color_series_int.append(next_color_int)
    return color_series_hex


def locate_shape(shape):
    """ Calculate the bounding box location, center and dimensions.
        x_org, y_org is the bottom-left corner, the origin.
        wid is the width of the bounding box, hgt is the height.
        and x_cen, y_cen is the center of the bounding box.
    """
    x_list = []
    y_list = []
    for i in range(int(len(shape)/2)):    # Separate out the x and components.
        x_list.append(shape[2*i])
        y_list.append(shape[2*i+1])
    x_org = min(x_list)
    y_org = min(y_list)
    wid = max(x_list) - x_org
    hgt = max(y_list) - y_org
    x_cen = x_org + wid/2.0
    y_cen = y_org + hgt/2.0
    xy_cen = [x_cen, y_cen]
    xy_size = [ wid, hgt]
    return xy_cen, xy_size
```

```
def amplify_2d_shape(shape, x_amplify, y_amplify):
    """ Expand or contract a shape about the center of its bounding box.
    """
    new_shape = []
    xy_bunch = locate_shape(shape)
    x_cen = xy_bunch[0][0]
    y_cen = xy_bunch[0][1]
    wid = xy_bunch[1][0]
    hgt = xy_bunch[1][1]
    x_org = x_cen - wid/2
    y_org = y_cen - hgt/2
    for i in range(int(len(shape)/2 )):
        x_ampd = (shape[2*i]   - x_org)*x_amplify + x_org - wid*(x_amplify - 1)/2
        y_ampd = (shape[2*i+1] - y_org)*y_amplify + y_org - hgt*(y_amplify -
1)/2
        new_shape.append(x_ampd)
        new_shape.append(y_ampd)
    return new_shape

def translate_shape(shape, x_shift, y_shift):
    """ Expand or contract a shape about a given point x_center, y_center.
        An enhancement could be to expand it about the mean of the coordinates.
    """
    new_shape = []
    for i in range(int(len(shape)/2) ):
        x_new = shape[2*i]  + x_shift
        y_new = shape[2*i+1] + y_shift
        new_shape.append(x_new)
        new_shape.append(y_new)
    return new_shape

def shrinking_series(shape, start_color, end_color, x_amplify, y_amplify,
number_layers):
    """ Shaded image assembly and display.
    """
    kulas = discrete_kula_series(start_color, end_color, number_layers)
    canvas_1.create_polygon(shape, outline='', fill=kulas[0], smooth=0 )
    for i in range(number_layers):
        shape = amplify_2d_shape(shape, x_amplify, y_amplify )
        canvas_1.create_polygon(shape, outline='', fill=kulas[i], smooth=0 )

#***********************************************************
# Execute and Demonstrate.
# ========================
```

```
# Initialization setup.
new_sun = amplify_2d_shape(sun,0.4, 0.4 )   # Starting Shape.

# Example 1 - Yellow-to-blue concentrics
new_sun = translate_shape(new_sun, -200, -200 )   # Starting Shape.
number_layers = 12
start_color = '#ffff00'
end_color   = '#0000ff'
x_amplify = 0.96
y_amplify = 0.96
shrinking_series(new_sun, start_color, end_color, x_amplify, y_amplify,
number_layers)

# Example 2 - Red-to-black cat's eye.
new_sun = translate_shape(new_sun, 300, 0 )   # Starting Shape.
start_color = '#ff0000'
end_color   = '#000000'
x_amplify = 0.7
y_amplify = 0.999
shrinking_series(new_sun, start_color, end_color, x_amplify, y_amplify,
number_layers)

# Example 2 - Purple glow.
new_sun = translate_shape(new_sun, 300, 0 )   # Starting Shape.
start_color = '#000000'
end_color   = '#8800ff'
x_amplify = 0.96
y_amplify = 0.8
shrinking_series(new_sun, start_color, end_color, x_amplify, y_amplify,
number_layers)

root.mainloop()
```

Discussion

We have now added the function *discrete_kula_series(...)* from the previous chapter and has given us versatile control of color texture.

To create the above three images we have shrunk the size of the object while at the same time filling it with the next color in a discrete transition color list. In the first image, the yellow-to-blue transition series, the shrinking action has been applied by the same amount in both the x and y directions. In the second red-to-black series only the horizontal x component od an oval has been shrunk. In the right-most purple-to-black image both x and y directions of an oval have been shrunk but the vertical y component has been shrunk faster.

Points to note

We are now able to create very subtle shading and color transitions to objects that have vertical or horizontal symmetry. If the objects do not have simple symmetries then more complicated techniques need to be used. For example how could we apply colored shading to the outline of the curvy python we have been using in this chapter. The axis of symmetry of a python follows it vertebrae – following the center of it upper back or dorsal side. Then realistic shading is dominated by the sources of light that illuminate the objects in a scene. These are considerations that occupy the artists and engineers who are constantly extending the boundaries of realism and visual appeal of video games.

What next?

In the next chapter we start to dip our toes in the beguiling world of visual creativity. It is a technical world where maths and art meet in unexpected and interesting ways.

5

Graphic Elements: Textured Color

In this chapter we will cover:

- the ideas of line slope and intercept
- the computation of slope and intercept parameters
- how to determine where lines intersected
- how to determine where segments of lines intersected
- how to determine if lines segments are inside polygons
- the occurrence of problems like triple intersections
- how to add random variations to lines
- how to guide the random positioning of circular spots

- how to guide streams of random bubbles
- the rotation of randomized (noisy) lines
- the rotation of jagged noisy lines
- daisy-wheel rotational effects
- high voltage electrified charge visual effects on lines
- high voltage electrified charge visual effects on complex shapes

Up to now we have filled in shapes with solid color. In Chapter 4 we experimented with ways of filling a shape with progressively smaller versions of the same shape to create more subtle shadings of color. Can we do more? The answer is yes, of course we can. The chief limitation is our own imagination and ability to express creativity using geometry. Geometry plus bits of algebra, trigonometry, linear algebra and some random statistics.

However the software is presented in a way that that means we do not have to know and understand the mathematics any more than a cyclist needs to know how to make steel tubing and rubber in order to ride a bicycle. The mathematics is not ignored but it is not central and you can ignore it without suffering deprivation.

Nevertheless if you want to become a creative master of the medium of computer graphics and game creation it will definitely give you a lead, an edge of speed and agility, if you can do new and unusual things using by harnessing mathematics to your purpose.

Drawing shapes using vector graphics has the great advantage that the shapes are preserved in software code rather than pixel-by-pixel files on a screen. This means that we can shift shapes, rotate them, squash them and skew them using well known algebra. These strategies are easily extended to three dimensions. 3-D transformations are dealt with in the book 7, "3D Concepts".
The pixel-by-pixel approach that is used in many 2D games need a separate drawing for each 'frame' of a movie on the screen (canvas). We use the term 'movie' to mean a controlled time sequence of separate images that create the sensation of smooth motion. When using vectors we only need to change some parameters in some lines of code to

achieve a similar thing. The disadvantage is that complex textures made of subtle color changes are difficult to achieve. However there are techniques to create color texture in vector shapes. This opens up a world of new artistic possibilities. This chapter demonstrates just a few of these possibilities.

What we explore here are techniques for achieving interesting effects on our basic shapes – lines and polygons.

Is algebra distasteful?

The strategies used in many of the programs in this chapter use high school geometry. Artistic people typically hate mathematics. We sympathize BUT... Mathematics is one of the most practical and useful tools the human race has conceived. The stunning dynamic imagery of video games uses mathematics at it's heart. In this book there is a tiny bit of trigonometry in the from of sine, cosine and tangent functions which we use without delving into their nature. We also use geometry in the form of straight line equations and the algebra that allows us to discover where exactly two lines intersect each other.

The good news is that we do not *need* to understand any mathematics to use the code. It is like carving wood using a carpenter's mallet and chisel. We do not need to be able to make a mallet from a log of timber and fabricate a chisel from a bar of steel in order to carve wood. We only need to know how to guide a chisel and strike it nicely with a mallet and understand how the grain of the carved work piece reacts to the edge of the chisel. So fear not the math. Just use it to hammer out your art. But if you become comfortable with the math then you can become a master craftsman and push the boundaries into new and unexplored territories.

With the aim of making the code understandable there are more than the usual number of comments in the code. In addition there are illustrations and explanations to make sure there is no confusion when we use terms like 'line' and 'segment' for similar but different things.

Where are we headed with the geometry?

Our aim is to be able to color and fill interesting shapes with textures other than pure colors. For example why shouldn't we be able to create the effect of an ink drawing where shading is achieved by lots of lines next to each other? Why not alternate the colors of the lines to make richer textures? Perhaps we could fill certain areas with dots of chosen size and color? These ideas are explored in this chapter. This is what the geometry is for.

The Intrinsic Nature of a Straight Line

All straight lines are infinitely long. We never see the whole line, only a *piece* or *segment* of it.
A pure straight line has two properties that make it unique and different. The first is it's slope or steepness. The second is where it cuts across the vertical, or y, axis. This cutting point is called "the intercept with the y-axis" or just "intercept" for short. If we know the slope and the intercept then we know everything necessary about the line.

In the first half of this chapter we work with the slope and intercept of straight lines because they are how we control the way we fill shapes with colored textures. In another book dealing with three dimensional geometry the ideas around slope and intercept are still vital.

Slope of a Straight Line

In vector graphics we represent straight lines as the coordinates of two points, one at each end of a segment of the line. To be precise when we draw a line using an instruction like *canvas_1.create_line(x1, y1, x2, y2)* we are only drawing a segment of a whole, infinitely long, line. Mathematically speaking the whole line is very, very long. Infinitely long in fact. We just need to be clear that when we draw lines on a canvas we are always dealing with *segments* – the short portion of the very long line that is shown on our canvas. Why is this important? Well in this chapter we are very concerned whether our line segments touch each other. When we try to figure out if two lines are intersecting we solve an equation and the result may be wrong for our purposes. The solution of the equation does not differentiate between the segments intersecting or the infinitely long lines intersecting somewhere outside the segments. One of the tasks we have with out Python code is to identify those results that are exclusive to segments of lines intersecting.

A key property of a line is it's slope. Slope is a measure of steepness which is a measure of how quickly it rises or falls as we progress horizontally. The slope is the vertical change divided by the horizontal change. This is shown in the illustration below.

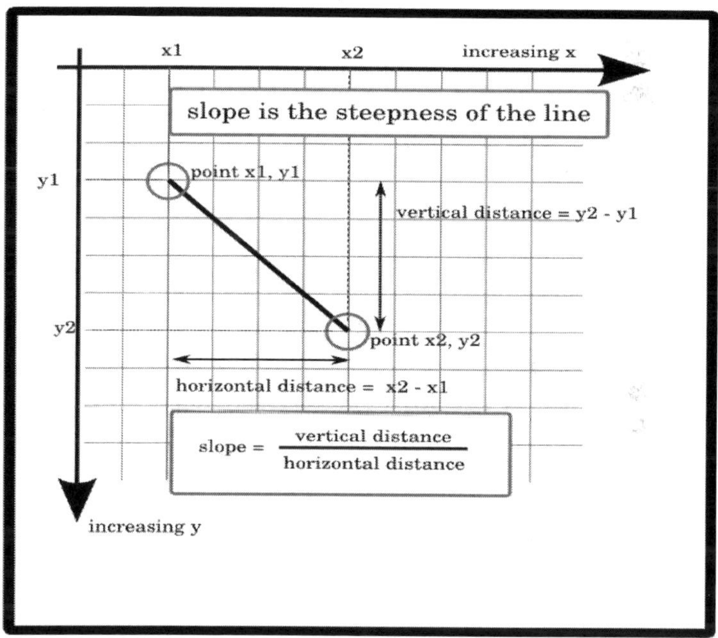

Intercept of a Straight Line

The second important property of a straight line is the intercept with the y-axis. Now here is a bit of mind magic to deal with. The intercept often lies outside of the segment we are drawing but it is nonetheless a critical property of that segment. It is the only property of our line segment that makes it different from the billions of other lines that have the same slope as our particular line.
The picture below shows what the intercept with the y axis looks like.

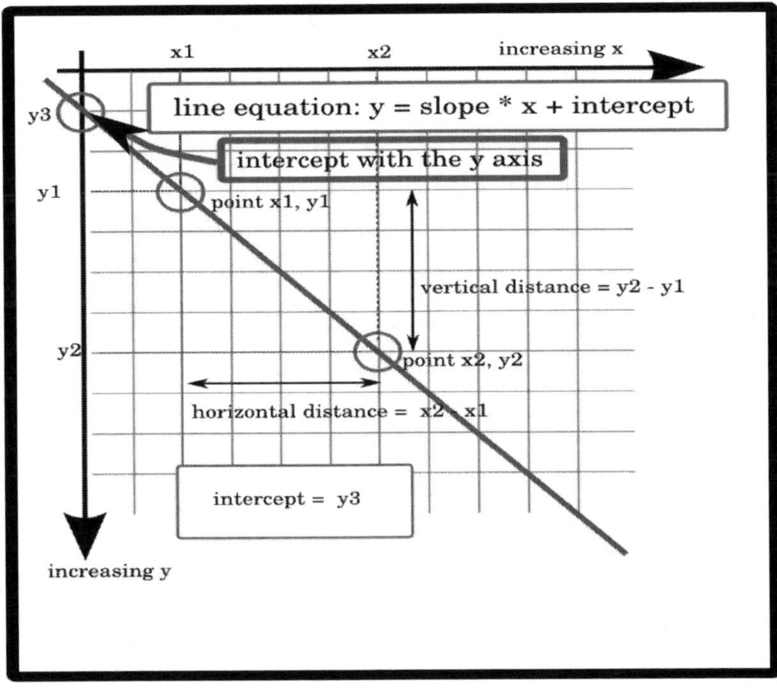

Intersection of two Straight Lines

In the art and science of creating and controlling images in the real-looking but totally imaginary world of video games it is vital to be able to differentiate between surfaces which are in front of other surfaces. Only the surfaces in front are drawn on the screen. The surfaces which should be hidden need to be figured out. Discovering hidden surfaces ultimately comes down to calculating where two lines intersect. In this chapter we deal with visible and hidden portions of lines in two dimensions (2D).
Just to be clear on concepts we use the picture shown below.

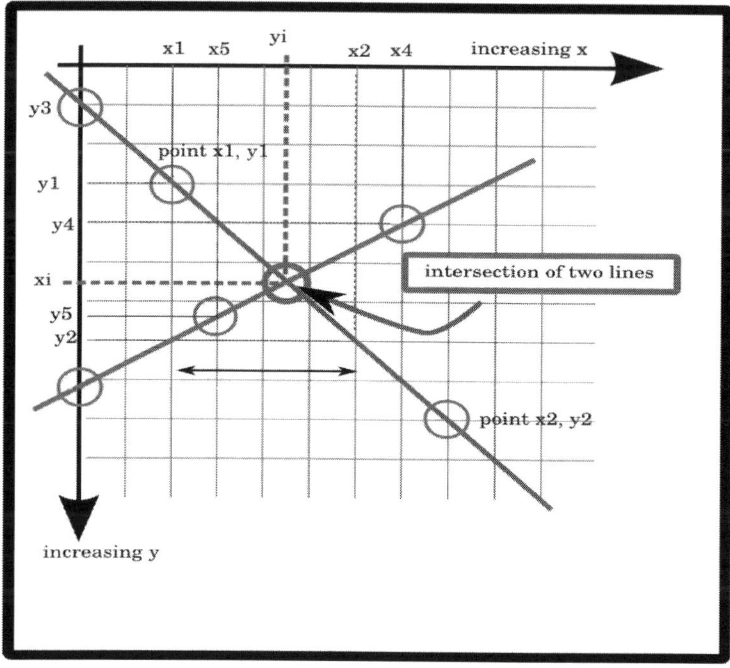

The point of intersection is the point defined by the coordinates xi, yi. When we solve the equation for the intersection of the two lines we are actually discovering what the numerical values of xi and yi are.
This what we do in the next two examples.

Parameters of a Straight Line

Here we draw two straight line segments and then calculate the slope and y-axis intercepts for each. These are the constant parameters that define any straight line. The two line-segments shown below are drawn using the two sets of points:
line_1 = [30.0, 140.0, 130.0, 30.0]
line_2 = [90.0, 120.0, 150.0, 180.0]

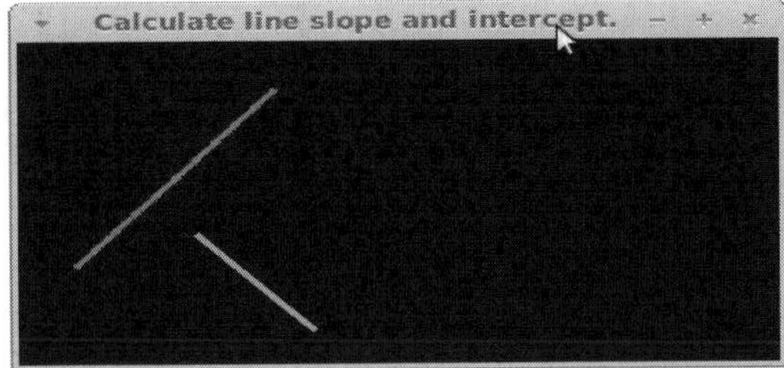

We use the two pairs of points given to calculate the slope and intercept for each line. And then test the validity of our calculations by drawing two new lines, the yellow segments, independently only using the line equations whose slope and intercept we have just worked out. If our new lines, the yellow ones here, lie exactly on top of the original line segments then our code has been proven correct and can be trusted.

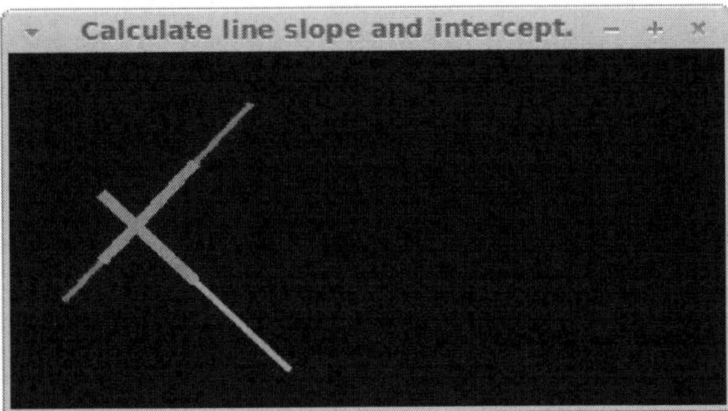


```
"""
Program name: line_parameters_1.py
```

Objective: Calculate the slope and intercept parameters of straight lines.
Prove the calculations are correct.

Keywords: polygons, line, slope, intercept, prove
===
Comments:

Tested on: Python 2.6, Python 2.7, Python 3.2.3
Author: Mike Ohlson de Fine
"""

```
from Tkinter import *
#from tkinter import *  # For Python 3.2.3 and higher.
root = Tk()
root.title(" Calculate line slope and intercept.")
cw = 380                              # canvas width
ch = 200                              # canvas height
canvas_1 = Canvas(root, width=cw, height=ch, background="#000088")
canvas_1.grid(row=0, column=1)

line_1 = [ 30.0, 140.0, 130.0, 30.0]
line_2 = [ 90.0, 120.0, 150.0, 180.0]


def get_line_params(line):
   """ Calculate straight line parameters from two given points (ie line as a
segment).
       The returned 'line' is in the form of slope and intercept and the segment
coordinates.
   """
   x1 = line[0]
   y1 = line[1]
   x2 = line[2]
   y2 = line[3]
   delt_y = y2 - y1
   delt_x = x2 - x1
   slope = delt_y/delt_x
   intercept = y1 - slope * x1
   return [slope, intercept, x1, y1, x2, y2]

def prove_line(x1, x2, line_n):
   """ A test and development utility.
       Verify that 'get_line_params' gives the correct slope and y-axis intercept.
       x1, x2 are the x-coordinates of the line segment to be shown.
   """
   y1 = line_n[0] * x1 + line_n[1]
```

```
    y2 = line_n[0] * x2 + line_n[1]
    canvas_1.create_line(x1, y1, x2, y2,  fill='orange', width =6)

canvas_1.create_line(line_1,  fill='green', width = 3)
canvas_1.create_line(line_2,  fill='grey', width = 3)

line_a = get_line_params(line_1)
prove_line(50, 100, line_a)
line_b = get_line_params(line_2)
prove_line(50, 100, line_b)

root.mainloop()
```

Discussion

The equation for a straight line is "y = slope* x + intercept". This means that for any pair of coordinates on the line the equation hold true. We use this to derive the slope and intercept parameters.

If we are given any two points on the line x1, y1 and x2, y2 then the slope is

(y2 – y1)/(x2 – x1). Once we have the slope we can use one of the points on the line, say x1, y1 in the equation of the line:

y1 = (y2 – y1)/(x2 – x1)*x1 + intercept.

Thus the intercept = y1 - (y2 – y1)/(x2 – x1)*x1.

Points to note

We are going to use the above code in more complex programs so we need to be absolutely confident that the answers are correct. That is why it was important to test the results.

What next?

The next level in our use of coordinate geometry of straight lines is to be able to discover where they intersect, if at all. We do this in the next exercise.

Calculate the Intersection Two Lines

To achieve multi-line shading of an area on a canvas we need to find points where lines intersect. The code of *line_intersection_1.py* below achieves this.
Program failure would occur if we look for intersection points of parallel lines. The program calculation will attempt to divide by zero but the Python interpreter catches this before it can happen and terminates execution of our program. We must take precautions against this ourselves if we want our code to work under all conditions that may arise normally. One the circumstances that would cause a divide by zero error is when the two lines whose intersection we are seeking, happen to be parallel to each other. They will never intersect.

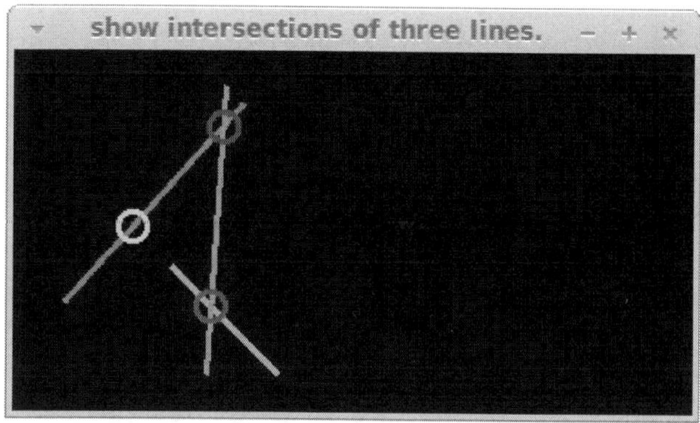

The picture above shows circles around the intersection points of three lines. In our program we have tried to prevent errors when lines cannot intersect because they are parallel. This is a special case or edge case that we should test and the picture below is the result.

This example highlights something we raised earlier regarding intersections points of long lines. Although they do intersect somewhere, the *segments* we happen to be interested in do not

intersect.
In the picture below we can see that the two yellow circles on the right of the picture show points of intersection that would occur if the lines were made longer. The lines intersect but the segments do not.

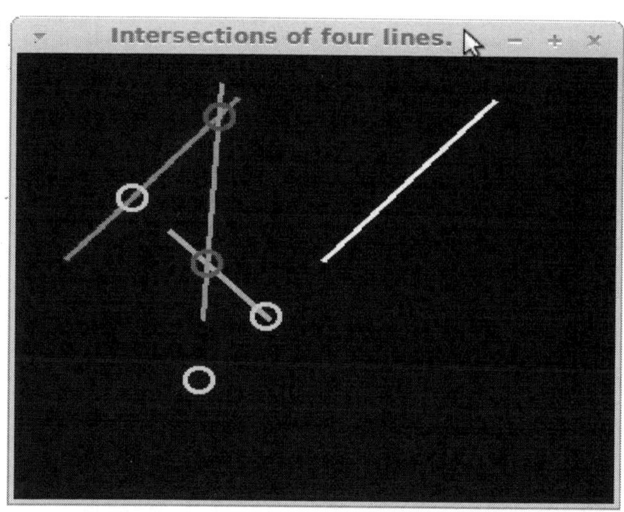


```
"""
Program name: line_intersections_1.py
Objective: Calculate the point of intersection of four straight lines.
Indicate the intersections with circles.

Keywords: polygons, line, intersections, intercepts, parallel
==================================================
Comments:

Tested on: Python 2.6, Python 2.7, Python 3.2.3
Author: Mike Ohlson de Fine

"""
from Tkinter import *
#from tkinter import *  # For Python 3.2.3 and higher.
root = Tk()
root.title(" Intersections of four lines.")
cw = 350                                # canvas width
ch = 300                                # canvas height
canvas_1 = Canvas(root, width=cw, height=ch, background="#000044")
canvas_1.grid(row=0, column=1)

line_1 = [ 30.0, 140.0, 130.0, 30.0]
line_2 = [ 90.0, 120.0, 150.0, 180.0]
line_3 = [ 110.0, 180.0, 120.0, 20.0]
line_4 = [ 180.0, 140.0, 280.0, 30.0]
```

```
def get_line_params(line):
    """ Calculate straight line parameters from two given points (ie line as a
segment).
        The returned 'line' is in the form of slope and intercept and the segment
coordinates.
    """
    x1 = line[0]
    y1 = line[1]
    x2 = line[2]
    y2 = line[3]
    delt_y = y2 - y1
    delt_x = x2 - x1
    slope = delt_y/delt_x
    intercept = y1 - slope * x1
    return [slope, intercept, x1, y1, x2, y2]

def prove_line(x1, x2, line_n):
    """ A test and development utility.
        Verify that 'get_line_params' gives the correct slope and y-axis intercept.
        x1, x2 are the x-coordinates of the line segment to be shown.
    """
    y1 = line_n[0] * x1 + line_n[1]
    y2 = line_n[0] * x2 + line_n[1]
    canvas_1.create_line(x1, y1, x2, y2,  fill='orange', width =6)

def line_intersection(line_1, line_2):
    """ Specify lines by their start and end positions.
        Returned: The x, y location of the intercept point.
    """
    line_a = get_line_params(line_1)  # Translate from start and end coordinates to
linear equation.
    line_b = get_line_params(line_2)  # Translate from start and end coordinates to
linear equation.
    # x_intercept = (intercept2-intercept1)/(slope1-slope2)
    if (line_a[0] - line_b[0]) == 0:
        print " Paralell lines may never connect."
        lines_parallel = 1
        return 0, 0, lines_parallel     # Parallel case. "lines_parallel" flag goes up.
    else:
        x_intercept = (line_b[1] - line_a[1]) / (line_a[0] - line_b[0])
        y_intercept = x_intercept * line_a[0] + line_a[1]
        lines_parallel = 0
        return x_intercept, y_intercept, lines_parallel
```

```
# Test each possibility.
# =====================
canvas_1.create_line(line_1,  fill='green', width = 3)
canvas_1.create_line(line_2,  fill='grey', width = 3)
canvas_1.create_line(line_3,  fill='orange', width = 3)
canvas_1.create_line(line_4,  fill='white', width = 3)

xy = line_intersection(line_1, line_2)
if xy[2] == 0:
   canvas_1.create_oval(xy[0]-8, xy[1]-8,  xy[0]+8, xy[1]+8, outline = 'yellow',
width = 3)
xy = line_intersection(line_1, line_3)
if xy[2] == 0:
   canvas_1.create_oval(xy[0]-8, xy[1]-8,  xy[0]+8, xy[1]+8, outline = 'red',
width = 3)
xy = line_intersection(line_3, line_2)
if xy[2] == 0:
   canvas_1.create_oval(xy[0]-8, xy[1]-8,  xy[0]+8, xy[1]+8, outline = 'purple',
width = 3)
xy = line_intersection(line_4, line_3)
if xy[2] == 0:
   canvas_1.create_oval(xy[0]-8, xy[1]-8,  xy[0]+8, xy[1]+8, outline = 'yellow',
width = 3)
xy = line_intersection(line_4, line_2)
if xy[2] == 0:
   canvas_1.create_oval(xy[0]-8, xy[1]-8,  xy[0]+8, xy[1]+8, outline = 'yellow',
width = 3)
xy = line_intersection(line_1, line_4)
if xy[2] == 0:
   canvas_1.create_oval(xy[0]-8, xy[1]-8,  xy[0]+8, xy[1]+8, outline = 'yellow',
width = 3)

root.mainloop()
```

Discussion

We will not explain here how derive the intersection points of lines. We do not want this to become an algebra textbook. Having said that the reader is encouraged to understand this for themselves and they will surely find the derivation in any reasonable high school book covering coordinate geometry. Youtube is a wonderful resource for high school mathematics lessons as well. Many skilled teachers have generously filmed excellent lessons for anyone in the world to view and learn from.

Points to note

Drawing with pencil on paper is the basic skill of all artists. The link from real world objects to the abstract representation of ideas about objects is most naturally expressed by drawing on paper. Geometric ideas are no different. Pencil and paper are the best way to record and examine ideas about lines and shapes. When we get stuck on code dealing with geometry it really, really helps to start trying to draw your ideas on paper. Different parts of our brain are aroused to help us solve our problems.

What next?

If a line lies across a polygon we need to identify the segment of the line that is inside the polygon. When two polygon shapes lie partially on top of each other we have to find out where their edges cross over each other. That is, where the line segments forming their edges intersect. This is what we explore in the next few examples.

Select Segment Intersection

Now we tackle the problem of identifying only those points of intersection that occur inside line segments and not those that occur outside, although they are still mathematically valid intersections for the portions of the line which extend beyond the segment.

The problem with the previous example is that it calculates the intersection of mathematical lines which are infinitely long. What we need are only the intersection points of line segments of interest. Remember a line-segment is just a portion of a line between two given points. So what we do here is use a method to test whether the intersection of two lines is inside particular segments of the two lines. We call this the 'inner box' test because the intersection will always be inside the smallest box we can make from the line segment start and end positions. If a point of intersection is inside the inner box then the segments intersect each other. In practice the test is even simpler: if the only the x-component of the point of intersection is inside the inner box then the segments intersect. The inner box is the smallest rectangular box that can be constructed from the coordinates of the segments being tested. This is illustrated in the drawing below.

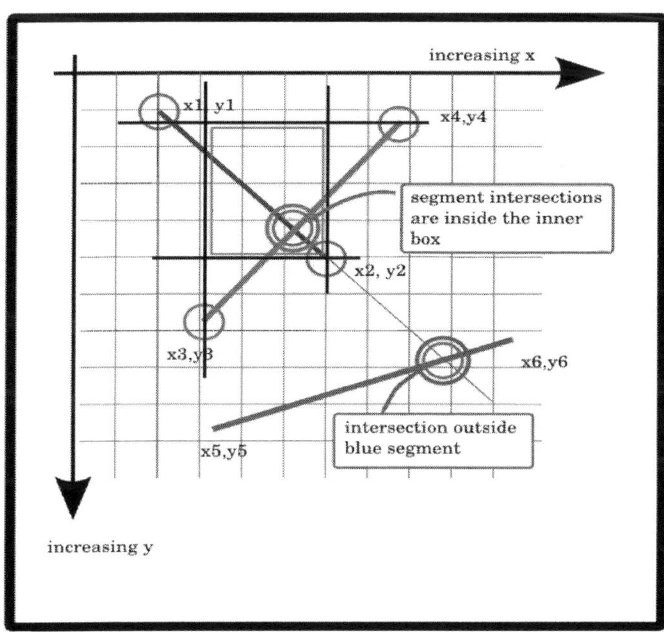

Applying this test criterion to all possible intersection points we get the correct results which are the intersection points indicated by the red circles in the diagram below.

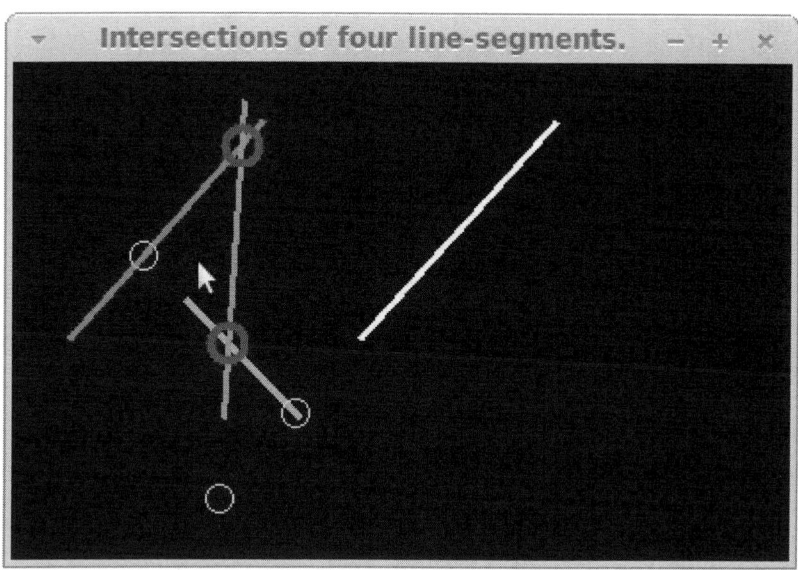


```
"""
Program name: line-segment_intersections_1.py
Objective: Calculate the point of intersection of four straight line-segments.
Differentiate between internal and external intersections.
Avoid parallel line errors.

Keywords: polygons, line, intersections, intercepts, parallel
==========================================================
Comments:

Tested on: Python 2.6, Python 2.7, Python 3.2.3
Author: Mike Ohlson de Fine

"""
from Tkinter import *
#from tkinter import *  # For Python 3.2.3 and higher.
root = Tk()
root.title(" Intersections of four line-segments.")
cw = 400                                # canvas width
ch = 250                                # canvas height
canvas_1 = Canvas(root, width=cw, height=ch, background="#000044")
canvas_1.grid(row=0, column=1)

line_1 = [ 30.0, 140.0, 130.0, 30.0]
line_2 = [ 90.0, 120.0, 150.0, 180.0]
line_3 = [ 110.0, 180.0, 120.0, 20.0]
```

```
line_4 = [ 180.0, 140.0, 280.0, 30.0]


def get_line_params(line):
    """ Calculate straight line parameters from two given points (ie line as a
segment).
        The returned 'line' is in the form of slope and intercept and the segment
coordinates.
    """
    x1 = line[0]
    y1 = line[1]
    x2 = line[2]
    y2 = line[3]
    delt_y = y2 - y1
    delt_x = x2 - x1
    slope = delt_y/delt_x
    intercept = y1 - slope * x1
    return [slope, intercept, x1, y1, x2, y2]

def prove_line(x1, x2, line_n):
    """ A test and development utility.
        Verify that 'get_line_params' gives the correct slope and y-axis intercept.
        x1, x2 are the x-coordinates of the line segment to be shown.
    """
    y1 = line_n[0] * x1 + line_n[1]
    y2 = line_n[0] * x2 + line_n[1]
    canvas_1.create_line(x1, y1, x2, y2,  fill='orange', width =6)

def inner_box(line_1, line_2):
    """ Purpose: Provide coordinates of inner-bow within which an intersection
point
        should lie is the line segments intersect.
        This function returns the coordinates of the inner box that would contain
        the intersection of both line segments (if they intersected).
        The lines are defined by their end points.
    """
    x1 = line_1[0]
    x2 = line_1[2]
    x3 = line_2[0]
    x4 = line_2[2]
    y1 = line_1[1]
    y2 = line_1[3]
    y3 = line_2[1]
    y4 = line_2[3]
    x_list = sorted([x1,x2,x3,x4])
```

```
    y_list = sorted([y1,y2,y3,y4])
    inner_box = x_list[1],y_list[1], x_list[2], y_list[2]
    return x_list, y_list

def line_intersection(line_1, line_2):
  """ Specify lines by their start and end positions.
     Returned: The x, y location of the intercept point.
  """
  line_a = get_line_params(line_1)  # Translate from start and end coordinates to
linear equation.
  line_b = get_line_params(line_2)  # Translate from start and end coordinates to
linear equation.
  # x_intercept = (intercept2-intercept1)/(slope1-slope2)
  if (line_a[0] - line_b[0]) == 0:
     print " Paralell lines may never connect."
     #print( " Paralell lines may never connect." )
     lines_parallel = 1
     return 0, 0, lines_parallel  # Parallel case. Raise "lines_parallel" flag.
  else:
     x_intercept = (line_b[1] - line_a[1]) / (line_a[0] - line_b[0])
     y_intercept = x_intercept * line_a[0] + line_a[1]
     lines_parallel = 0
     return x_intercept, y_intercept, lines_parallel

def inner_intersection(line_1, line_2):
  """ Specify lines as slope=m and Y intercept c
     Returned: The x, y location of the intercept point AND "seg_intersect".
     If the segments do not intersect then "seg_intersect" = FALSE, otherwise
TRUE.
  """
  line_a = get_line_params(line_1)  # Translate from start and end coordinates to
linear equation.
  line_b = get_line_params(line_2)  # Translate from start and end coordinates to
linear equation.
  # x_intercept = (intercept2-intercept1)/(slope1-slope2)
  if (line_a[0] - line_b[0]) == 0:   # Are the two lines parallel?
     print " Paralell lines: ", line_1," and ", line_2
     #print " Paralell lines: ", line_1," and ", line_2
     lines_parallel = 1
     return 0, 0, 0, lines_parallel  # Parallel case. Raise "lines_parallel" flag and
exit function.
  else:                         # Non-parallel case.
     lines_parallel = 1      # Lower the "lines_parallel" flag.
     x_intercept = (line_b[1] - line_a[1]) / (line_a[0] - line_b[0])
     y_intercept = x_intercept * line_a[0] + line_a[1]
```

```
    xy = x_intercept, y_intercept
    # Is the intersection inside x components of each segment? Get the smallest
rectangle.
    xy_box = inner_box(line_1, line_2)
    if (xy_box[0][1] <= x_intercept) and ( x_intercept <= xy_box[0][2]):
        seg_intersect = TRUE    # Intersection of segments.
        canvas_1.create_oval(xy[0]-9, xy[1]-9,  xy[0]+9, xy[1]+9, outline = 'red',
width = 4)
    else:
        seg_intersect = FALSE    # Intersection is external to the segments.
        canvas_1.create_oval(xy[0]-7, xy[1]-7,  xy[0]+7, xy[1]+7, outline =
'yellow', width = 2)
    return x_intercept, y_intercept, seg_intersect, lines_parallel

# Test each possibility.
# =====================
canvas_1.create_line(line_1,  fill='green', width = 3)
canvas_1.create_line(line_2,  fill='grey', width = 3)
canvas_1.create_line(line_3,  fill='orange', width = 3)
canvas_1.create_line(line_4,  fill='white', width = 3)

xy = inner_intersection(line_1, line_2)
xy = inner_intersection(line_1, line_3)
xy = inner_intersection(line_3, line_2)
xy = inner_intersection(line_4, line_3)
xy = inner_intersection(line_4, line_2)
xy = inner_intersection(line_1, line_4)

root.mainloop()
```

Discussion

The key function in the above program is *inner_intersection(line_1, line_2)*. This function applies two tests to the intersection points of the two lines passed to it. The first test is *if (line_a[0] - line_b[0]) == 0: # Are the two lines parallel?*

If the slopes are equal (the values *line_a[0]* and *line_b[0]*) then the function is terminated but the search for other intersections can continue. The program does not stop. A warning message is printed and a warning flag in the code is raised then the function exited.

```
print " Paralell lines: ", line_1," and ", line_2
lines_parallel = 1
return 0, 0, 0, lines_parallel  # Parallel case. Raise "lines_parallel" flag and exit function.
```

The second test is whether the intersection point found is inside the inner box:

```
# Is the intersection inside x components of each segment? Get the smallest rectangle.
xy_box = inner_box(line_1, line_2)
if (xy_box[0][1] <= x_intercept) and ( x_intercept <= xy_box[0][2]):
    seg_intersect = TRUE     # Intersection of segments.
    canvas_1.create_oval(xy[0]-9, xy[1]-9,  xy[0]+9, xy[1]+9, outline = 'red', width = 4)
```

Here the function *inner_box* returns the coordinates of the inner box sorted out from all possible possible coordinates defining the start and end of each line segment. There is some saving of effort because we do not have to test each corner of the box but only the x components.

Points to note

These complicated types of tests are tricky things to program. Firstly it takes a fair amount of head scratching and mistake making to clarify our thinking about what exactly it is we are trying to solve. It is an iterative process and we have to be doggedly persistent to get to a solution. The sense of triumph and achievement when we do have a solution is hard to beat. However we usually need to make additions and modifications to the code to accommodate all edge cases. The edge cases are situations at the outer limits of regions where the code obviously works well.

What next?

Next we apply our discoveries to the tricky task of filling the interiors of a bunch of polygons with colored line segments.

Fill a set of Polygons with Colored Line Segments

Here we pull the previous three programs together to draw groups of lines through groups of polygons

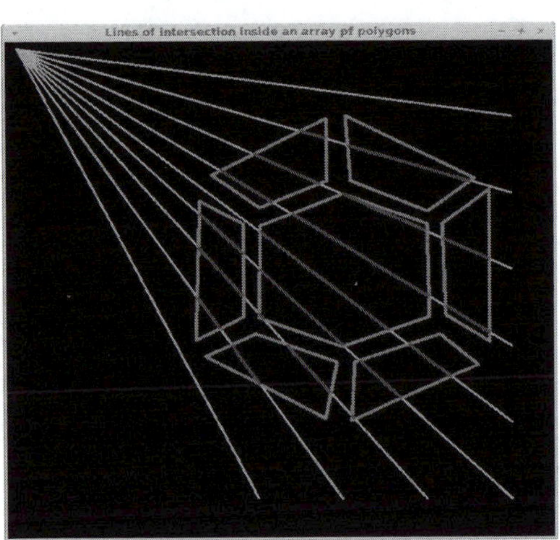


```
"""
Program name: polygon_intercepts_4.py
Objective: Draw the internal portion lines where they penetrate polygons.

Keywords: polygons, line, intercepts, segments, polygons
==================================================
Comments:
A polygon is made by joining a sequence of x-y points,
with the last point automatically joined to the first by a line to close
the polygon.

Tested on: Python 2.6, Python 2.7, Python 3.2.3
Author: Mike Ohlson de Fine
"""
from Tkinter import *
#from tkinter import *  # For Python 3.2.3 and higher.
root = Tk()
root.title(" Lines of intersection inside an array of polygons")
```

```
cw = 650                    # canvas width
ch = 650                    # canvas height
canvas_1 = Canvas(root, width=cw, height=ch, background="black")
canvas_1.grid(row=0, column=1)


poly_1 =[ 402.0, 201.0, 303.0, 243.0, 301.0, 363.0, 400.0, 401.0, 504.0, 362.0,
501.0, 241.0, 402.0, 201.0]
poly_2 =[382.0, 103.0, 383.0, 184.0, 302.0, 219.0, 245.0, 176.0, 382.0, 103.0 ]
poly_3 =[231.0, 210.0, 283.0, 241.0, 282.0, 362.0, 226.0, 392.0, 231.0, 210.0 ]
poly_4 =[237.0, 413.0, 297.0, 384.0, 394.0, 421.0, 380.0, 495.0, 237.0, 413.0 ]
poly_5 =[411.0, 498.0, 415.0, 421.0, 516.0, 385.0, 561.0, 425.0, 411.0, 498.0 ]
poly_6 =[575.0, 395.0, 523.0, 360.0, 519.0, 241.0, 574.0, 196.0, 575.0, 395.0 ]
poly_7 =[557.0, 181.0, 502.0, 224.0, 411.0, 184.0, 405.0, 99.0, 557.0, 181.0 ]
sun_poly = [poly_1, poly_2, poly_3, poly_4,poly_5, poly_6, poly_7]

line_1 = [ 15.0, 10.0, 600.0, 100.0]
line_2 = [ 15.0, 10.0, 600.0, 200.0]
line_3 = [ 15.0, 10.0, 600.0, 300.0]
line_4 = [ 15.0, 10.0, 600.0, 400.0]
line_5 = [ 15.0, 10.0, 600.0, 500.0]
line_6 = [ 15.0, 10.0, 600.0, 600.0]
line_7 = [ 15.0, 10.0, 500.0, 600.0]
line_8 = [ 15.0, 10.0, 400.0, 600.0]
line_9 = [ 15.0, 10.0, 300.0, 600.0]
lines = [line_1, line_2, line_3, line_4, line_5 , line_6, line_7, line_8, line_9]


def get_line_params(line):
   """ Calculate straight line parameters from two given points (ie line as a
segment).
       The returned 'line' is in the form of slope and intercept and the segment
coordinates.
   """
   x1 = line[0]
   y1 = line[1]
   x2 = line[2]
   y2 = line[3]
   delt_y = y2 - y1
   delt_x = x2 - x1
   slope = delt_y/delt_x
   intercept = y1 - slope * x1
   return [slope, intercept, x1, y1, x2, y2]
```

```
def inner_box(line_1, line_2):
  """ Purpose: Provide coordinates of inner-bow within which an intersection
point
      should lie is the line segments intersect.
      This function returns the coordinates of the inner box that would contain
      the intersection of both line segments (if they intersected).
      The lines are defined by their end points.
  """
  x1 = line_1[0]
  x2 = line_1[2]
  x3 = line_2[0]
  x4 = line_2[2]
  y1 = line_1[1]
  y2 = line_1[3]
  y3 = line_2[1]
  y4 = line_2[3]
  x_list = sorted([x1,x2,x3,x4])
  y_list = sorted([y1,y2,y3,y4])
  inner_box = x_list[1],y_list[1], x_list[2], y_list[2]
  return x_list, y_list


def inner_intersection(line_1, line_2):
  """ Specify lines as slope=m and Y intercept c
      Returned: The x, y location of the intercept point AND "seg_intersect".
      If the segments do not intersect then "seg_intersect" = FALSE, otherwise
TRUE.
  """
  line_a = get_line_params(line_1)  # Translate from start and end coordinates to
linear equation.
  line_b = get_line_params(line_2)  # Translate from start and end coordinates to
linear equation.
  # x_intercept = (intercept2-intercept1)/(slope1-slope2)
  x_intercept = (line_b[1] - line_a[1]) / (line_a[0] - line_b[0])
  y_intercept = x_intercept * line_a[0] + line_a[1]
  # Is the intersection inside x components of each segment? Get the smallest
rectangle.
  xy_box = inner_box(line_1, line_2)
  if (xy_box[0][1] <= x_intercept) and ( x_intercept <= xy_box[0][2]):
     seg_intersect = TRUE
  else:
     seg_intersect = FALSE     # Default assumption that intersection is external
to the segments.
  return x_intercept, y_intercept, seg_intersect
```

```
def internal_segment(lines, polygons):
    """  Draw segments of intersection where arrays of lines cut arrays of
polygons.
        The polygons could be other sets of lines ( ie not necessarily polygons).

    """
    xy_intercepts = []  # The set of intersection points within each segment-
internal box.
    for i in range(0, len(polygons)/2-1):
        line_temp = [polygons[2*i], polygons[2*i+1], polygons[2*i+2],
polygons[2*i+3] ]
        x, y, seg_intersect = inner_intersection(lines, line_temp)
        if seg_intersect == 1:
            xy_intercepts.append(x)
            xy_intercepts.append(y)
        if len(xy_intercepts)==4:
            canvas_1.create_line(xy_intercepts,  fill='red', width =4)

# Execute and Demonstrate.
# ===========================
for m in range(len(lines)):
    canvas_1.create_line(lines,  fill='grey', width = 3)
for n in range(len(sun_poly)):
    canvas_1.create_line(sun_poly[n],  fill='green', width = 4)

for i in range(len(lines)):
    for j in range(len(sun_poly)):
        internal_segment(lines[i], sun_poly[j])

root.mainloop()
```

Discussion

Our example proves that our code works where the lines have a range of slopes and intercept parameters. It also seems to handle a whole set of polygon shapes. However we have not yet experimented with vertical lines which we know are likely to cause difficulties.

Points to note

This example seems to do what is expected. The function: *internal_segment(lines, polygons)* is designed specifically to cycle through every polygon belonging to a list of polygons. For single polygons we would eliminate the loop *for i in range(0, len(polygons)/2-1):* to process a single polygon. A weakness in our code is the stalement *if len(xy_intercepts)==4:* This says in effect "when two coordinate points have been accumulated draw the segment and exit the function. What happens if there are more pairs of points to be accumulated? We do not have instructions that explicitly deal with such situations. They would make our program much more complicated. This situation is addressed later when trying to fill the interior of a multi-looped python shape with colored lines. This is where tesselation or tiling comes to the rescue.

Program Layout

Starting with the program above we have begun to split our code into two distinct sections. There is the uppers section where the canvas is created and dimensioned and all the general purpose functions are defined. We say general purpose because some of these functions will be used repeatedly in other programs. Then there is the lower section which follows after the comment lines:

```
# Execute and Demonstrate.
# ========================
```

These are lines of code to test and use the functions defined above. This is code that is probably only going to be used once for this specific example. We will use this structure repeatedly in order to save space and avoid excessive repetition.

What next?

We shall examine the behavior of our strategy for triple junctions. A triple junction is where three lines intersect at the same position. We did not plan for this in our code so it will not come as a surprise if triple junctions do not work out.

Another problem we have avoided so far, in the interest of simplicity, are vertical lines. The problem with a vertical line is it has a slope which is infinitely large because the denominator of slope = change in vertical/ change in horizontal is zero. There is no change in horizontal when the the line is vertical.

The Problem of the Triple Junction

Here we attempt to completely fill the polygons with horizontal lines to see what will happen at any triple junctions. The code for this program is identical to that in the above program except for the portion below the comment line:

```
# Execute and Demonstrate – dense raster of horizontal lines..
# ==========================================
```

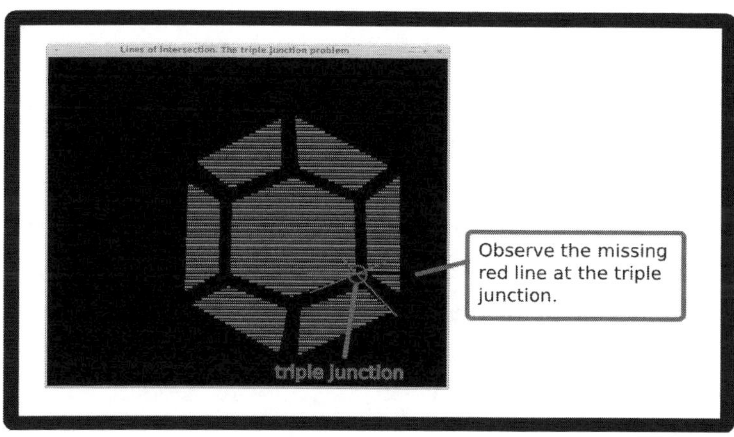


```
"""
Program name: poly_triple_junction_1.py
Objective: Draw the internal portion of lines where they penetrate polygons.
```

```
{ The code inserted here are the numerical list composing the set of polygon
sun_poly
and the functions:
def get_line_params(line): ...
def inner_box(line_1, line_2): ...
def inner_intersection(line_1, line_2): ...
def internal_segment(lines, polygons): ...
- all the above are identical to those in the example above }

# Execute and Demonstrate – dense raster of horizontal lines..
# ==================================================
x_start, y_start, line_length, gap = 10, 10, 630, 10
new_line = [x_start, y_start, x_start+line_length, y_start]
for i in range(60):
    for j in range(len(sun_poly)):
        internal_segment(new_line, sun_poly[j],'red')
    new_line =  [x_start, y_start+i*gap, x_start+line_length, y_start+i*gap]

y_start = 15
new_line = [x_start, y_start, x_start+line_length, y_start]
for i in range(60):
    for j in range(len(sun_poly)):
        internal_segment(new_line, sun_poly[j],'green')
    new_line =  [x_start, y_start+i*gap, x_start+line_length, y_start+i*gap]

root.mainloop()
```

Discussion

Examining the the illustration above it appears superficially that a triple junction will not prevent our code from working and the missing red segment could be tolerated as a minor visual flaw which could be worked around by re-positioning the horizontals by one or two pixels. The problem with this kind of approach is the same as it is like trying to hide cracks in a brick wall by covering them with wall paper. The crack is still there and is going to get worse as time progresses. Re-positioning our horizontal is likely to create another triple junction somewhere else on the canvas.

There are also problems that come to light when we have

complex shapes that require good code navigation tests and actions. Some of these problems are demonstrated in the illustration shown below.

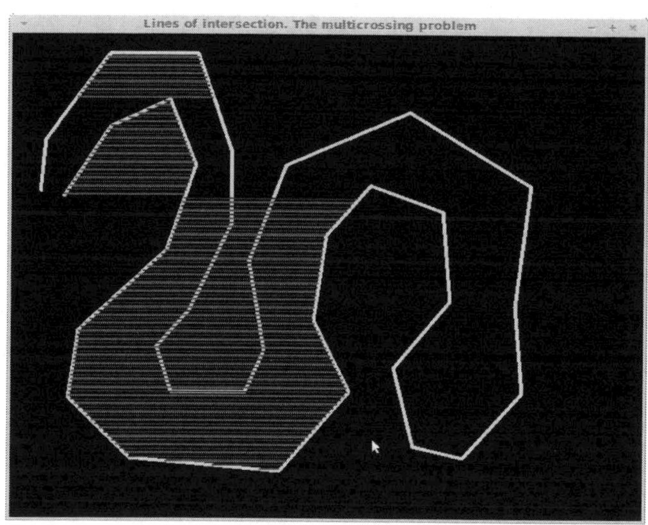

We can see here that our code starts off behaving as expected at the top but things go wrong when it encounters the first instance where are more than two segments that need to be drawn.
This did not occur when we were filling the "sun_poly" shape previously and this offers a clue to a solution. What would happen if we made up our python shape as a collection of simpler shapes? The central issue is that our original code was not designed to deal with complex shapes. The obvious solution is to keep adding tests to our code until we have a robust collection of tests that covers all possibilities. The code will rapidly become too complicated to understand. Although our algorithm needs improvement we must start from a position of reduced complexity. We must try to make the problem simpler.

One way to make our task simpler is to break up the

troublesome python outline into much simpler shapes. Shapes that are easier to work with.
We have split our python shape into a collection of three and four sided figures as shown below.

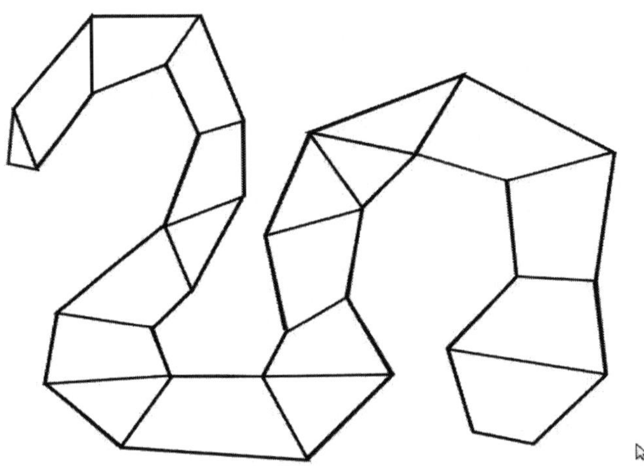

This process is called tesselation and is well established in producing high quality images in video games as well as massive scientific computations such as those that predict weather and the dynamics of galaxies to mention only two. In the scientific field the concept of breaking complex 3 dimensional fields into simpler shapes is called finite element analysis.

The tesselated variable lists are shown here.

```
py_0 = [ 33.3,195.7 , 59.5,202.8 , 37.8,130.5, 33.3,195.7]
py_1 = [ 38.3,132.1 , 109.6,25.5 , 109.5,114.9 , 59.04,200.8, 38.3,132.1]
py_2 = [ 110.6,24.5 , 206.5,25.0 , 175.2,82.6 , 110.1,114.4  ,110.6,24.5]
py_3 = [ 207.5,25.0 , 244.9,147.7 , 205.0,162.9 , 176.2,82.1, 207.5,25.0]
py_4 = [ 243.9,149.7 , 244.9,235.6 , 173.2,270.5 , 206.0,162.9, 243.9,149.7 ]
py_5 = [ 242.9,237.6 , 197.4,344.7 , 173.7,269.9 , 242.9,237.6]
py_6 = [ 196.4,344.7 , 162.6,387.1 , 75.71,369.4 , 173.2,268.9,  196.4,344.7]
py_7 = [ 160.1,386.1 , 177.2,443.2 , 64.6,451.8 , 76.2,370.5, 160.1,386.1]
py_8 = [ 178.2,445.2 , 133.8,524.5 , 65.1,451.3 , 65.6,452.3, 178.2,445.2]
py_9 = [ 133.8,525.5 , 299.5,541.7 , 259.6,444.7 , 175.7,443.7, 133.8,525.5]
```

```
py_10 = [ 299.5,538.1 , 374.7,444.2 , 258.5,444.7,  299.5,538.1]
py_11 = [ 374.7,445.2 , 334.8,353.8 , 280.8,394.2 , 260.6,444.2 , 374.7,445.2]
py_12 = [ 279.8,391.7 , 263.1,281.6 , 350.0,251.8 , 334.3,355.3, 279.8,391.7]
py_13 = [ 350.0,250.8 , 303.0,162. , 263.1,280.6,  350.0,250.8]
py_14 = [ 304.0,161.9 , 397.4,188.6 , 349.0,251.8, 304.0,161.9]
py_15 = [ 396.9,188.1 , 302.5,161.9 , 441.4,96.2, 396.9,188.1]
py_16 = [ 398.0,188.1 , 441.4,97.2 , 575.2,187.1 , 479.3,219.9 , 477.8,219.4]
py_17 = [ 576.2,187.6 , 558.1,336.6 , 487.3,331.1 , 479.8,219.9, 398.0,188.1]
py_18 = [ 557.0,338.1 , 566.6,445.2 , 425.2,415.4 , 487.3,331.6, 557.0,338.1 ]
py_19 = [ 567.7,445.2 , 501.0,525.0 , 446.9,510.4 , 425.7,416.9, 567.7,445.2]
pyth = [py_0,  py_1,  py_2,  py_3,  py_4,  py_5,  py_6,  py_7,  py_8,  py_9,
py_10,  py_11,  py_12,  py_13,  py_14,  py_15,  py_16,  py_17,  py_18,  py_19]
```

When this code is used in the poly_triple_junction_1.py program above it produces the following image.

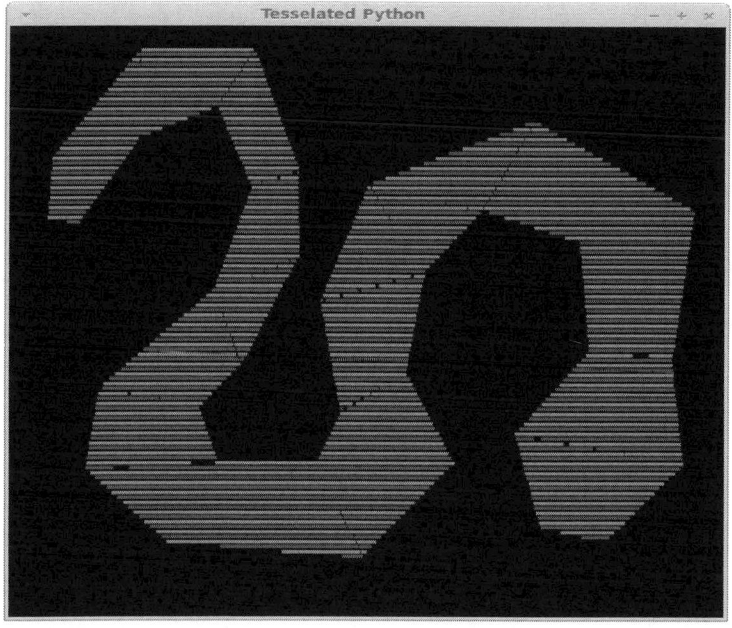

Although this image is not flawless it seems to be a better approach compared to the untesselated form.

This raises an important idea when trying to solve complex computer programming problems. *The correct approach to solving complex programming problems is to make the problem simpler rather than the solution more complex.*

Points to note

A far more serious problem is how to handle vertical lines, whose slope is infinite because of the 'divide-by-zero' explosion they cause. This is a definite show stopper. Any polygon shape is likely to have vertical lines. This is definitely a problem that cannot be ignored. The obvious approach would be to devise code tests that detect perfectly vertical lines and then invent specialized functions using new algebraic expressions to calculate where points of intersection are. It is simple enough to determine if a line is vertical. The divisor for the slope calculation will be zero. However finding an expression for the intersection that avoids slope calculations is not obvious.

Using the idea of making the problem simpler rather than making the solution more complex we could change vertical lines to horizontal ones by rotating the lines whose intersection we are seeking. When we have found the intersection coordinates then we simply rotate the point back to where it would have been before the rotation.
It turns out that this tactic also helps us with a completely different problem later on in this chapter under the heading "Smooth Symmetrical Chaos"

What next?

In the next example we deal with the vertical line issue.

The Problem of Vertical Lines and their Infinite Slope

There is more than one way to tackle problems of inconvenient geometry in software code.
There are two main possibilities. One is to trap a divide by zero before it occurs by performing a test and then if the test fails (the divide by zero condition) take suitable alternate action. This alternate may turn out to be complicated. The second possibility is to 'move the earth' by rotating the local geometry temporarily, working out slopes and intersections on the rotated system, and rotating everything back the way it was. This sounds like a large amount of work for what seems to be a small problem. Firstly it is not a little problem. It is a guaranteed show stopper for every vertical line. In any picture of man-made objects such as buildings and furniture there are many, many verticals. Secondly, as we have already created reliable rotation functions, part of the problem has already been solved. It is a simple matter to rotate any shape, including line segments, perform some operations on them. We us this idea in the section headed "Rough Symmetrical Chaos".

Randomness and Controlled Chaos

Now we are going to use random numbers to add new types of texture to our images.
Images appear flat and poster-like when uniform colors are used to fill shapes. Although we have solved part of this problem in the previous chapter using gradually varied color transitions while changing shape size, we always want to know what more can we do. How can we produce textures that are partially transparent like dust or mist. These are huge problems that challenge the large video game production companies and we certainly do not solve them here and now. However what we *do* explore here are ways to

introduce random variation into our images with the object of enriching texture and thus making the images more interesting.

Control of Randomness

Python provides a wonderful module named *random* which generates random numbers in various families of statistical distributions. We will not be exploring them from a mathematical point of view. Using a previous analogy we do not want to discover how to manufacture chisels and mallets. We just want to use the tools to achieve our purpose which is to enrich our images.

The best way to demystify randomness is to draw pictures of what it looks like and how it behaves. We start by drawing lines between two points. We add controlled amounts of random variation or noise to these lines. The key idea is that we draw a series of short line segments joined to each other without knowing *exactly* where each point will be. There a component of almost pure chance determining where the next point on the line will be. However we control the amount or size of the random component. It is not completely random because we progressively add quantities that consistently move our noisy line toward a precisely defined end position. We fix the beginning and end but allow a controlled amount of random noise to the segment between the end points.

Line Randomness

Here we draw two columns of noisy lines with the amount of noise increasing as we move down the canvas. The amount of noise is controlled by a number called the *standard deviation*. The column of noisy line segments on the left is where we have not allowed the x-component of the line to be noisy. Only the y-component has a random quantity added to it. On the other hand the column lines on the right has a random component added to both the x and the y components. The consequence of both will have a profound effect on the character of drawings made using them.

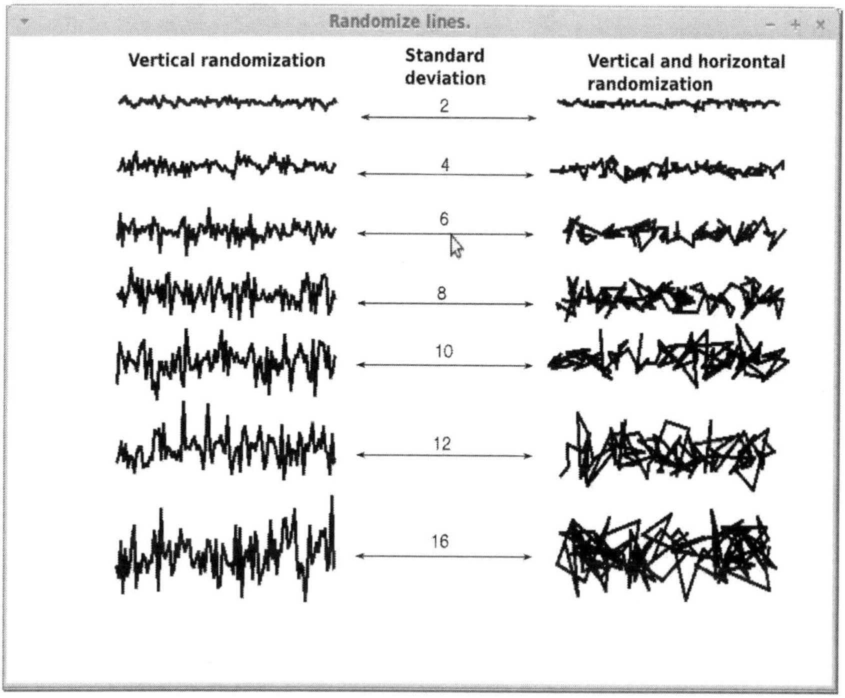

Randomize lines.

Vertical randomization | Standard deviation | Vertical and horizontal randomization

2

4

6

8

10

12

16

```
"""
Program name: line_randomize_1.py
Objective: Draw two segmented sets of lines with a confined but random
(Gaussean)components.
```

```
Keywords: random vertical, distribution
=====================================================
Comments:  We draw a set of segmented line with partially random
vertical components using the function line_randomize_vertical(...).
 We also draw a set of segmented line with partially random vertical
as well as horizontal components using the function line_randomize_xy(...).

A gaussean random distribution is used.

Tested on: Python 2.6, Python 2.7.3, Python 3.2.3
Author: Mike Ohlson de Fine
"""
from Tkinter import *
#from tkinter import *  # For Python 3.2.3 and higher.
from random import *

root = Tk()
root.title(" Randomize lines.")
cw = 750                              # canvas width
ch = 500                              # canvas height
canvas_1 = Canvas(root, width=cw, height=ch, background="white")
canvas_1.grid(row=0, column=1)

def line_randomize_vertical(xy_line, x_delta, standard_deviation):
    """ Draw a segmented line with randomized vertical component
        added.
    """
    num_steps = int((xy_line[2] - xy_line[0])/x_delta)
    xy_list = []
    for i in range(num_steps):
        y_randomized = xy_line[1] + gauss(mean, standard_deviation)
        x_next = xy_line[0] + i * x_delta
        xy_list.append(x_next)
        xy_list.append(y_randomized)
    canvas_1.create_line(xy_list, width = 3)

def line_randomize_xy(xy_line, x_delta, standard_deviation):
    """ Draw a segmented line with randomized vertical component
        added.
    """
    num_steps = int((xy_line[2] - xy_line[0])/x_delta)
    xy_list = [] line_randomize_1.py
    for i in range(num_steps):
        y_randomized = xy_line[1] + gauss(mean, standard_deviation)
        x_randomized  = xy_line[0] + i * x_delta + gauss(mean,
```

```
standard_deviation)
        xy_list.append(x_randomized)
        xy_list.append(y_randomized)
    canvas_1.create_line(xy_list, width = 3)


# Execute and Demonstrate.
# ==========================
x_delta = 2.0
mean = 1.0
standard_deviation = 2.0
xy_line = 100.0, 50.0, 300.0, 50.0
line_randomize_vertical(xy_line, x_delta, standard_deviation)
standard_deviation = 4.0
xy_line = 100.0, 100.0, 300.0, 100.0
line_randomize_vertical(xy_line, x_delta, standard_deviation)
standard_deviation = 6.0
xy_line = 100.0, 150.0, 300.0, 150.0
line_randomize_vertical(xy_line, x_delta, standard_deviation)
standard_deviation = 8.0
xy_line = 100.0, 200.0, 300.0, 200.0
line_randomize_vertical(xy_line, x_delta, standard_deviation)
standard_deviation = 10.0
xy_line = 100.0, 250.0, 300.0, 250.0
line_randomize_vertical(xy_line, x_delta, standard_deviation)
standard_deviation = 12.0
xy_line = 100.0, 320.0, 300.0, 320.0
line_randomize_vertical(xy_line, x_delta, standard_deviation)
standard_deviation = 16.0
xy_line = 100.0, 400.0, 300.0, 400.0
line_randomize_vertical(xy_line, x_delta, standard_deviation)

standard_deviation = 2.0
xy_line = 500.0, 50.0, 700.0, 50.0
line_randomize_xy(xy_line, x_delta, standard_deviation)
standard_deviation = 4.0
xy_line = 500.0, 100.0, 700.0, 100.0
line_randomize_xy(xy_line, x_delta, standard_deviation)
standard_deviation = 6.0
xy_line = 500.0, 150.0, 700.0, 150.0
line_randomize_xy(xy_line, x_delta, standard_deviation)
standard_deviation = 8.0
xy_line = 500.0, 200.0, 700.0, 200.0
line_randomize_xy(xy_line, x_delta, standard_deviation)
standard_deviation = 10.0
```

```
xy_line = 500.0, 250.0, 700.0, 250.0
line_randomize_xy(xy_line, x_delta, standard_deviation)
standard_deviation = 12.0
xy_line = 500.0, 320.0, 700.0, 320.0
line_randomize_xy(xy_line, x_delta, standard_deviation)
standard_deviation = 16.0
xy_line = 500.0, 400.0, 700.0, 400.0
line_randomize_xy(xy_line, x_delta, standard_deviation)

root.mainloop()
```

Discussion

What we have created here is a new way of drawing lines between two points. It can be used in a similar way that the *create_line(..)* function.

Points to note

We have added random variations to lines. The lines that artists draw on canvas and paper are never perfectly straight. Much of the vitality of images created by artists comes from the fact that the lines they create are not perfectly smooth. The lines we see in nature are seldom smooth and regular. Every leaf on a tree is a different size and shape. So if we want to create appealing shapes a random wobble is usually a good thing.

What next?

Why not draw outlines of objects using scatterings of shapes like circles or stars? The example below explores this with ovals.

Spot Randomness

Here we use a different randomization function to draw randomly scattered circles or spots between the end positions of our given line segments. As we did above with the randomized lines we make two sets of lines. The first set has vertical random noise added and the second set has both vertical and horizontal noise. The main difference between the two is that overlapping of circles cannot be avoided where there is both vertical and horizontal scatter. Where there is only vertical scatter it is possible to avoid overlap of any circles by ensuring that the minimum increment in x, the quantity *x_delta* is larger the the radius of the circle being drawn.

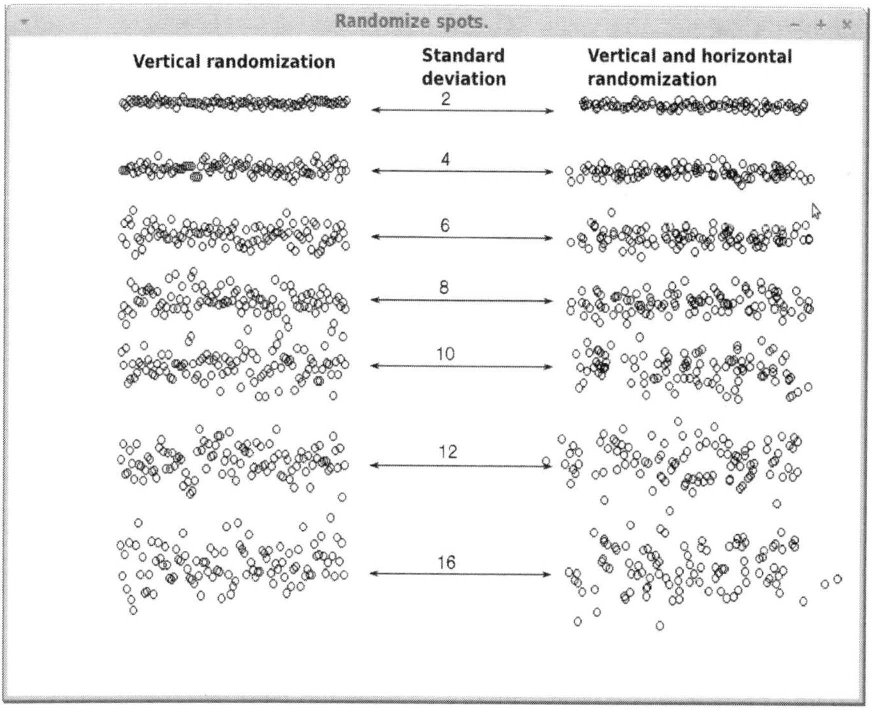

```
"""
Program name: spot_randomize_1.py
Objective: Draw a random scattering of spots between two points.

Keywords: random vertical, random horizontal, spots, gaussean distribution
=======================================================================
Comments: One set with a random (Gaussean) vertical component.
A second set with a random component in both vertical and horizontal directions.

Tested on: Python 2.6, Python 2.7.3, Python 3.2.3
Author: Mike Ohlson de Fine
"""
from Tkinter import *
#from tkinter import *  # For Python 3.2.3 and higher.
from random import *

root = Tk()
root.title(" Randomize spots.")
cw = 750                              # canvas width
ch = 500                              # canvas height
canvas_1 = Canvas(root, width=cw, height=ch, background="white")
canvas_1.grid(row=0, column=1)

def spot_randomize_vertical(xy_line, x_delta, standard_deviation):
    """ Draw a segmented line with randomized vertical component
        added.
    """
    num_steps = int((xy_line[2] - xy_line[0])/x_delta)
    for i in range(num_steps):
        y_randomized = xy_line[1] + gauss(mean, standard_deviation)
        x_next = xy_line[0] + i * x_delta
        canvas_1.create_oval(x_next-3,  y_randomized-3, x_next+3,
y_randomized+3)

def spot_randomize_xy(xy_line, x_delta, standard_deviation):
    """ Draw a segmented line with randomized horizontal and vertical
components
        added.
    """
    num_steps = int((xy_line[2] - xy_line[0])/x_delta)
    for i in range(num_steps):
        y_randomized = xy_line[1] + gauss(mean, standard_deviation)
        x_randomized  = xy_line[0] + i * x_delta + gauss(mean,
standard_deviation)
```

```
    canvas_1.create_oval(x_randomized-3,  y_randomized-3, x_randomized+3,
y_randomized+3)


# Execute and Demonstrate.
# ==========================
x_delta = 2.0
mean = 1.0
standard_deviation = 2.0
xy_line = 100.0, 50.0, 300.0, 50.0
spot_randomize_vertical(xy_line, x_delta, standard_deviation)
standard_deviation = 4.0
xy_line = 100.0, 100.0, 300.0, 100.0
spot_randomize_vertical(xy_line, x_delta, standard_deviation)
standard_deviation = 6.0
xy_line = 100.0, 150.0, 300.0, 150.0
spot_randomize_vertical(xy_line, x_delta, standard_deviation)
standard_deviation = 8.0
xy_line = 100.0, 200.0, 300.0, 200.0
spot_randomize_vertical(xy_line, x_delta, standard_deviation)
standard_deviation = 10.0
xy_line = 100.0, 250.0, 300.0, 250.0
spot_randomize_vertical(xy_line, x_delta, standard_deviation)
standard_deviation = 12.0
xy_line = 100.0, 320.0, 300.0, 320.0
spot_randomize_vertical(xy_line, x_delta, standard_deviation)
standard_deviation = 16.0
xy_line = 100.0, 400.0, 300.0, 400.0
spot_randomize_vertical(xy_line, x_delta, standard_deviation)

standard_deviation = 2.0
xy_line = 500.0, 50.0, 700.0, 50.0
spot_randomize_xy(xy_line, x_delta, standard_deviation)
standard_deviation = 4.0
xy_line = 500.0, 100.0, 700.0, 100.0
spot_randomize_xy(xy_line, x_delta, standard_deviation)
standard_deviation = 6.0
xy_line = 500.0, 150.0, 700.0, 150.0
spot_randomize_xy(xy_line, x_delta, standard_deviation)
standard_deviation = 8.0
xy_line = 500.0, 200.0, 700.0, 200.0
spot_randomize_xy(xy_line, x_delta, standard_deviation)
standard_deviation = 10.0
xy_line = 500.0, 250.0, 700.0, 250.0
spot_randomize_xy(xy_line, x_delta, standard_deviation)
```

```
standard_deviation = 12.0
xy_line = 500.0, 320.0, 700.0, 320.0
spot_randomize_xy(xy_line, x_delta, standard_deviation)
standard_deviation = 16.0
xy_line = 500.0, 400.0, 700.0, 400.0
spot_randomize_xy(xy_line, x_delta, standard_deviation)

root.mainloop()
```

Discussion

The major difference between this example using randomly positioned circles and the previous example using randomly positioned line segments is that we need to store the sequence of points making up the noisy line because each point in the line is not independent of it immediate neighbors. Each point has to be connected to it's immediate neighbor by an invisible line segment. That is why we save the whole sequence in the list *xy_list* inside the functions.

What next?

Can we randomize the size of the spots as well as their position? The answer is yes, of course, and we demonstrate that next.

Bubble Randomness

Here we also make the size of the circles random.

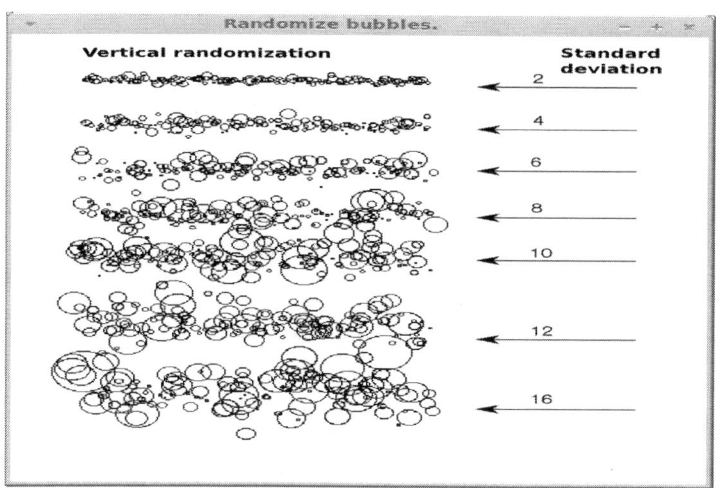


```
"""
Program name: bubbles_randomize_1.py
Objective: Draw a random scattering of randomly sized circles between two
points.

Keywords: random vertical, random horizontal, spots, gaussean distribution
=============================================================
Comments:  We want draw a set of circular spots line with random radii (size)
as well as vertical position components.

Tested on: Python 2.6, Python 2.7.3, Python 3.2.3
Author: Mike Ohlson de Fine
"""
from Tkinter import *
#from tkinter import *  # For Python 3.2.3 and higher.
from random import *

root = Tk()
root.title(" Randomize bubbles.")
cw = 500                          # canvas width
ch = 500                          # canvas height
canvas_1 = Canvas(root, width=cw, height=ch, background="white")
canvas_1.grid(row=0, column=1)

def spot_randomize_vertical(xy_line, x_delta, standard_deviation):
    """ Draw a segmented line with randomized vertical component
      added.
```

```
  """
  num_steps = int((xy_line[2] - xy_line[0])/x_delta)
   for i in range(num_steps):
       radius = gauss(mean, standard_deviation)
       y_randomized = xy_line[1] + gauss(mean, standard_deviation)
       x_next = xy_line[0] + i * x_delta
       canvas_1.create_oval(x_next-radius,  y_randomized-radius, x_next+3,
y_randomized+3)


# Execute and Demonstrate.
# ==========================
x_delta = 2.0
mean = 1.0
standard_deviation = 2.0
xy_line = 50.0, 50.0, 300.0, 50.0  # The Seed line for randomization.
spot_randomize_vertical(xy_line, x_delta, standard_deviation)
standard_deviation = 4.0
xy_line = 50.0, 100.0, 300.0, 100.0
spot_randomize_vertical(xy_line, x_delta, standard_deviation)
standard_deviation = 6.0
xy_line = 50.0, 150.0, 300.0, 150.0
spot_randomize_vertical(xy_line, x_delta, standard_deviation)
standard_deviation = 8.0
xy_line = 50.0, 200.0, 300.0, 200.0
spot_randomize_vertical(xy_line, x_delta, standard_deviation)
standard_deviation = 10.0
xy_line = 50.0, 250.0, 300.0, 250.0
spot_randomize_vertical(xy_line, x_delta, standard_deviation)
standard_deviation = 12.0
xy_line = 50.0, 320.0, 300.0, 320.0
spot_randomize_vertical(xy_line, x_delta, standard_deviation)
standard_deviation = 16.0
xy_line = 50.0, 400.0, 300.0, 400.0
spot_randomize_vertical(xy_line, x_delta, standard_deviation)

root.mainloop()
```

Discussion

In the previous three examples we have experimented with methods of using random numbers to add a quantity of variation to objects like lines and circles. This is just a start. Real world objects like leaves on a tree or pebbles on a beach are all different from each other. There something like a random component to their size and shape. The possibilities are endless.

Points to note

We should be aware that in the first example line_randomize_1.py we were able to control and confine the degree of noise applied to straight lines by allowing one dimension only to be randomized, the vertical component in our example. Where both were allowed to vary randomly we saw an jarring, kind of insane character to the lines.
The Python code to achieve these effects assumed that the lines would be mainly horizontal.

What next?

What happens if we rotate the lines created by the randomization functions in
line_randomize_1.py ?
The diagram below is the result.

Rotation of Randomized Lines

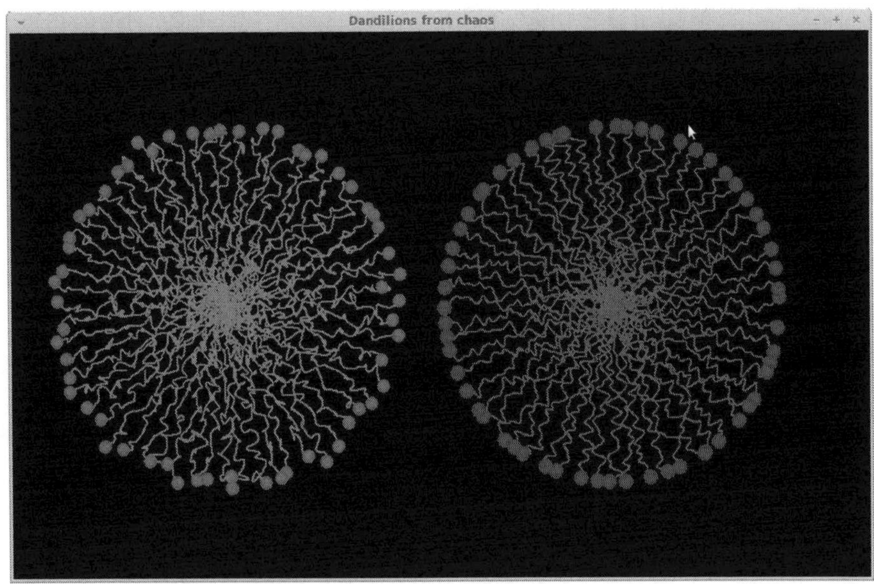


```
"""
Program name: line_rotation_randomization_1.py
Objective: Add random components to a line between two points and then
rotate the line through a full circle.

Keywords: line, random, chaotic.
====================================================
Comments:
A Straight line between two points has a random 'wobble' added to it.
Two styles of randomization are used. The leftmost is random in both
vertical and horizontal components. The rightmost is only random in the
vertical component.

Tested on: Python 2.6, Python 2.7.3, Python 3.2.3
Author: Mike Ohlson de Fine

"""
from Tkinter import *
#from tkinter import *  # For Python 3.2.3 and higher.
from random import *
import math
root = Tk()
root.title(" Dandilions from chaos")
cw = 1000                          # canvas width
ch = 600                           # canvas height
canvas_1 = Canvas(root, width=cw, height=ch, background="black")
```

```
canvas_1.grid(row=0, column=1)

def rotate_shape(shape, xy_center, angle_degrees):
    """ Rotate any shape about a cetner point xy_center.
    """
    angle_rad = math.radians(angle_degrees)
    x_cen = xy_center[0]
    y_cen = xy_center[1]
    new_shape = []
    for i in range(len(shape)/2 ):
        x_temp = shape[2*i]  - x_cen
        y_temp = shape[2*i+1] - y_cen
        radian_temp  = math.atan2(y_temp, x_temp )
        length_temp = math.sqrt( y_temp**2 + x_temp**2)
        new_angle = angle_rad + radian_temp
        new_x = length_temp * math.cos(new_angle) + x_cen
        new_y = length_temp * math.sin(new_angle) + y_cen
        new_shape.append(new_x)
        new_shape.append(new_y)
    return   new_shape   # angle_deg = post rotation angle

def line_randomize_vertical(xy_line, x_delta, standard_deviation):
    """ Draw a segmented line with randomized vertical component
        added.
    """
    num_steps = int((xy_line[2] - xy_line[0])/x_delta)
    xy_list = []
    for i in range(num_steps):
        y_randomized = xy_line[1] + gauss(mean, standard_deviation)
        x_next = xy_line[0] + i * x_delta
        xy_list.append(x_next)
        xy_list.append(y_randomized)
    return xy_list

def line_randomize_xy(xy_line, x_delta, standard_deviation):
    """ Draw a segmented line with randomized vertical component
        added.
    """
    num_steps = int((xy_line[2] - xy_line[0])/x_delta)
    xy_list = []
    for i in range(num_steps):
        y_randomized = xy_line[1] + gauss(mean, standard_deviation)
        x_randomized  = xy_line[0] + i * x_delta + gauss(mean,
standard_deviation)
        xy_list.append(x_randomized)
```

```
        xy_list.append(y_randomized)
    return xy_list

# Execute and Demonstrate.
# ========================
mean = 1.0
standard_deviation = 6.0
x_delta = 5.0
angle_degrees = 6.0

kula = '#ff8800'
xy_line = [250.0, 300.0, 450.0, 300.0]   # The Seed line for randomization.
xy_center = xy_line[0], xy_line[1]

for j in range(60):
    # Orange flower. Random in both x and y
    xy_list = line_randomize_xy(xy_line, x_delta, standard_deviation)
    xy_list = rotate_shape(xy_list, xy_center, angle_degrees*j)
    canvas_1.create_line(xy_list, smooth = 1, fill=kula, width = 2)
    x_tip = xy_list[len(xy_list)-2]
    y_tip = xy_list[len(xy_list)-1]
    canvas_1.create_oval(x_tip -6, y_tip -6,x_tip +6, y_tip +6, fill='#ff6600',
outline= '#ff4400',width = 3)

kula = '#0088ff'
xy_line = [700.0, 300.0, 900.0, 300.0]   # The Seed line for randomization.
xy_center = xy_line[0], xy_line[1]

for j in range(60):
    # Blue Flower. Random in y component only
    xy_list = line_randomize_vertical(xy_line, x_delta, standard_deviation)
    xy_list = rotate_shape(xy_list, xy_center, angle_degrees*j)
    canvas_1.create_line(xy_list, smooth = 1, fill=kula, width = 2)
    x_tip = xy_list[len(xy_list)-2]
    y_tip = xy_list[len(xy_list)-1]
    canvas_1.create_oval(x_tip -7, y_tip -7,x_tip +7, y_tip +7, fill='#0066ff',
outline= '#0044ff',width = 3)

root.mainloop()
```

Discussion

The randomization functions have slightly modified from the form they had in line_randomize_1.py . The difference is that the create_line(...) functions have not been included inside the *line_randomize_vertical(...)* and the *line_randomize_xy(...)* functions. This means that the randomized line list should be returned from the function so that it can be used externally by the rotation function.

Points to note

A “seed pod” has been added to the tip of each rotated line. This makes it clearly apparent how the character of drawn objects is influenced by the type of randomization applied. The orange flower on the left looks more natural than the one on the right in some respects.

A weakness to the way we have coded these randomized and rotated images is that the seed line *xy_line* to which the randomization is applied has to be horizontal. As the seed line *xy_line* becomes more vertical the intended randomization breaks down because of the way the x-component of the line is divided up.

What next?

In the next example we eliminate the requirement that the seed line be horizontal and change the code so that it does not matter what the original orientation of *xy_line* is.

Rough Symmetrical Chaos

There is a trick to ensure that the angle of our randomized lines will not be influenced their original orientation. We use a method of transforming the geometric space that we see on the canvas into an unseen alternate workshop space where we have better control of our environment. After doing tool work on the line we restore it to it's original orientation. A descriptive name for this trick or technique could be *rotate-reshape-restore* because this how it works for any particular line we might be working on:

1. Rotate the line so that is lies horizontal.
2. Re-shape and randomize the line in a suitably controlled fashion.
3. Restore the altered line to it original orientation by negatively rotating by the same amount as the original rotation.

This technique is useful in other situations. One that springs to the fore is the problem of finding the intersection of vertical lines with the boundaries of polygons mentioned earlier in this chapter. We would take the vertical line and the polygon being explored for intersection points and rotate both by ninety degrees. This would transform the vertical line into a horizontal one whose intersection points could be discovered using the functions we had already created for the purpose. Once the line segments inside the polygon and the polygon edge are restored to their original orientation everything will be where it should and the problem is solved.

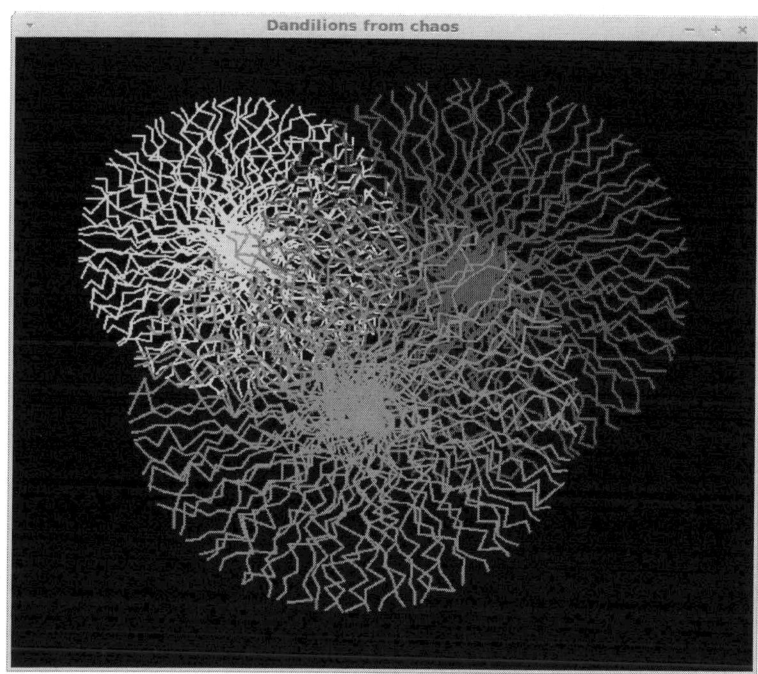


```
"""
Program name: line_rough_randomization_1.py
Objective: Add jagged random components to a line between two points.

Keywords: line, jagged, random, chaotic.
=====================================================
Comments:
A Straight line between two points has a random 'wobble' added to it.
To confine the randomness to being deviations on either side of the line
without overlap or looping a strategy or rotation to the x-axis,
randomization and restore the rotation was used.

Tested on: Python 2.6,
Author: Mike Ohlson de Fine

"""
from Tkinter import *
from random import *
import math
root = Tk()
root.title(" Dandilions from chaos")
```

```
cw = 650                        # canvas width
ch = 600                        # canvas height
canvas_1 = Canvas(root, width=cw, height=ch, background="black")
canvas_1.grid(row=0, column=1)

def rotate_shape(shape, xy_center, angle_degrees):
    """ Rotate any shape about a center point xy_center.
    """
    angle_rad = math.radians(angle_degrees)
    x_cen = xy_center[0]
    y_cen = xy_center[1]
    new_shape = []
    for i in range(len(shape)/2 ):
        x_temp = shape[2*i]  - x_cen
        y_temp = shape[2*i+1] - y_cen
        radian_temp  = math.atan2(y_temp, x_temp )
        length_temp = math.sqrt( y_temp**2 + x_temp**2)
        new_angle = angle_rad + radian_temp
        new_x = length_temp * math.cos(new_angle) + x_cen
        new_y = length_temp * math.sin(new_angle) + y_cen
        new_shape.append(new_x)
        new_shape.append(new_y)
    return   new_shape   # angle_deg = post rotation angle


def gauss_y_scatter(xy_line, mean, std_dev, num_steps, factor):
    """ Generate a list of points randomly scattered about a straight line.
        xy_line are the start and end coordintes of the line and should be
        given as floats.
        Strategy: rotate line to the horizontal, create the scatter in y only,
        rotate line back to original angle.
    """
    xx = xy_line[2] - xy_line[0]
    yy = xy_line[3] - xy_line[1]
    len_1 = math.sqrt( xx*xx + yy*yy)  # Length of the line.
    alpha = math.atan2(yy,xx)          # Angle of line with the horizontal.

    # Generate the randomization. Assume the line is horizontal and of length
len_1
    x_delta = len_1/num_steps
    xy_list = [xy_line[0] + factor* gauss(mean, std_dev), xy_line[1] + factor*
gauss(mean, std_dev)]
    for i in range(num_steps):             # Generate the list of horizontal randomize
points.
        y_rand =  factor* gauss(mean, std_dev) # random.gauss(mean, sigma)
```

```
        x_progressive =  i * x_delta
        beta = math.atan2(y_rand, x_progressive)
        len_2 =  math.sqrt( x_progressive *x_progressive + y_rand * y_rand)

        # Restore the horizontal randomized line to it's original position.
        x_3 = xy_line[0] + len_2 * math.cos(alpha - beta)
        y_3 = xy_line[1] + len_2 * math.sin(alpha - beta)
        xy_list.append(x_3)
        xy_list.append(y_3)
    return xy_list


# Execute and Demonstrate.
# ===========================
mean = 1.0
std_dev = 0.5
factor = 3
num_steps = 20
kula = 'red'
diameter = 2
angle_degrees = 4.0

factor = 10
kula = 'yellow'
xy_line = [200.0, 200.0, 350.0, 200.0]
xy_center = xy_line[0], xy_line[1]

for j in range(90):
    xy_list = rotate_shape(xy_line, xy_center, angle_degrees*j)
    xy_list = gauss_y_scatter(xy_list, mean, std_dev, num_steps, factor)
    canvas_1.create_line(xy_list, fill=kula, smooth=0, width = 2)

factor = 12
kula = 'red'
xy_line = [400.0, 230.0, 600.0, 200.0]   # The Seed line for randomization.
xy_center = xy_line[0], xy_line[1]

for j in range(90):
    xy_list = rotate_shape(xy_line, xy_center, angle_degrees*j)
    xy_list = gauss_y_scatter(xy_list, mean, std_dev, num_steps, factor)
    canvas_1.create_line(xy_list, fill=kula, smooth=0, width = 2)

factor = 15
kula = 'green'
xy_line = [300.0, 350.0, 500.0, 300.0]   # The Seed line for randomization.
```

```
xy_center = xy_line[0], xy_line[1]

for j in range(90):
   xy_list = rotate_shape(xy_line, xy_center, angle_degrees*j)
   xy_list = gauss_y_scatter(xy_list, mean, std_dev, num_steps, factor)
   canvas_1.create_line(xy_list, fill=kula, smooth=0, width = 2)

root.mainloop()
```

Discussion

We need to randomize the line in a way that only randomizes the position at right angles to the line segment. We do this by by calculating the length and angle of the line. Then we treat it as horizontal and randomize the vertical y component only. The we simply rotate the resulting set of points back to their original angle.

Points to note

We calculate the original angle of the line using the *atan2()* trigonometric tangent function from the Python math module. This is because the older atan() function cannot handle certain angles. It loses its bearings when angles approach 90%.

What next?

Can we smooth a chaotic line and does it make a difference? Yes and yes. See the next example.

Smooth Symmetrical Chaos

In this example we have applied smoothing to the randomized line through the parameter smooth=1 in the *create_line(...)* function.

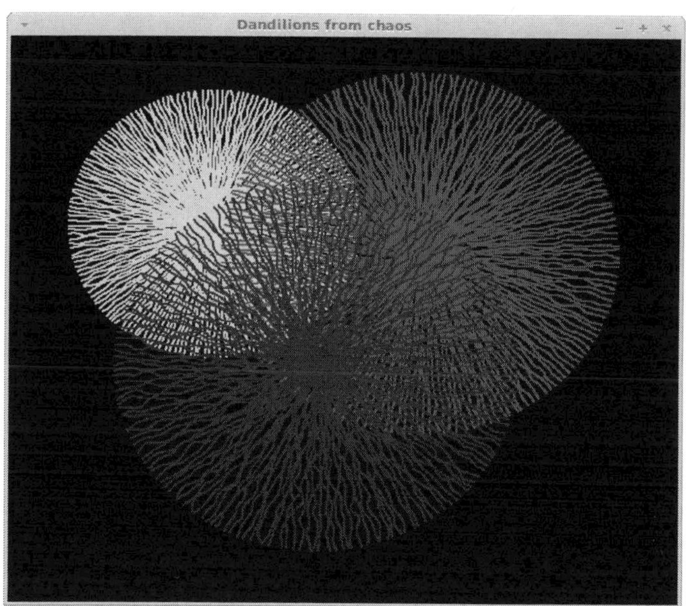

Discussion

Although the lines are still constructed using controlled chaos they look more like a natural plant that would grow in nature when compared to the sharply jagged lines of the previous example.

Chaos in Disguise

In this final example we randomize the seed line once only

and then rotate the same line through a full circle. The result is a circular shape with symmetrical patterns with apparent bands of fluorescence.

The functions used are identical to those in the previous example. Only the **Execute and Demonstrate** part is different and is given below the diagram.

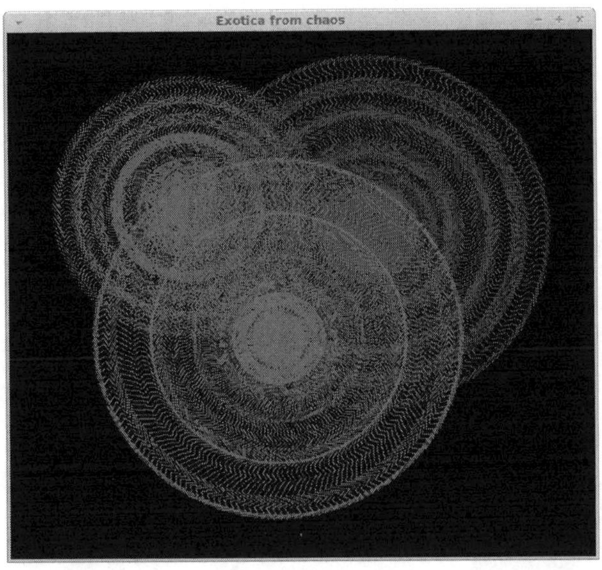


```
"""
Program name: daisywheel_randomization_1.py
...

# Execute and Demonstrate.
# ==========================
mean = 1.0
std_dev = 0.5
factor = 9.0
num_steps = 32
kula = 'red'
diameter = 2
angle_degrees = 2.0

factor = 10
kula = '#888800'  # Dark yellow.
```

```
xy_line = [200.0, 200.0, 350.0, 200.0]
xy_center = xy_line[0], xy_line[1]
xy_list = gauss_y_scatter(xy_line, mean, std_dev, num_steps, factor)
for j in range(180):
    xy_list = rotate_shape(xy_list, xy_center, angle_degrees)
    canvas_1.create_line(xy_list, fill=kula, smooth=0, width = 1)

factor = 12
kula = 'red'
xy_line = [400.0, 230.0, 600.0, 200.0]
xy_center = xy_line[0], xy_line[1]
xy_list = gauss_y_scatter(xy_line, mean, std_dev, num_steps, factor)
for j in range(180):
    xy_list = rotate_shape(xy_list, xy_center, angle_degrees)
    canvas_1.create_line(xy_list, fill=kula, smooth=0, width = 1)

factor = 15
kula = '#00dd00'
xy_line = [300.0, 350.0, 500.0, 300.0]
xy_center = xy_line[0], xy_line[1]
xy_list = gauss_y_scatter(xy_line, mean, std_dev, num_steps, factor)
for j in range(180):
    xy_list = rotate_shape(xy_list, xy_center, angle_degrees)
    canvas_1.create_line(xy_list, fill=kula, smooth=0, width = 1)

root.mainloop()
```

What next?

How can we get closer to the kind of line an artist might draw on paper. We end the chapter by exploring this question.

Electrocution of Lines

Now we attempt something special which is to draw in a style that is intended to be more human and spontaneous. We want to draw outlines that have squiggles, fuzz and fur. Or outlines that look like a cartoon impression of something connected to high voltage electricity. The sort of thing a graphic design student might try when experimenting with different styles. Except in our case here there is nothing spontaneous about our effort. The effort is considerable and requires the solution of some knotty problems.

So our aim is to be able to embellish any chosen shape with the kind of random noise we have been developing. One the problems we cannot avoid now is the one mentioned earlier of dealing with vertical lines. The slope of a vertical line is a number that is infinitely large and so when we attempt to calculate the slope of vertical lines we must develop code that will handle it without crashing, freezing or causing unwanted visual effects.

A second problem is that we have not dealt with lines that have negative slope.

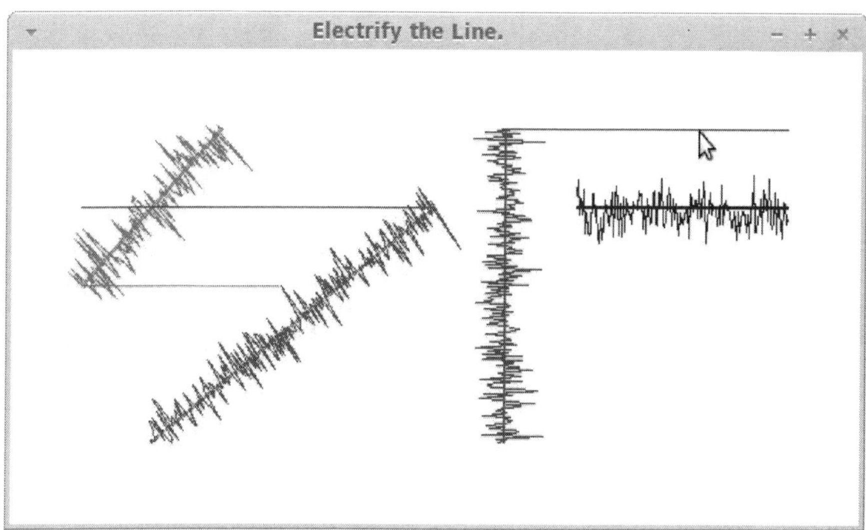


```
"""
Program name:  line_electrify_randomization_1.py
Objective: Add random components to line segments.
Test edge conditions.

Keywords: line, random, edge cases.
============================================================
Comments:
A Straight line between two points has a random 'wobble' added to it.
1. Each segment is first made horizontal and the angle and length noted.
2. A vertical random noise component is added to the segment.
3. The segment is restored to it's original orientation.

There are test shapes that include verticals,horizontals, positive slopes
and negative slopes.

Tested on: Python 2.6, Python 2.7.3, Python 3.2.3
Author: Mike Ohlson de Fine
"""
from Tkinter import *
#from tkinter import *  # For Python 3.2.3 and higher.
from random import *
import math
root = Tk()
root.title(" Electrify the Line.")
```

```
cw = 600                           # canvas width
ch = 300                           # canvas height
canvas_1 = Canvas(root, width=cw, height=ch, background="white")
canvas_1.grid(row=0, column=1)

def rotate_shape(shape, xy_center, angle_rad):
    """ Rotate any shape about a cetner point xy_center.
    """
    #angle_rad = math.radians(angle_degrees)
    x_cen = xy_center[0]
    y_cen = xy_center[1]
    new_shape = []
    for i in range(int(len(shape)/2 )):
        x_temp = shape[2*i]  - x_cen
        y_temp = shape[2*i+1] - y_cen
        radian_temp  = math.atan2(y_temp, x_temp )
        length_temp = math.sqrt( y_temp**2 + x_temp**2)
        new_angle = angle_rad + radian_temp
        new_x = length_temp * math.cos(new_angle) + x_cen
        new_y = length_temp * math.sin(new_angle) + y_cen
        new_shape.append(new_x)
        new_shape.append(new_y)
    return   new_shape   # angle_deg = post rotation angle

def make_horizontal(segment):
    """ Rotate to the horizontal.
        Detect if a line is positive going right ( direction = 1),
        negative going left ( direction = -1) or if slope is infinite.
        The atan2() function should take care of verticals.
    """
    x1 = segment[0]
    y1 = segment[1]
    x2 = segment[2]
    y2 = segment[3]
    delt_y = y2-y1
    delt_x = x2-x1
    if delt_x > 0:         # Normal - x increasing, slope.
        x_direction = 1
    if delt_x < 0:         # Negative moving line.
        x_direction = -1
    if delt_x == 0:         # Vertical line, slope infinite.
        x_direction = 0
    angle = math.atan2(delt_y, delt_x)   # Angle to make line horizontal.
    length = math.sqrt(delt_y**2 + delt_x**2)
    return   length, angle, x_direction
```

```
def line_randomize_vertical(xy_line, x_direction, x_delta, standard_deviation):
    """ Draw a segmented line with randomized vertical component
        added.
    """
    going_positive = 1
    if xy_line[2] < xy_line[0]:  # Negative going line.
        going_positive = -1
    if xy_line[2] > xy_line[0]:  # Normal positive going line.
        going_positive = 1

    num_steps = int(going_positive * (xy_line[2] - xy_line[0])/x_delta)  # A
positive number.
    xy_list = []
    for i in range(num_steps):
        y_randomized = xy_line[1] + gauss(mean, standard_deviation)
        x_next = xy_line[0] + going_positive * x_direction * i * x_delta
        xy_list.append(x_next)
        xy_list.append(y_randomized)
    return xy_list

def electrocute_line(xy_line):
    """ Add a vertical (normal) component of random noise to a line segment.
    """
    canvas_1.create_line(xy_line, fill='gray')
    length, angle, x_direction  = make_horizontal(xy_line)                #
Horizontalization parameters.
    temp_line = [xy_line[0], xy_line[1], xy_line[0] + x_direction * length,
xy_line[1]] # Pure horizontal line
    canvas_1.create_line(temp_line, fill=kula)
    temp_line = line_randomize_vertical(temp_line, x_direction, x_delta,
standard_deviation)
    xy_center = [ xy_line[0], xy_line[1] ]
    temp_line = rotate_shape(temp_line, xy_center, angle)
    canvas_1.create_line(temp_line, fill=kula)

# Execute and Demonstrate.
# ========================

# Edge case test lines.
diagonal_rising_right = [ 50.0,150.0 , 150.0,50.0 ]
diagonal_dropping_left= [ 300.0,100.0 , 100.0,250.0 ]
horizontal_line = [ 400.0,100.0 , 550.0,100.0  ]
vertical_line = [ 350.0,50.0 , 350.0,250.0  ]
```

```
# Randomization parameters.
mean = 1.0
standard_deviation = 10.0
x_delta = 1.0       # If this is smaller than the length of a line there are not enough
randomized points to plot.
''' Problem Alert! Still to be solved: What if a point is repeated?  There should be
a 'hedge' in the code:
    Skip over the repeated point or take some other suitable measure.
'''
#Original and electrified/noisified lines.
kula = '#00dd00'
canvas_1.create_line( diagonal_rising_right, width=2, fill='#00dd00') # Positive
slope.
electrocute_line( diagonal_rising_right)

kula = 'red'
canvas_1.create_line( diagonal_dropping_left, width=2, fill='red')     # Negative
slope.
electrocute_line(diagonal_dropping_left)
canvas_1.create_line( vertical_line, width=2, fill='red')              # Infinite
slope.
electrocute_line( vertical_line)

kula = 'blue'
canvas_1.create_line( horizontal_line,width=2, fill='blue')            # Zero
slope.
electrocute_line(horizontal_line)

root.mainloop()
```

Discussion

In this program we handle troublesome line slopes inside the function *make_horizontal(segment).* This function has a single straight line segment as the input argument and returns the the length and angle with the horizontal and a third variable called *x_direction* which says if the line has x increasing or decreasing or not varying at all (a vertical line).

Electrocution of Shapes

Now that we have sorted out how to handle negative slope and infinite slope we want to apply the solution to a complex drawing on any shape. As we have just done in the previous example we use test cases that include instances that were known to cause failure previously – the instances of line segments that have negative and infinite slope.

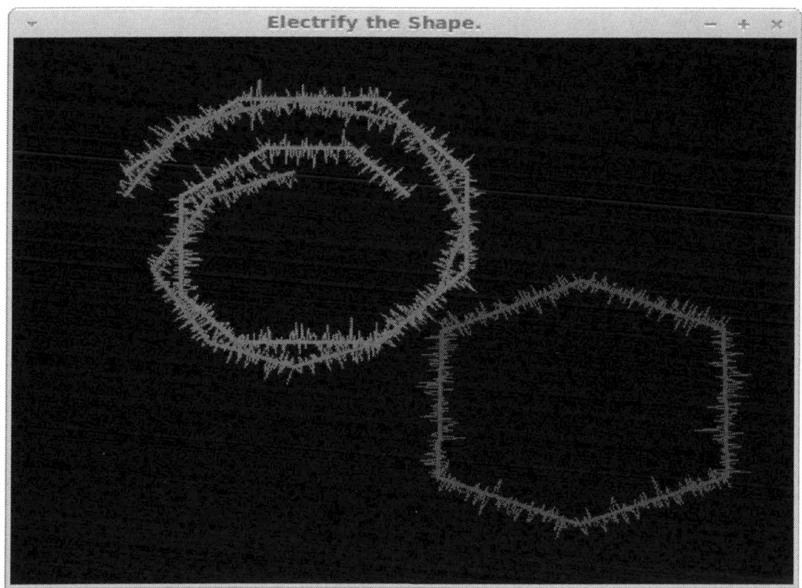

The program used here is identical to *line_electrify_randomization_1.py* above except that the following function was added:

```
def electrocute_shape(shape):
    """ Add a vertical (normal) component of random noise to each line segment
      of a polygon shape.
    """
    for i in range(int(len(shape)/2 -1)):
      xy_line = [ shape[2 *i],  shape[2 *i+1], shape[2 *i+2], shape[2 *i+3] ]
      length, angle, x_direction  = make_horizontal(xy_line)            #
```

Horizontalization parameters.

```
    temp_line = [xy_line[0], xy_line[1], xy_line[0] + x_direction * length,
xy_line[1]] # Pure horizontal line
    temp_line = line_randomize_vertical(temp_line, x_direction, x_delta,
standard_deviation)
    if len(temp_line) <= 2:
      temp_line = [ temp_line[0], temp_line[1],  temp_line[0]+1,
temp_line[1] ] # Hedge for x_delta too small.
    # Rotate back to original position.
    xy_center = [ xy_line[0], xy_line[1] ]
    temp_line = rotate_shape(temp_line, xy_center, angle)
    canvas_1.create_line(temp_line, fill=kula)
```

The shapes used to test how well the function *electrocute_shape(shape)* were the following:

```
# Execute and Demonstrate.
# ==========================

# Edge case test lines.
# Closed hexagon
hexagon_1 =[ 402.0, 201.0, 303.0, 243.0, 301.0, 363.0, 400.0, 401.0, 504.0,
362.0, 501.0, 241.0, 402.0, 201.0]

# Curl with pure horizontals and verticals.
electra_1 = [ 80,112.3 , 160,52.3 , 260,52.3 , 320,112.3 , 320,192.3 , 260,252.3 ,
160,252.36218 , 120,212.3 , 120,132.3 , 180,92.3 , 240,92.3 , 280,132.3 ]

# Curl no horizontals or veticals.
electra_2 = [80,132.36218 , 120,72.362183 , 200,52.362183 , 280,72.362183 ,
320,152.36218 , 300,212.36218 , 260,252.36218 , 200,272.36218 ,
140,252.36218 , 100,192.36218 , 140,132.36218 , 200,112.36218 ]

# Randomization parameters.
mean = 1.0
standard_deviation = 6.0
x_delta = 1.0          # If this is smaller than the length of a line there are not
enough randomized points to plot.
''' Problem Alert! Still to be solved: What if a point is repeated?  There should be
a 'hedge' in the code:
  Skip over the repeated point or take some other suitable measure.
'''
kula = '#0044cc'
electrocute_shape(hexagon_1)
```

```
canvas_1.create_line(hexagon_1, width=3, fill=kula)
kula = '#00dd00'
electrocute_shape(electra_1)
canvas_1.create_line(electra_1, width=3, fill=kula)
kula = '#ff4400'
electrocute_shape(electra_2)
canvas_1.create_line(electra_2, width=3, fill=kula)
```

Discussion

The logo at the start of this chapter is is drawing of a cat whose outline is made of the edges of polygons which have been 'electrified'.

6

Graphic Elements: Text Control

"*I am the story teller. My words burn like flame in the darkness. I speak and hearts beat high.*" Jim Fitzpatrick, The Silver Arm.

In this chapter we will cover:

- default text on a canvas
- control of font size
- how line overflow affects layout
- font placing using anchor points

- default center anchoring of text
- anchoring text at bottom-left (south-west)
- anchoring text at top-right (north-east)
- alignment of text by right or left justification
- use of unusual fonts
- creation of custom fonts
- discovery of all operating system fonts
- acquistition and installation of TrueType web fonts

This chapter is about the placement of text on a Tkinter canvas in a similar fashion to lines, ovals and polygons. We also cover how to create unique fonts as polygons. This offers potent artistic freedom and makes animation of text possible.

The use of text in a graphic context involves:

- choice of font,
- size and color,
- placement of whole columns of text – anchoring the columns to the north, south, east or west of the canvas.
- alignment of the text - right-justified, left-justified or centered.
- discovering what fonts are available.
- acquiring new and unusual fonts.
- creating original fonts of our own.

Placing Blocks of Text on the Canvas

First we need to understand the terms used to describe and specify the placement of text.
The placement of blocks of text are described using the same ideas of compass direction that we use to navigate on our planet except that we use the flat surface of a canvas as our 'world', not the round ball of planet earth.

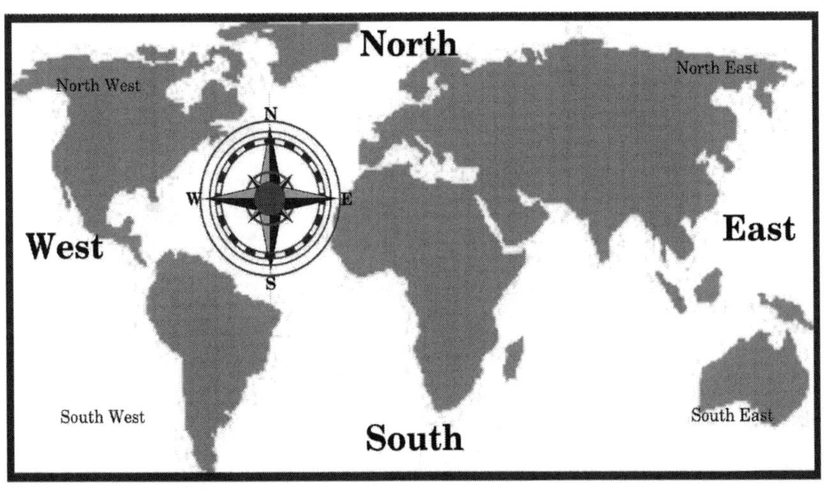

Simple Text to a Canvas

The Python instruction that draws text on canvas is
canvas_1.create_text(xy, text=" What is the default text size and style?")

The result is shown below.

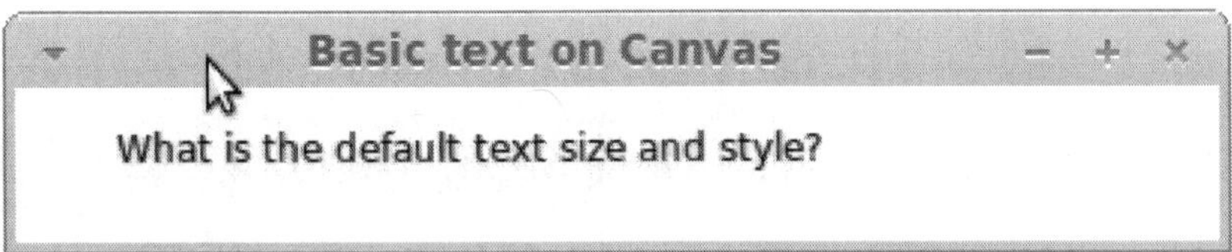

"""
Program name: text_1.py
Objective: Place text on a canvas.

Keywords: canvas, text
===
Comments: Using all default settings this is the bare minimum code
to place text onto a canvas.

```
Tested on: Python 2.6, Python 2.7.3, Python 3.2.3
Author:         Mike Ohlson de Fine
"""
from Tkinter import *
#from tkinter import *  # For Python 3.2.3 and higher.
root = Tk()
root.title('Basic text on Canvas')

cw = 400                          # canvas width
ch = 50                           # canvas height
canvas_1 = Canvas(root, width=cw, height=ch, background="white")
canvas_1.grid(row=0, column=1)

xy = 150, 20
canvas_1.create_text(xy, text=" What is the default text size and style?")
root.mainloop()
```

Discussion

Text is a graphic object with special characteristics. Because it has a history inherited from the printing industry the font style, properly called typeface, is measured in a peculiar unit called 'point'. There are 72 points in one inch. This makes a point 0.3527 millimeters. That is close to one third of a millimeter.

In the instructions

xy = 150, 20
canvas_1.create_text(xy, text=" text large, Arial 20 point", fill='red', width=200, font='Arial 20')

- The starting position of the area where our text is going to be is the canvas coordinate xy = 150, 20. This is in *pixels.*
- However the *font size* is not in pixels it is in *points*, 20 in this example.
- The font style or family is called Ariel.
- The width of the invisible box inside of which the text will be placed is 200 pixels.

We also need to decide whether the text must be positioned to the right, to the left or in the middle of the 200 pixel wide invisible box. The default choice, when we specify nothing, is center. This is specified by the *anchor* parameter which we will deal with later on.

A typeface (also known as font family) is a set of characters that share common design features. A font family refers to the three separate but similar fonts of normal, bold and italic, that go by the same name. A single typeface is represented by a specific weight (thickness), style, inter-character spacing, width, slant, italicization, ornamentation, but not size. We specify size independently. We also decide what color we want our text to be.
Common usage has the terms font and typeface used interchangeably with font probably being used most frequently. We will use *font* to refer to style of text.

Points to note

On the graphic canvas on which we write all measurements are pixels. Pixel size depends on monitor screen manufacture. Pixels are definitely not printer's *points* and this makes the control of text a bit frustrating at times.

Default choice.

If we do not make an explicit selection of certain parameters then Tkinter graphic system will choose defaults on our behalf. Font type, size and color can be specified explicitly but it may happen thaqt a particular font style was not installed on your operating system. When this happens Tkinter will apply a 'best-guess' font and size if the exact font we specified is not available on the platform.

What next?

The next three examples illustrate various fonts, point sizes, color and position coordinates. In these examples some deliberate mistakes have been made in order to illustrate things that should be avoided.

Font Size

Here we get an idea of what a selection of different font sizes, in typesetting *point* measure, look like.

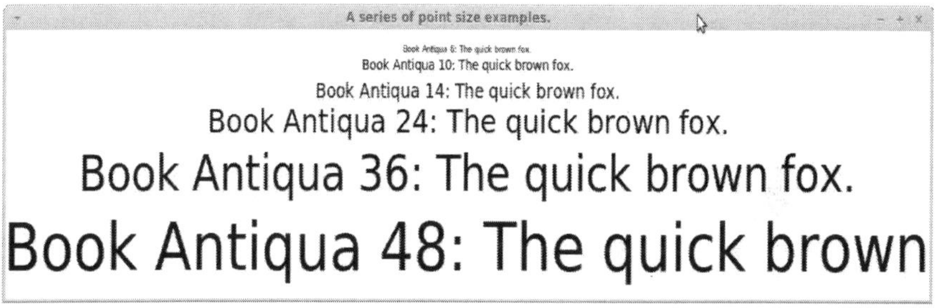

```
"""
Program name: text_font_size_1.py
Objective: Demonstrate a series of text sizes.

Keywords: canvas, text, point, size.
=============================================================
Comments:

Tested on: Python 2.6, Python 2.7.3, Python 3.2.3
Author: Mike Ohlson de Fine
"""
from Tkinter import *
#from tkinter import *  # For Python 3.2.3 and higher.
root = Tk()
root.title("A series of point size examples.")

cw = 1100                              # canvas width
ch = 260                               # canvas height
canvas_1 = Canvas(root, width=cw, height=ch, background="white")
canvas_1.grid(row=0, column=1)

fox = "The quick brown fox."
point_6 = 'Book Antiqua 6: '
```

```
font_6 = 'Bookantiqua 6'
point_10 = 'Book Antiqua 10: '
font_10 = 'Bookantiqua 10'
point_14 = 'Book Antiqua 14: '
font_14 = 'Bookantiqua 14'
point_24 = 'Book Antiqua 24: '
font_24 = 'Bookantiqua 24'
point_36 = 'Book Antiqua 36: '
font_36 = 'Bookantiqua 36'
point_48 = 'Book Antiqua 48: '
font_48 = 'Bookantiqua 48'

x = 550
y = 20
column_width = 1200
offset = 0
canvas_1.create_text(x,y+offset, text=point_6+fox,  width=column_width,
font=font_6)
offset = 15
canvas_1.create_text(x,y+offset, text=point_10+fox,  width=column_width,
font=font_10)
offset = 40
canvas_1.create_text(x,y+offset, text=point_14+fox,  width=column_width,
font=font_14)
offset = 70
canvas_1.create_text(x,y+offset, text=point_24+fox,  width=column_width,
font=font_24)
offset = 120
canvas_1.create_text(x,y+offset, text=point_36+fox,  width=column_width,
font=font_36)
offset = 230
canvas_1.create_text(x,y+offset, text=point_48+fox,  width=column_width,
font=font_48)

root.mainloop()
```

Discussion

The example above provides a convenient means of testing the look of any fonts we may wish to try. Note that 6 point size is too small to read comfortably. In this book 10.5 has been used for the Python code and 12 point for normal text. The font family for the Python code is Liberation Serif and the normal text is Century Schoolbook L.

Text too Large for Specified Width

In the example below we see what happens if there is too much text to fit in the 200 pixel width we specified in our *create_text* instruction. The text overflows and continues on the next line below. This next line will conform to the 200 pixel width as specified. If there is a lot more text then it continues on to the next line below that and continues on to fill the space like a newspaper column. The bottom of the last line remains anchored to the xy coordinate of 150, 100 and the column expands upward to accommodate the text to be displayed.

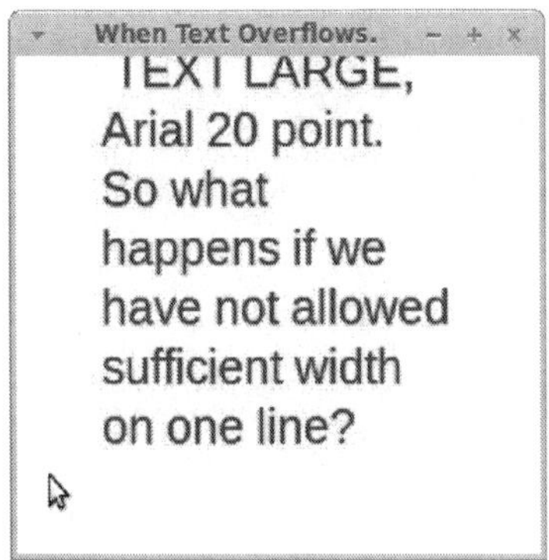


```
"""
Program name: text_width_overflow_1.py
Objective: Draw text onto the canvas at a chosen location.

Keywords: canvas,text
==================================================
 Comments: The text is written starting at co-ordinate location (x,y) = 200,20.
The "width=200" is the horizontal size of the writing area. The text column
grows upwards with each
new line..

Tested on: Python 2.6, Python 2.7.3, Python 3.2.3
Author: Mike Ohlson de Fine.
"""
from Tkinter import *
#from tkinter import *  # For Python 3.2.3 and higher.
root = Tk()
root.title("When Text Overflows.")

cw = 300                              # canvas width
ch = 260                              # canvas height
canvas_1 = Canvas(root, width=cw, height=ch, background="white")
canvas_1.grid(row=0, column=1)

xy = 150, 100
canvas_1.create_text(xy, text=" TEXT LARGE, Arial 20 point. So what happens
if we have not allowed sufficient width on one line?", fill='red', width=200,
font='Arial 20')
```

```
root.mainloop()
```

Discussion

We see here that size and space matter if we want our text to look professional. We should not leave too much to default settings.

What next?

Next we explore how different font families occupy different amounts of space even if their point size specifications are identical.

Bad Spacing when certain Font Families are used

In this example we compare the space occupying properties of different font families of the same typset point size. All the text is 20 point (7 millimeters) high. Clearly bold Courier is noticeably smaller than normal Sans Serif. The width and spacing of BookAntiqua results in column width overflow with consequent upward overlapping of the previous text.

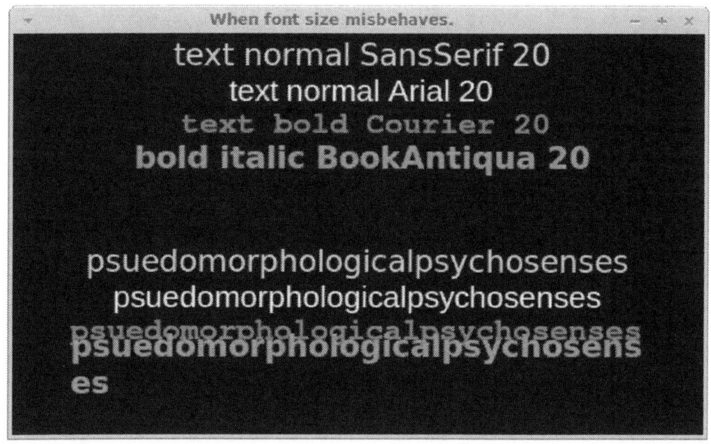

```
"""
Program name: text_font_space_1.py
Objective: Draw text onto the canvas at a chosen location.

Keywords: canvas, text, font size, overlap.
============================================================
Comments: The text is written starting at co-ordinate location x= 200
with y progressing down the canvas in steps of 30 pixels.
The default position has the text string centered at x= 200 which can
look messy.
The "width=500" is the horizontal size of the writing area,
in pixels (not typeset point measure).

ested on: Python 2.6, Python 2.7.3, Python 3.2.3
Author: Mike Ohlson de Fine
"""
from Tkinter import *
#from tkinter import *  # For Python 3.2.3 and higher.
root = Tk()
root.title("When font size misbehaves.")

cw = 600                              # canvas width
ch = 350                              # canvas height
canvas_1 = Canvas(root, width=cw, height=ch, background="#000066")
canvas_1.grid(row=0, column=1)

x = 300

# Font Family descriptions.
canvas_1.create_text(x, 20,  text=" text normal SansSerif 20",   fill='yellow',
width=500, font='SansSerif 20 ')
canvas_1.create_text(x, 50,  text=" text normal Arial 20",       fill='white',
width=500, font='Arial 20 ')
canvas_1.create_text(x, 80,  text=" text bold Courier 20",       fill='green',
width=500, font='Courier 20 bold')
canvas_1.create_text(x, 110, text=" bold italic BookAntiqua 20", fill='violet',
width=500, font='Bookantiqua 20 bold')

# Size comparisons.
canvas_1.create_text(x, 200, text="psuedomorphologicalpsychosenses",
fill='yellow', width=500, font='SansSerif 20 ')
canvas_1.create_text(x, 230, text="psuedomorphologicalpsychosenses",
fill='white', width=500, font='Arial 20 ')
canvas_1.create_text(x, 260, text="psuedomorphologicalpsychosenses",
fill='green', width=500, font='Courier 20 bold')
```

```
canvas_1.create_text(x, 290, text="psuedomorphologicalpsychosenses",
fill='violet', width=500, font='Bookantiqua 20 bold')

root.mainloop()
```

Discussion

This example emphasizes the need to experiment and discover the attributes of different fonts that we may use.

Points to note

It is noteworthy that if we specify a particular point size like 20, it is just an *approximate* measure.

Using Anchors to Establish Position

Now we start using anchor positions to exert better control of our text positioning.
Referring to the map of the world diagram at the start of this chapter we use abbreviations of compass points to denote the location of text columns on a canvas.
The anchor positions must be one of the four corners of the map (canvas) as follows.
NE = North-East = Top left of the canvas.
SW = South-West = Bottom right of the canvas.
NW = North-West = Top right of the canvas.
SE = South-East = Bottom left of the canvas.

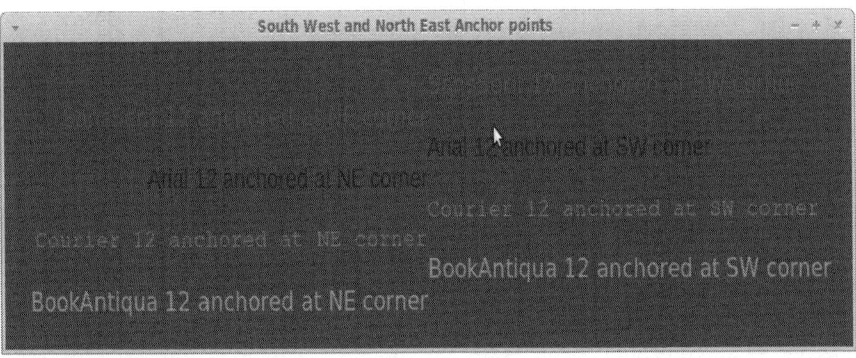

..

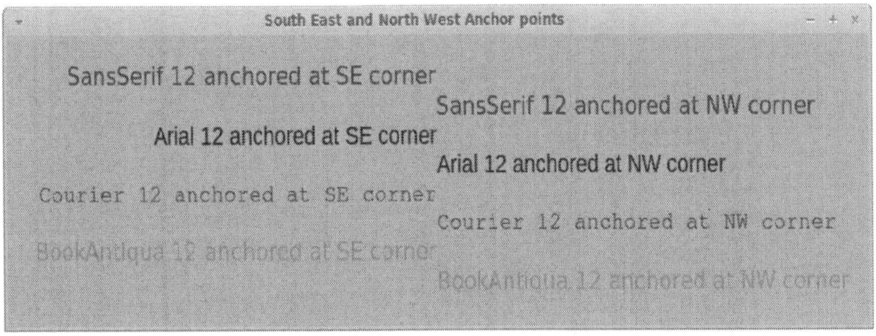

```
""" Program name: text_anchored_1.py
Objective: Draw text onto the canvas using anchor points for location.

Keywords: canvas, text, arial, courier, sans serif, book antiqua, anchor.
==================================================
Comments: The text is written starting at co-ordinate location x= 600, with y
progressing down the canvas
 in steps of 30 pixels.
The default position has the text string anchored by it SW (bottom-left) or NE
(top right corner).

Tested on: Python 2.6, Python 2.7, Python 3.2,
Author:       Mike Ohlson de Fine

"""
from Tkinter import *
#from tkinter import *  # For Python 3.2.3 and higher.
root = Tk()
```

```
root.title('South West and North East Anchor points')

cw = 900                              # canvas width
ch = 250                              # canvas height
canvas_1 = Canvas(root, width=cw, height=ch, background="dark green")
canvas_1.grid(row=0, column=1)

xy = 200, 20

################      South West (SW) anchored
##################################################
canvas_1.create_text(450, 50,  text="SansSerif 12 anchored at SW corner",
fill='red', width=600, font='SansSerif 16 ',     anchor= SW)
canvas_1.create_text(450, 100,  text="Arial 12 anchored at SW corner",
fill='blue', width=600, font='Arial 16',         anchor= SW)
canvas_1.create_text(450, 150, text="Courier 12 anchored at SW corner",
fill='green', width=600, font='Courier 16',      anchor= SW)
canvas_1.create_text(450, 200, text="BookAntiqua 12 anchored at SW corner",
fill='violet', width=600, font='Bookantiqua 16', anchor= SW)
#=====================================================

#################   North East (NE)
anchored##################################################
canvas_1.create_text(450, 50,  text="SansSerif 12 anchored at NE corner",
fill='red', width=600, font='SansSerif 16',      anchor= NE)
canvas_1.create_text(450, 100,  text="Arial 12 anchored at NE corner",
fill='blue', width=600, font='Arial 16',         anchor= NE)
canvas_1.create_text(450, 150, text="Courier 12 anchored at NE corner",
fill='green', width=600, font='Courier 16',      anchor= NE)
canvas_1.create_text(450, 200, text="BookAntiqua 12 anchored at NE corner",
fill='violet', width=600, font='Bookantiqua 16', anchor= NE)
#=====================================================
root.mainloop()
```

Discussion

We have tried out all four anchor position. From previous experience we know that long strings of text will overlap one another if care is not exercised.

Unfortunate color combinations

We can see that good choices of background color and text

color are important.
For example pure red on a dark green background is an awful combination. Blue is not much better. In general, for text, light colored backgrounds are better than dark ones.
Many websites use black as a background because it is looks dramatic. Dramatic but almost unreadable. Often the text on such websites is difficult and off-putting to read.

What next?

Next we must get to grips with controlling text sensibly when the strings are substantially long.
Here we use a variable named dsn (an abbreviation for “dark and stormy night”) to isolate the overriding effect of column width on text layout.

Default (Center) Positioning of Long Text Strings

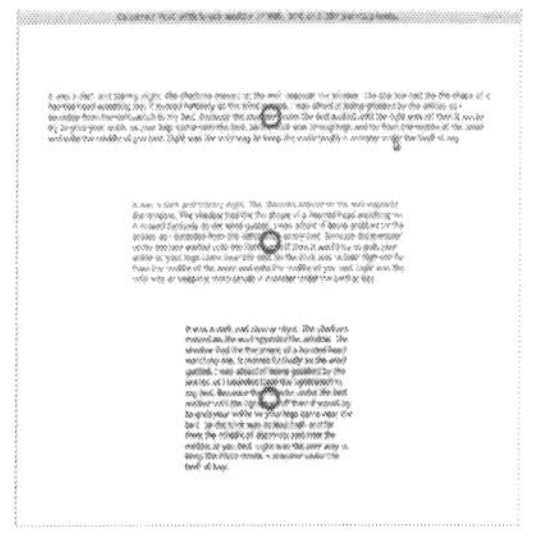
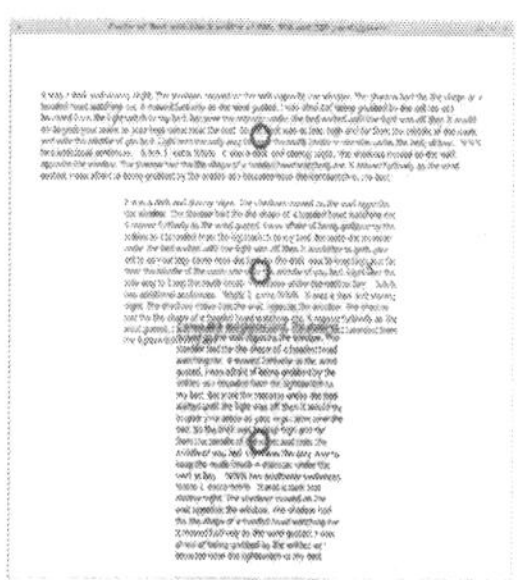
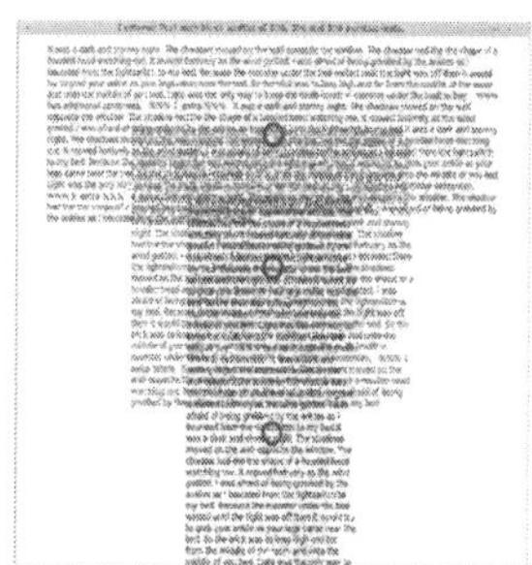

```
"""
Program name: text_sw_anchored_1.py
Objective: Place different colored texts anchored south-west on a canvas.

Keywords: canvas, text, color, font
============================================================
Comments:
1. Text position orig_x, orig_y.
2. anchor=SW. South-West.

Tested on: Python 2.6, Python 2.7, Python 3.2.3
Author:        Mike Ohlson de Fine
"""

from Tkinter import *
#from tkinter import *  # For Python 3.2.3 and higher.
root = Tk()
root.title('Text anchored SW with block widths of 800, 500 and 300
points/pixels.')

cw = 900                              # canvas width
ch = 630                              # canvas height
canvas_1 = Canvas(root, width=cw, height=ch, background="white")
canvas_1.grid(row=0, column=1)

dsn= "It was a dark and stormy night; the rain fell in torrents - except at
```

occasional intervals, when it was checked by a violent gust of wind which swept up the streets, rattling along the housetops, and fiercly agitating the scanty flame of the lamps that struggled against the darkness. In her attic bedroom Margaret Muray, wrapped in an old patchwork quilt, sat on the foot of her bed and watched the trees tossing in the frenzied lashing of the wind. Behind the trees clouds scudded frantically across the sky. Every few moments the moon ripped through them, creating wraithlike shadows that raced along the ground."

```
orig_x = 50
orig_y  = 140

canvas_1.create_text(orig_x, orig_y,   anchor= SW, text=dsn,   fill='red',\
                         width=800, font='SansSerif 10 ')
canvas_1.create_oval(orig_x-16, orig_y-16,  orig_x+16, orig_y+16, outline='red',
width =6)

orig_y = 320
canvas_1.create_text(orig_x, orig_y,   anchor= SW, text=dsn,   fill='brown',\
                         width=500, font='SansSerif 10 ')
canvas_1.create_oval(orig_x-16, orig_y-16,  orig_x+16, orig_y+16, outline='red',
width =6)

orig_y = 600
canvas_1.create_text(orig_x, orig_y,   anchor= SW, text=dsn,   fill='blue',\
                         width=300, font='SansSerif 10 ')
canvas_1.create_oval(orig_x-16, orig_y-16,  orig_x+16, orig_y+16, outline='red',
width =6)

root.mainloop()
```

Discussion

The diagram above shows how the parameter values in the create_text instructions

orig_x = 450
orig_y = 70
like canvas_1.create_text(orig_x, orig_y, text=dasn, fill='red', width=800, font='SansSerif 10 ')

relate to the coordinate positions on the canvas.

The default anchor postions for the text columns have been shown as red circles drawn by each *canvas_1.create_oval(orig_x-16, orig_y-16, orig_x+16, orig_y+16, outline='red', width =6)* instruction.

What we see in each of the three result illustrations is that no matter how tall the column of text is, it's geometric center remains always in the same position. That is the anchor point is in the center of the column and as the column grows it's lowest point moves downward and it's highest point moves upward.

What next?

Most often we need to fix the position of either the top or the bottom rather than the center. In the next example we fix the bottom-left corner of the text column to the canvas.

Bottom-Left (South-West) Anchor for Text Columns

As before we show the position of the text anchor points by means of a red circle created with the *canvas_1.create_oval(orig_x-16, orig_y-16, orig_x+16, orig_y+16, outline='red', width =6)* instruction.

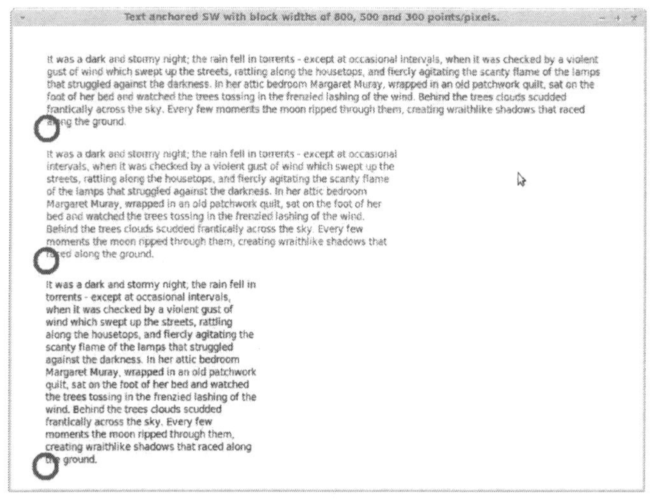

```
"""
Program name: text_sw_anchored_1.py
Objective: Place different colored texts anchored south-west on a canvas.

Keywords: canvas, text, color, font
=============================================================
Comments:
1. Text position orig_x, orig_y.
2. anchor=SW. South-West.

Tested on: Python 2.6, Python 2.7, Python 3.2.3
Author:          Mike Ohlson de Fine
"""

from Tkinter import *
#from tkinter import *  # For Python 3.2.3 and higher.
root = Tk()
root.title('Text anchored SW with block widths of 800, 500 and 300
points/pixels.')

cw = 900                              # canvas width
ch = 630                              # canvas height
canvas_1 = Canvas(root, width=cw, height=ch, background="white")
canvas_1.grid(row=0, column=1)

dsn= "It was a dark and stormy night; the rain fell in torrents - except at
occasional intervals, when it was checked by a violent gust of wind which swept
up the streets, rattling along the housetops, and fiercly agitating the scanty flame
of the lamps that struggled against the darkness. In her attic bedroom Margaret
Muray, wrapped in an old patchwork quilt, sat on the foot of her bed and watched
the trees tossing in the frenzied lashing of the wind. Behind the trees clouds
scudded frantically across the sky. Every few moments the moon ripped through
them, creating wraithlike shadows that raced along the ground."

orig_x = 50
orig_y  = 140

canvas_1.create_text(orig_x, orig_y,   anchor= SW, text=dsn,   fill='red',\
                      width=800, font='SansSerif 10 ')
canvas_1.create_oval(orig_x-16, orig_y-16,  orig_x+16, orig_y+16, outline='red',
width =6)

orig_y = 320
canvas_1.create_text(orig_x, orig_y,   anchor= SW, text=dsn,   fill='brown',\
```

```
                    width=500, font='SansSerif 10 ')
canvas_1.create_oval(orig_x-16, orig_y-16,  orig_x+16, orig_y+16, outline='red',
width =6)

orig_y = 600
canvas_1.create_text(orig_x, orig_y,   anchor= SW, text=dsn,   fill='blue',\
                    width=300, font='SansSerif 10 ')
canvas_1.create_oval(orig_x-16, orig_y-16,  orig_x+16, orig_y+16, outline='red',
width =6)

root.mainloop()
```

Discussion

In this example the column will grow upward while the bottom remains fixed.

Points to note

Note that in both the previous examples the text on each line is neat and tight up against the left (west) of the column. This is called a "left justified' text column. Later we will see how to make our columns left or right justified.

Top-Right (North-East) Anchor for Text Columns

Again we show the position of the text anchor points by means of a red circle created with the *canvas_1.create_oval(orig_x-16, orig_y-16, orig_x+16, orig_y+16, outline='red', width =6)*

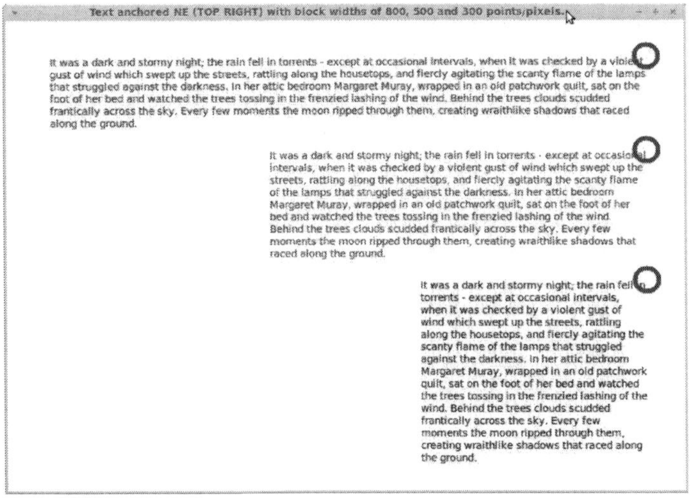

```
"""
Program name: text_ne_anchored_1.py
Objective: Place different colored texts anchored south-west on a canvas.

Keywords: canvas, text, color, font, anchor ne, top right.
============================================================
Comments:
1. Text position orig_x, orig_y.
2. anchor=NE. North-East.
3. justify=LEFT. Default is LEFT.

Tested on: Python 2.6, Python 2.7, Python 3.2.3
Author:       Mike Ohlson de Fine
"""
from Tkinter import *
#from tkinter import *  # For Python 3.2.3 and higher.
root = Tk()
root.title('Text anchored NE (TOP RIGHT) with block widths of 800, 500 and
300 points/pixels.')

cw = 900                        # canvas width
ch = 650                        # canvas height
canvas_1 = Canvas(root, width=cw, height=ch, background="white")
canvas_1.grid(row=0, column=1)

dasn= "It was a dark and stormy night; the rain fell in torrents - except at
occasional intervals, when it was checked by a violent gust of wind which swept
```

up the streets, rattling along the housetops, and fiercly agitating the scanty flame of the lamps that struggled against the darkness. In her attic bedroom Margaret Muray, wrapped in an old patchwork quilt, sat on the foot of her bed and watched the trees tossing in the frenzied lashing of the wind. Behind the trees clouds scudded frantically across the sky. Every few moments the moon ripped through them, creating wraithlike shadows that raced along the ground."

```
orig_x = 850
orig_y  = 50
canvas_1.create_text(orig_x, orig_y,   anchor= NE, text=dasn,   fill='red',\
                        width=800, font='SansSerif 10 ')
canvas_1.create_oval(orig_x-16, orig_y-16,  orig_x+16, orig_y+16, outline='red',
width =6)
orig_y  = 180
canvas_1.create_text(orig_x, orig_y,   anchor= NE, text=dasn,   fill='brown',\
                        width=500, font='SansSerif 10 ')
canvas_1.create_oval(orig_x-16, orig_y-16,  orig_x+16, orig_y+16, outline='red',
width =6)
orig_y  = 360
canvas_1.create_text(orig_x, orig_y,   anchor= NE, text=dasn,   fill='blue',\
                        width=300, font='SansSerif 10 ')
canvas_1.create_oval(orig_x-16, orig_y-16,  orig_x+16, orig_y+16, outline='red',
width =6)

root.mainloop()
```

Discussion

Note that the fact that although the anchor point is on the right, the right-hand side of the column is not nice and straight like the left. The test is left justified by default.

What next?

In the next example we see how to control text justification within the column.

Left and Right Justification of Text in a Column

Various justifications with NW anchor points. Column widths of 300 pixels.

It was a dark and stormy night; the rain fell in torrents - except at occasional intervals, when it was checked by a violent gust of wind which swept up the streets, rattling along the housetops, and fiercly agitating the scanty flame of the lamps that struggled against the darkness. In her attic bedroom Margaret Muray, wrapped in an old patchwork quilt, sat on the foot of her bed and watched the trees tossing in the frenzied lashing of the wind. Behind the trees clouds scudded frantically across the sky. Every few moments the moon ripped through them, creating wraithlike shadows that raced along the ground.

It was a dark and stormy night; the rain fell in torrents - except at occasional intervals, when it was checked by a violent gust of wind which swept up the streets, rattling along the housetops, and fiercly agitating the scanty flame of the lamps that struggled against the darkness. In her attic bedroom Margaret Muray, wrapped in an old patchwork quilt, sat on the foot of her bed and watched the trees tossing in the frenzied lashing of the wind. Behind the trees clouds scudded frantically across the sky. Every few moments the moon ripped through them, creating wraithlike shadows that raced along the ground.

It was a dark and stormy night; the rain fell in torrents - except at occasional intervals, when it was checked by a violent gust of wind which swept up the streets, rattling along the housetops, and fiercly agitating the scanty flame of the lamps that struggled against the darkness. In her attic bedroom Margaret Muray, wrapped in an old patchwork quilt, sat on the foot of her bed and watched the trees tossing in the frenzied lashing of the wind. Behind the trees clouds scudded frantically across the sky. Every few moments the moon ripped through them, creating wraithlike shadows that raced along the ground.

It was a dark and stormy night; the rain fell in torrents - except at occasional intervals, when it was checked by a violent gust of wind which swept up the streets, rattling along the housetops, and fiercly agitating the scanty flame of the lamps that struggled against the darkness. In her attic bedroom Margaret Muray, wrapped in an old patchwork quilt, sat on the foot of her bed and watched the trees tossing in the frenzied lashing of the wind. Behind the trees clouds scudded frantically across the sky. Every few moments the moon ripped through them, creating wraithlike shadows that raced along the ground.

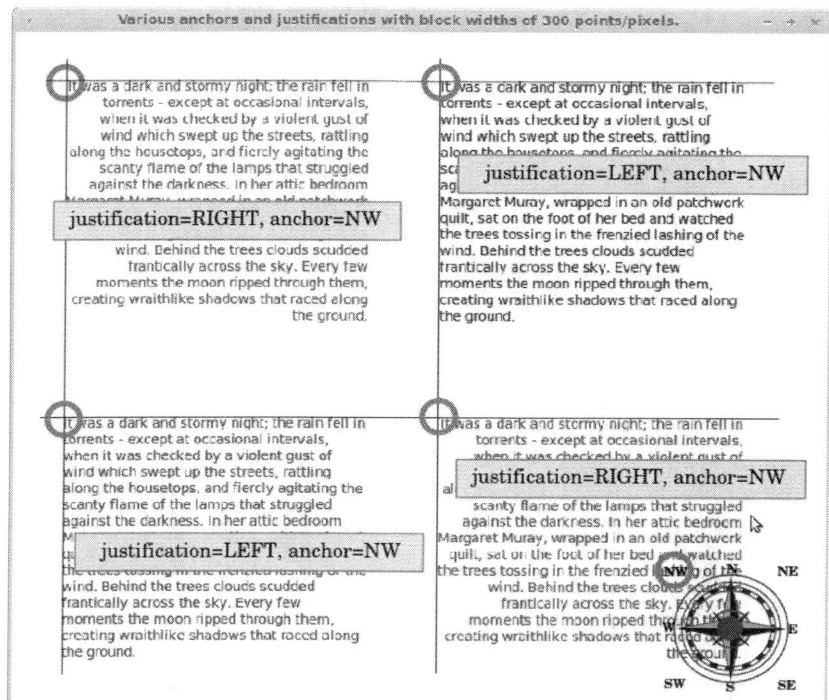

"""

Program name: text_justify_align_1.py

Objective: Place different colored texts and font types on a canvas.

Keywords: canvas, text, color, font

==

Comments:

1. Font type, size and color can be specified. Tkinter will
apply a 'best-guess' font if the exact font specified is not available
on your platform.

2. anchor=anchorPos: Text position orig_x, orig_y is where the text is centered (by default).
   This can be overriden by anchor options like "anchor= NW".

2. anchor=anchorPos
AnchorPos Specifies which part of the text (the text's bounding box, more exactly) that should be placed at the given position.
Use one of N, NE, E, SE, S, SW, W, NW or CENTER. Default is CENTER.

justify=how (ACTIVE WHEN LINE OVERFLOWS OCCUR)
Specifies how to justify the text within its bounding region. How must be one of

the values "LEFT", "RIGHT", or "CENTER". This option will only matter if the text is displayed as multiple lines. If the option is omitted, it defaults to left.

3. tags=tagList
Specifies a set of tags to apply to the item. TagList consists of a list of tag names, which replace any existing tags for the item. TagList may be an empty list.

4. width=lineLength
Specifies a maximum line length for the text. If this option is zero (the default) the text is broken into lines only at newline characters. However, if this option is non-zero then any line that would be longer than lineLength is broken just before a space character to make the line shorter than lineLength; the space character is treated as if it were a newline character.

Tested on: Python 2.6, Python 2.7, Python 3.2.3
Author: Mike Ohlson de Fine
"""

```
from Tkinter import *
#from tkinter import *  # For Python 3.2.3 and higher.
root = Tk()
root.title('Various justifications with NW anchor points. Column widths of 300
pixels.')

cw = 800                                  # canvas width
ch = 700                                  # canvas height
canvas_1 = Canvas(root, width=cw, height=ch, background="white")
canvas_1.grid(row=0, column=1)

dasn= "It was a dark and stormy night; the rain fell in torrents - except at
occasional intervals, when it was checked by a violent gust of wind which swept
up the streets, rattling along the housetops, and fiercly agitating the scanty flame
of the lamps that struggled against the darkness. In her attic bedroom Margaret
Muray, wrapped in an old patchwork quilt, sat on the foot of her bed and watched
the trees tossing in the frenzied lashing of the wind. Behind the trees clouds
scudded frantically across the sky. Every few moments the moon ripped through
them, creating wraithlike shadows that raced along the ground."


orig_y = 50
orig_x = 50
canvas_1.create_text(orig_x, orig_y,  anchor= NW,  justify= RIGHT, text=dasn,
fill='brown',\
                              width=300, font='SansSerif 10 ')
canvas_1.create_oval(orig_x-16, orig_y-16,  orig_x+16, orig_y+16, outline='red',
width =6)
```

```
orig_y = 50
orig_x = 420
canvas_1.create_text(orig_x, orig_y,    anchor= NW, justify= LEFT, text=dasn,
fill='blue',\
                         width=300, font='SansSerif 10 ')
canvas_1.create_oval(orig_x-16, orig_y-16,  orig_x+16, orig_y+16, outline='red',
width =6)

orig_y = 400
orig_x = 50
canvas_1.create_text(orig_x, orig_y,  anchor= NW,  justify= LEFT, text=dasn,
fill='dark green',\
                         width=300, font='SansSerif 10 ')
canvas_1.create_oval(orig_x-16, orig_y-16,  orig_x+16, orig_y+16, outline='red',
width =6)
orig_y = 400
orig_x = 420
canvas_1.create_text(orig_x, orig_y,    anchor= NW, justify= RIGHT, text=dasn,
fill='red',\
                         width=300, font='SansSerif 10 ')
canvas_1.create_oval(orig_x-16, orig_y-16,  orig_x+16, orig_y+16, outline='red',
width =6)

root.mainloop()
```

Unusual and Creative Fonts

For compete control of font attributes like font family (Helvetica, Times Roman, etc.), weight (bold or normal), slant (italic or normal), size (points) we should a specified in the create_text(..) method that looks like *font = (font_family, size_points, bold_norm, slant)*
where:

- *font_family* is the font family name as a string. Example: 'Helvetica'
- *size_points* is the height of the font in the printers unit of measure that is points. One point = 0.353

millimeters. See Note 1

- *bold_norm* = '*bold*' for boldface or '*normal*' or regular print thickness.
- *Slant* = '*italic*' for slanted italic or '*roman*' for unslanted.

Note 1: In Typography (the art and craft of typesetting) a point is the smallest unit of measure. There are 72 points to an inch. One point = 0.353 mm.

In the examples that follow we demonstrate how to structure font parameters using unusual fonts that are not normally supplied with an operating system. These fonts are easily obtained as shown in the section that follows after this one.

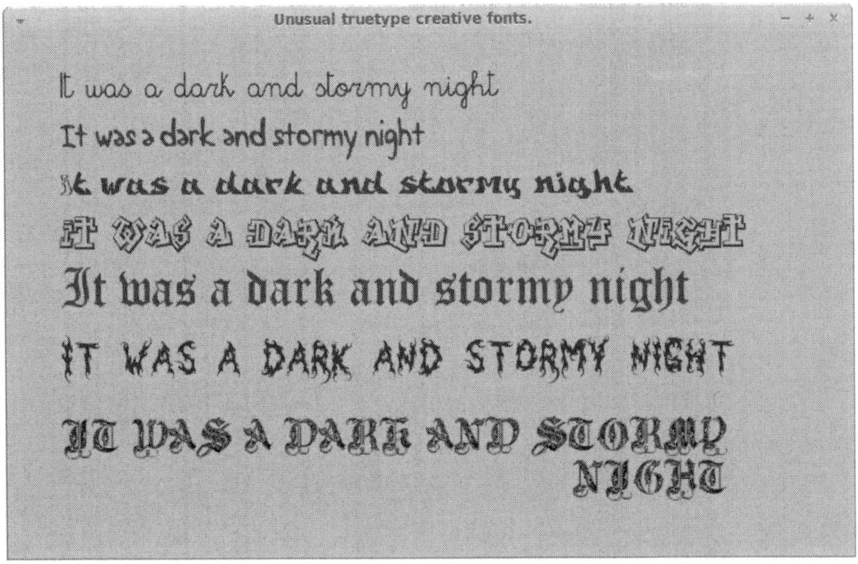

```
"""
Program name: strange_fonts_text_1.py
Objective: Display unusual and creative fonts.

Keywords: canvas, text, color, font family, size, style
=============================================================
Comments: The value of defining font specification parameters via a
```

```
function definition is that any of the parameter can become an effective
for the duration when the program is run - they whole group of parameters
not not need to re-declared every time new text is displayed.

Tested on: Python 2.6, Python 2.7, Python 3.2.3
Author:        Mike Ohlson de Fine
"""
from Tkinter import *
#from tkinter import *  # For Python 3.2.3 and higher.
root = Tk()
root.title('Unusual truetype creative fonts.')

cw = 800                          # canvas width
ch = 600                          # canvas height
canvas_1 = Canvas(root, width=cw, height=ch, background="white")
canvas_1.grid(row=0, column=1)

dasn= "It was a dark and stormy night; the rain fell in torrents - except at
occasional intervals."

# Unusual Fonts
darkgarden = 'Dark Garden'
lenka      = 'Lenka'
onthewall  = 'OnTheWall'
katam      = 'Katamotzikasi'
purisa     = 'Purisa'
graffititreat = 'Graffiti Treat'
oldenglish = 'Old English Text MT'
royal = 'Royal'
chancery   = 'URW Chancery L'

# Colours
kula_bg = '#d8f800'
kula_1  = '#4c10ae'
kula_2  = '#de0052'
kula_3  = '#9303a7'
kula_4  = '#7109aa'
kula_5  = '#cd0074'
kula_6  = '#3914af'
kula_7  = '#150873'

def make_font(font_family, size_points, bold_norm, slant):
   make_font = (font_family, size_points, bold_norm, slant)
   return make_font
```

```
orig_x = 50

#1
font_family = katam
bold_norm = 'bold'
slant = 'normal'
size_points = 24
orig_y = 30
do_font = make_font(font_family, size_points, bold_norm, slant)
canvas_1.create_text(orig_x, orig_y,  anchor= NW,  justify= RIGHT, text=dasn,
fill=kula_1,\
                          width=700, font=do_font)
#2
font_family = lenka
size_points = 20
orig_y = 80
do_font = make_font(font_family, size_points, bold_norm, slant)
canvas_1.create_text(orig_x, orig_y,  anchor= NW,  justify= RIGHT, text=dasn,
fill=kula_2,\
                          width=700, font= do_font)
#3
font_family = onthewall
size_points = 20
orig_y = 120
do_font = make_font(font_family, size_points, bold_norm, slant)
canvas_1.create_text(orig_x, orig_y,  anchor= NW,  justify= RIGHT, text=dasn,
fill=kula_3,\
                          width=700, font= do_font)
#4
font_family = graffititreat
size_points = 24
orig_y = 160
do_font = make_font(font_family, size_points, bold_norm, slant)
canvas_1.create_text(orig_x, orig_y,  anchor= NW,  justify= RIGHT, text=dasn,
fill=kula_4,\
                          width=700, font= do_font)
#5
font_family = oldenglish
size_points = 36
orig_y = 200
do_font = make_font(font_family, size_points, bold_norm, slant)
canvas_1.create_text(orig_x, orig_y,  anchor= NW,  justify= RIGHT, text=dasn,
fill=kula_5,\
                          width=700, font= do_font)
#6
```

```
font_family = darkgarden
size_points = 28
orig_y = 260
do_font = make_font(font_family, size_points, bold_norm, slant)
canvas_1.create_text(orig_x, orig_y,  anchor= NW,  justify= RIGHT, text=dasn,
fill=kula_6,\
                    width=700, font= do_font)
#7
font_family = royal
size_points = 28
orig_y = 340
rdasn= "IT WAS A DARK AND STORMY NIGHT"
do_font = make_font(font_family, size_points, bold_norm, slant)
canvas_1.create_text(orig_x, orig_y,  anchor= NW,  justify= RIGHT, text=rdasn,
fill=kula_7,\
                    width=700, font= do_font)

root.mainloop()
```

Custom Made Fonts

Up till now we have used fonts provided as part of our basic operating system. If we need text as graphic objects that we can resize and rotate as well as embellish with edge effects, then we can create or own shapes that just happen to text fonts. It is not simple to have complete and easy control over size, position and orientation. We will not deal with those details here as we only wish to indicate that it is possible and that we already have the basic capability to do so.

```
"""
Program name: python_text_banner_1.py
Objective: Display a banner with DIY fonts.

Keywords: canvas, polygon, diy fonts.
==============================================================
Comments:

Tested on: Python 2.6, Python 2.7, Python 3.2.3
Author: Mike Ohlson de Fine
"""
from Tkinter import *
#from tkinter import *  # For Python 3.2.3 and higher.
root = Tk()
root.title("Python Banner.")
canvas_1 = Canvas(root, width=750, height=400, background="#000044")
canvas_1.grid(row=0, column=1)

p_1 = [15.7,340.2  , 39.3,250.2  , 39.3,119.5   , 135.0,116.6 ,
      167.1,139.5 , 181.4,165.2 , 181.4,209.5  , 163.6,231.6 ,
      134.3,248.1 , 85.7,253.1  , 102.1,339.5  ]

p_2 = [85.7,168.8  , 106.4,168.8 , 117.9,175.9 ,
      117.1,187.4 , 107.1,196.6 , 91.4,196.6]

t_1 = [192.1,84.5  , 264.3,115.9 , 299.3,118.1  , 369.3,85.9  ,
      367.9,136.6 , 306.4,156.6 , 331.4,338.8  , 254.3,340.9 ,
```

```
    275.7,158.1 , 189.3,121.6  ]

o_1 = [492.1,118.1 , 459.3,158.1 , 456.4,228.8 , 468.6,278.8 ,
    489.3,320.9 , 507.9,337.4 , 528.6,338.1 , 541.4,324.5 ,
    569.3,278.8 , 579.3,221.6 , 577.1,151.6 , 559.3,126.6 ,
    538.6,117.4 , 505.7,117.4  ]

o_2 = [519.3,170.9 , 510.7,174.5 , 506.4,181.6 , 509.3,193.1 ,
    524.3,196.6 , 533.6,187.4 , 532.9,176.6 , 527.9,171.6  ]

n_1 = [561.4,335.9 , 592.9,295.9 , 603.6,119.5 , 637.9,127.4 ,
    664.3,201.6 , 674.3,127.4 , 717.1,113.1 , 697.9,271.6 ,
    725.0,341.6 , 669.3,338.8 , 631.4,232.4 , 624.3,337.4  ]

y_1 = [198.6,145.2 , 200.0,229.5 , 157.1,312.4 , 122.1,340.9 ,
    236.4,338.1 , 200.0,310.2 , 231.4,228.8 , 259.3,169.5 ,
    235.7,160.2 , 222.9,190.9 , 221.4,156.6]

h_1 = [361.4,153.8 , 383.6,145.9 , 384.3,198.1 , 405.0,193.8 ,
    403.6,140.2 , 432.9,130.2 , 439.3,338.8 , 414.3,338.8 ,
    410.0,255.9 , 388.6,258.8 , 387.9,338.1 , 359.3,339.5]

# Dark glow.
canvas_1.create_polygon(p_1, outline='#640000', fill='', width=16 )
canvas_1.create_polygon(y_1, outline='#640000', fill='', width=16 )
canvas_1.create_polygon(t_1, outline='#640000', fill='', width=16 )
canvas_1.create_polygon(h_1, outline='#640000', fill='', width=16 )
canvas_1.create_polygon(o_1, outline='#640000', fill='', width=16 )
canvas_1.create_polygon(n_1, outline='#640000', fill='', width=16 )

# Main body.
canvas_1.create_polygon(p_1, outline='red', fill='#880000', width=6 )
canvas_1.create_polygon(p_2, outline='red', fill="#000044", width=6 )
canvas_1.create_polygon(y_1, outline='red', fill='#880000', width=6 )
canvas_1.create_polygon(t_1, outline='red', fill='#880000', width=6 )
canvas_1.create_polygon(h_1, outline='red', fill='#880000', width=6 )
canvas_1.create_polygon(o_1, outline='red', fill='#880000', width=6 )
canvas_1.create_polygon(o_2, outline='red', fill="#000044", width=6 )
canvas_1.create_polygon(n_1, outline='red', fill='#880000', width=6 )

# Inner incandescence.
canvas_1.create_polygon(p_1, outline='#ff8888', fill='', width=2 )
canvas_1.create_polygon(p_2, outline='#ff8888', fill='', width=2 )
canvas_1.create_polygon(y_1, outline='#ff8888', fill='', width=2 )
canvas_1.create_polygon(t_1, outline='#ff8888', fill='', width=2 )
```

```
canvas_1.create_polygon(h_1, outline='#ff8888', fill='', width=2 )
canvas_1.create_polygon(o_1, outline='#ff8888', fill='', width=2 )
canvas_1.create_polygon(o_2, outline='#ff8888', fill='', width=2 )
canvas_1.create_polygon(n_1, outline='#ff8888', fill='', width=2 )

root.mainloop()
```

Discussion

The shapes shown above for the banner were created and edited with the help of the open source drawing program "Inkscape" which produces SVG (Scaled Vector Graphics) format files. Inkscape was used only as a sketchpad. It is a good tool for producing because we can easily edit, tweak and improve the drawing. It is a refined, bug-free, sophisticated drawing tool that is well worth the effort of learning to use. It is also Open Source so it costs nothing and is not owned by any commercial company. The methods of converting SVG files into Python shapes is detailed in the next book in this series titled Python Graphics for Games: Animation".

All Fonts Available on Your Computer

Up till now we have used fonts provided as part of our basic operating system. How can we discover what fonts are available and what they look like? Just run the program shown below.

```
"""
Program name: fonts_available_1.py
Objective: Discover, list and demonstrate all fonts available on your
platform.

Keywords: canvas, text, font inventory
===================================================
Comments: To specify fonts precisely you need to know what fonts are
available and what they look like. The tkfont module is used here to
do that.
```

```
Tested on: Python 2.6, Python 2.7, Python 3.2.3
Author:        Mike Ohlson de Fine
"""
from Tkinter import *
#from tkinter import *  # For Python 3.2.3 and higher.
import tkFont   # This does not work with Python v3
#from tkinter import font as tkFont
root = Tk()
root.title('Fonts available on this Computer')

canvas_1 = Canvas(root, width =1500, height=800, background='white')
canvas_1.grid(row=0, column=1)

fonts_available = list( tkFont.families() )
fonts_available.sort()
text_sample = '  :  abcdefghij_HIJK_12340'
# list the font names on the system console first.
for this_family in fonts_available :
   # print( this_family)
   print this_family
# Show first third on left side of the screen .
for i in range(int(len(fonts_available)/3)):
    texty = fonts_available[i]
    canvas_1.create_text(50,30 + i*20, text= texty + text_sample,\
                   fill='black', font=(texty, 12), anchor= "w")

# Show second third in the middle of the screen .
for j in range(int(len(fonts_available)/3), int(2*len(fonts_available)/3)):
    texty = fonts_available[j]
    canvas_1.create_text(500,30 + ( j - int(len(fonts_available)/3))*20, text=
texty+ text_sample,\
 fill='black',font=(texty, 12),anchor= "nw")

# Show second third on the right of screen .
for i in range( int(2*len(fonts_available)/3), len(fonts_available)):
    texty = fonts_available[i]
    canvas_1.create_text(1000,30 + (i  - 2*int(len(fonts_available)/3))*20, text=
texty+ text_sample,\
 fill='black',font=(texty, 12),anchor= "w")

root.mainloop()
```

Finding and Installing New Fonts

Up till now we have used fonts provided with our basic operating system. If we have a word processor these will be the set from which we can make selections. Now we look at how we can extent that selection. There are hundreds of interesting fonts available for free and for purchase on the internet. What you will see now is a sequence of screen shots which show how to find and install one font called "OhNo". It is a TrueType font. TrueType fonts were originally developed by apple and have become the most widespread type in use and therefore the effective worldwide standard.

Acquiring fonts

1. Google "Download Free Fonts".

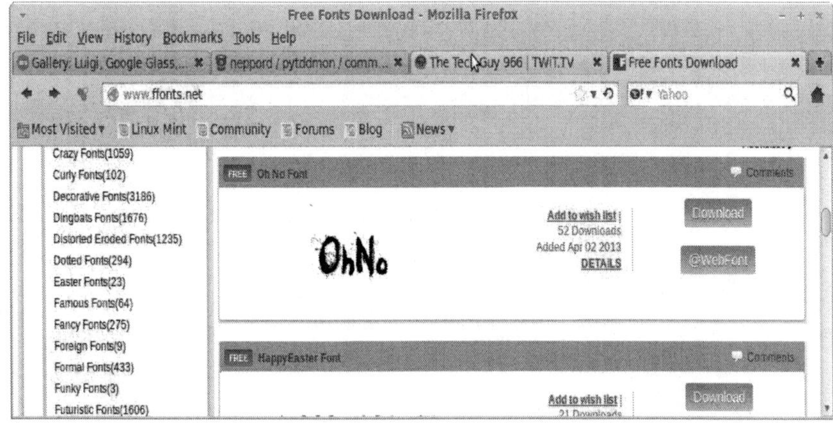

2. Select the font you want.

3. Press Download.

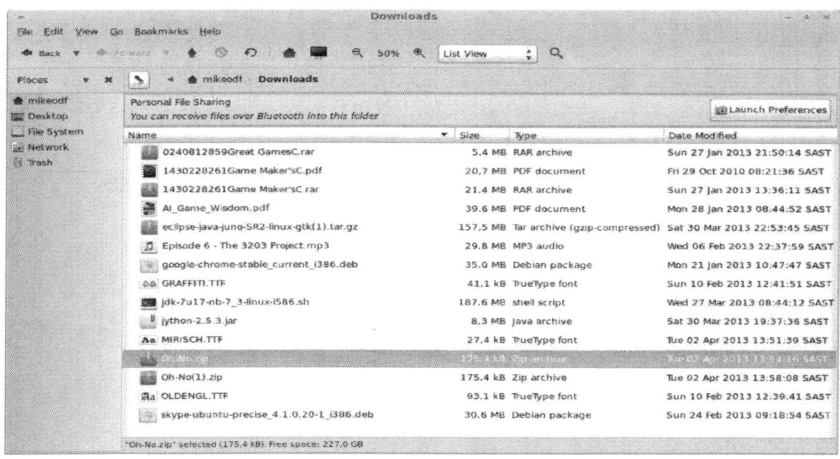

4. Double click on the zip to open it up.

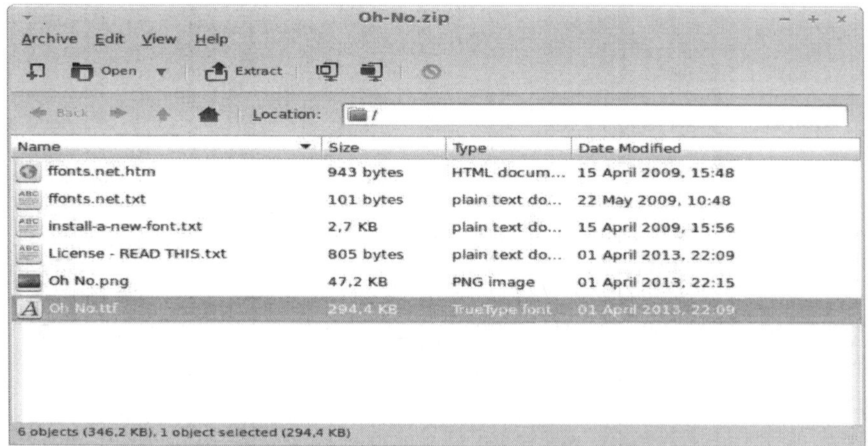

5. Doubleclick on the .ttf file. This will open up an install dialog window.

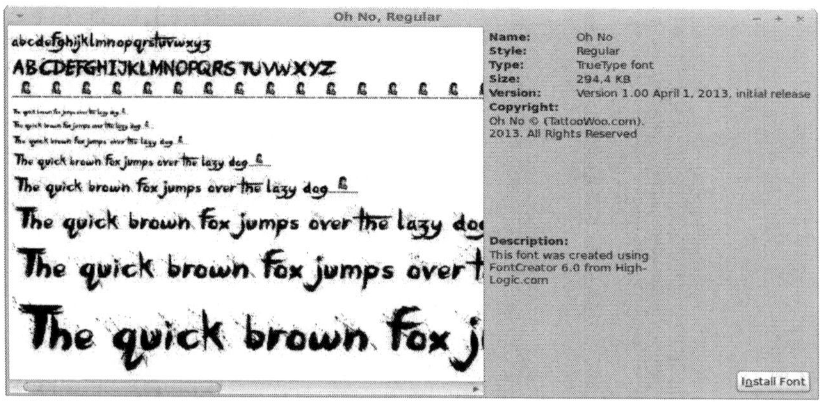

6. Click on stall in the "Install Font" button.

7. Open your Word processor and use the fonts.
If you do see them in the list of available fonts, then re-boot your system and they will be there.

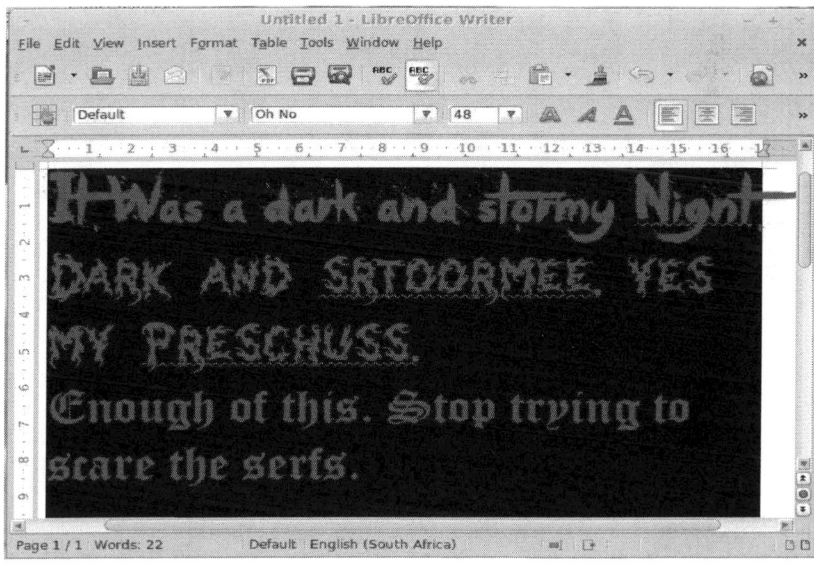

We end off this chapter showing the two samples of line textures that could be used on our custom designed fonts.

Appendix: Getting started with Python

a) How to find out all about Python.

Go to http://www.python.org/about/gettingstarted/
and read the page that is displayed. This page will tell you just about everything you need to get started even if you know nothing about Python or how to write programs.

If you are new to programming go to
http://wiki.python.org/moin/BeginnersGuide/NonProgrammers.

If you want a good book from which to learn Python then one of the best, in my humble opinion, is "A Primer on Scientific Programming with Python" by Hans Petter Lantegan. It is written for smart novices and is readable, interesting and pretty comprehensive.

However if you are cash limited *everything* you ever need to know about about Python is out there on the web. Because there is so much out there it can be confusing to find specific information that you might need. A good source for specific detailed information is http://python-forum.org/.
If you register and login there are many experts who are amazingly generous with their useful advice. There are also a few less than polite characters there but you must not let their presence inhibit you – the nice guys more than compensate for the rowdy fools.

b) Advice for Linux users.

1. **Check that Python is installed on your computer.**

The popular Linux distributions already have Python installed. Ubuntu Version 13.04 has two versions of Python installed – Python 2.7.4 as well as Python 3.3.1.
To check if Python is already in your computer, just type the word "python" into a command line terminal. The operating system will respond with a few lines stating which version is available and some hints on how get more information as shown here.

```
Terminal
File Edit View Search Terminal Help
mikeodf@mikeodf-HP-500B-Microtower ~ $ python
Python 2.7.3 (default, Sep 26 2012, 21:53:58)
[GCC 4.7.2] on linux2
Type "help", "copyright", "credits" or "license" for more information.
>>>
```

Here the Terminal dialog is telling us that Python version 2.7.3 is installed on the system.

2. **How to install Python if it is not present.**
For Linux Ubuntu and its derivatives, such as Mint, type "*sudo apt-get install python*".

3. **Check that Tkinter is installed.**
Type "python" and then "import Tkinter" into a terminal (ie. A command line terminal) and you may see the following.

```
mikeodf@mikeodf-HP-500B-Microtower: ~
mikeodf@mikeodf-HP-500B-Microtower:~$ python
Python 2.7.4 (default, Apr 19 2013, 18:32:33)
[GCC 4.7.3] on linux2
Type "help", "copyright", "credits" or "license" for more information.
>>> import Tkinter
Traceback (most recent call last):
  File "<stdin>", line 1, in <module>
  File "/usr/lib/python2.7/lib-tk/Tkinter.py", line 42, in <module>
    raise ImportError, str(msg) + ', please install the python-tk package'
ImportError: No module named _tkinter, please install the python-tk package
>>>
```

In this case we are informed that Python version 2.7.4 is installed on the system but the response to the instruction “import Tkinter” is an *Import Error* because Tkinter cannot be found. We are urged to ***please install the python-tk package*** which contains Tkinter.

4. **Installing Tkinter.**
We can install the Tkinter package by typing “sudo apt-get install python-tk” into the Terminal.
We will need to type in our system administrator password for authorization to install Tkinter as shown in the captured dialog below.

```
mikeodf@mikeodf-HP-500B-Microtower: ~
mikeodf@mikeodf-HP-500B-Microtower:~$ sudo apt-get install python-tk
[sudo] password for mikeodf:
Reading package lists... Done
Building dependency tree
Reading state information... Done
The following packages were automatically installed and are no longer required:
  gir1.2-json-1.0 gir1.2-timezonemap-1.0 gir1.2-xkl-1.0 gksu libgksu2-0
Use 'apt-get autoremove' to remove them.
The following extra packages will be installed:
  blt libxss1 tcl8.5 tcl8.5-lib tk8.5 tk8.5-lib
Suggested packages:
  blt-demo tix python-tk-dbg tcl-tclreadline
The following NEW packages will be installed
  blt libxss1 python-tk tcl8.5 tcl8.5-lib tk8.5 tk8.5-lib
0 upgraded, 7 newly installed, 0 to remove and 0 not upgraded.
Need to get 3,259 kB of archives.
After this operation, 9,514 kB of additional disk space will be used.
Do you want to continue [Y/n]?
```

When we reply 'Y' Tkinter and any files it depends on are downloaded and installed from the appropriate repositories on a server somewhere in the internet and the terminal output completes it mission with the reassuring response “*ldconfig deferred processing now taking place*” as shown below.

```
mikeodf@mikeodf-HP-500B-Microtower: ~
Processing 1 added doc-base file...
Setting up libxss1:i386 (1:1.2.2-1) ...
Setting up tcl8.5-lib:i386 (8.5.13-1ubuntu4) ...
Setting up tk8.5-lib:i386 (8.5.11-2ubuntu4) ...
Setting up tcl8.5 (8.5.13-1ubuntu4) ...
update-alternatives: using /usr/bin/tclsh8.5 to provide /usr/bin/tclsh (tclsh) in
 auto mode
Setting up tk8.5 (8.5.11-2ubuntu4) ...
update-alternatives: using /usr/bin/wish8.5 to provide /usr/bin/wish (wish) in au
to mode
Setting up blt (2.4z-5ubuntu2) ...
Setting up python-tk (2.7.4-0ubuntu1) ...
Processing triggers for libc-bin ...
ldconfig deferred processing now taking place
mikeodf@mikeodf-HP-500B-Microtower:~$
```

c) Advice for Microsoft Windows Users.

A Microsoft Windows installation will not have Python or Tkinter installed by default. However it is easy to fix this.

1. Go to http://www.python/org/download/ and look for the “Python 2.7.5 Windows Installer” as shown in the screenshot below. Click on this and follow the installation process. The Python binary file is 15.4 megaBytes which is relatively small considering that it also includes Tkinter automatically.

```
C:\Python27\python.exe
Python 2.7.5 (default, May 15 2013, 22:43:36) [MSC v.1500 32 bit (Intel)] on win
32
Type "help", "copyright", "credits" or "license" for more information.
>>> import Tkinter
>>>
```

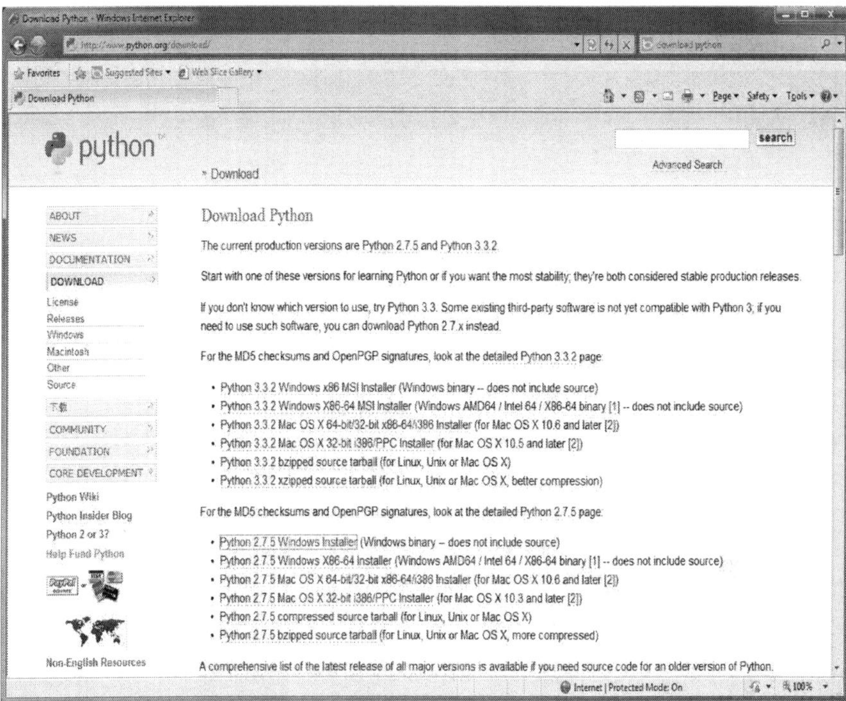

You will be shown the following two windows when the process has completed sucessfully.

Note that this last window shows you Python up and running inside a command line terminal and we have proved that Tkinter is present by typing “import Tkinter” and not getting any error message.

Other books in this series:

The books in this series will be:

Python Graphics for Games #1: Line, Shape and Color

Python Graphics for Games #2: Animation

Python Graphics for Games #3: Working in 3 Dimensions

Python Graphics for Games #4: Game Elements

Made in the USA
Middletown, DE
11 November 2015